Health and the Media

Sociology of Health and Illness Monograph Series

Edited by Jonathan Gabe
Department of Social and Political Science
Royal Holloway
Egham
Surrey
TW20 0EX
UK

Current titles:

- **Health and the Media (2004),**
  edited by *Clive Seale*
- **Partners in Health, Partners in Crime: Exploring the boundaries of criminology and sociology of health and illness (2003),**
  edited by *Stefan Timmermans and Jonathan Gabe*
- **Rationing: Constructed Realities and Professional Practices (2002),**
  edited by *David Hughes and Donald Light*
- **Rethinking the Sociology of Mental Health (2000),**
  edited by *Joan Busfield*
- **Sociological Perspectives on the New Genetics (1999),**
  edited by *Peter Conrad and Jonathan Gabe*
- **The Sociology of Health Inequalities (1998),**
  edited by *Mel Bartley, David Blane and George Davey Smith*
- **The Sociology of Medical Science (1997),**
  edited by *Mary Ann Elston*
- **Health and the Sociology of Emotion (1996),**
  edited by *Veronica James and Jonathan Gabe*
- **Medicine, Health and Risk (1995),**
  edited by *Jonathan Gabe*

Forthcoming titles:

- **Social Movements in Health,**
  edited by *Phil Brown*

- **The Social Organisation of Healthcare Work,**
  edited by *Davina Allen, Alison Pilnick and Carolyn Wiener*

Health and the Media

Edited by
Clive Seale

Blackwell
Publishing

First published as a special issue of *Sociology of Health and Illness* Vol.25 No. 6

350 Main Street, Malden, MA 02148-5018, USA
108 Cowley Road, Oxford OX4 1JF, UK
550 Swanston Street, Carlton, Victoria 3053, Australia

First published 2004 by Blackwell Publishing Ltd

Library of Congress Cataloging-in-Publication Data has been applied for

ISBN 1-4051-1244-1

A catalogue record for this title is available from the British Library.

Set by Graphicraft Limited, Hong Kong
Printed and bound in the United Kingdom
by MPG Books Ltd, Bodmin, Cornwall

For further information on
Blackwell Publishing, visit our website:
http://www.blackwellpublishing.com

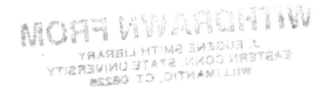

Contents

Chapter 1

Health and media: an overview
Clive Seale

Why should medical sociologists study the media? Accounts of the experience of illness are common in medical sociology (see, for example, recent reviews of this field by Pierret 2003 and Lawton 2003). The information these provide has been helpful over the years in re-orienting the vision of health care providers away from a biomedical and reductionist view of patienthood, towards a more holistic understanding of the meanings of illness for those who experience it. In this way many sociologists have contributed to a more widespread construction of 'patients' (passive) as being instead 'consumers' (active), promoting recognition of the psychosocial element of biopsychosocial care. Thus the medical gaze has been extended to parts of life previously hidden from view, so that a new knowledge of illness has come to dominate thinking in certain health care arenas – perhaps particularly so in primary care and in nursing (Armstrong 1983a, 1984).

In tandem with these developments has been the emergence of media and cultural studies as new disciplines. These have taken the (mass) mediated nature of personal experience to be an important topic. This can be understood as a component of the broader project of understanding what it is to be a person in late or postmodern social conditions. Thus it is very common, in these fields, to see accounts of media representations of gender, class or race (for example, Dines and Humez 2002), because these are felt to be important factors in understanding issues of identity, over which mass media have considerable influence. Personal identity is, to a great extent, a cultural construction (Rose 1999). Systems of knowledge, or discourses, are promoted in mass media and influence audiences in various ways. New media, such as the Internet, allow a new kind of experience (Castells 1996). We must, therefore, understand popular media if we are to understand experience and its rendering in narrative forms.

Yet these two fields of study – media studies and the sociology of health and illness – appear to stand at a distance from one another. There are, of course, studies of medical knowledge itself as a cultural system (Armstrong 1983b, Lupton 1994) and historical accounts may reveal the role of medical and other scientific knowledge in constructing, say, gendered subject identities (Showalter 1987). In this respect, medical sociologists draw upon the same broad theoretical perspective as many sociologists of science and technology, in so far as the truth claims of other sciences are temporarily bracketed, or held in suspense, in order to understand the role of scientific knowledge in the social construction of its subject. Yet medical sociology does not generally reveal very much about the mass mediated nature of scientific knowledge, which has largely been studied as a separate field (for example, Nelkin 1995).

To understand the potential relationship between media studies and medical sociology – at least where issues of identity and experience are concerned – we must address the issue of where experience comes from. On the whole, the discipline of psychology has a particular view of this, which many sociologists call an 'essentialist' vision of human nature. Sociologists must understand human experience differently from this, as at least in part a social construction rather than something that emanates from an inner essence. In constructing the self, modern culture makes available to individuals a great many options and resources. The resources might be understood as cultural scripts, or discourses, and modern self identity is formed in a manner that is sometimes quite reflexive (Giddens 1991), drawing on culturally available narratives, stories, scripts, discourses, systems of knowledge or, in more politically oriented analyses, ideologies.

Perhaps the greatest repository of stories in late modern societies is made up from the various organs of the mass media – television, newspapers, magazines, radio and, increasingly, the Internet. Here, people find a rich collection of resources to draw upon in telling the story of their selves. When people get sick, or make decisions about health, or visit their health service providers, or decide what to think and vote about health care policy and finance, their behaviour may be formulated in large part from resources drawn from various mass media. These can include depictions of what it is like to be sick, what causes illness, health and cure, how health care providers behave (or ought to) and the nature of health policies and their impact. Particular stories may be promoted by particular interest groups seeking to exert influence over populations.

Mass media depictions, of course, are not 'true'. At best, they are partial truths. Sometimes we may even feel they are collections of lies! The producers of mass mediated messages about health have particular agendas, and this is likely to influence what is shown. As ordinary people we must decide to trust or distrust media messages in much the same way as we decide to trust or distrust medical advice or other expertise. As sociologists interested in the experience of illness, and in health care and health policy, we ought to be interested in which stories get told and which are suppressed, and in how members of the media audience (which includes health policy makers and health care providers themselves of course) respond to mediated health messages. Because I think this is important, I have provided an overview of the media and health research field (Seale 2003). I have also edited this monograph which contains some of the best examples of media studies of health that I have been able to elicit from the research community, in a process of selection that was unusually competitive.

In this introduction, therefore, I have first discussed why I believe it to be important to bring together the fields of media studies and the sociology of health and illness. In the sections that follow I outline a general account of the media and health field, focusing first on different conceptualisations of the media audience, then on the general formal structure of popular mass media health representations. I feel that there is now sufficient knowledge to propose a general account of representations that can guide future research studies and assist those concerned to understand the underlying logic that produces particular media health stories[1].

Following this, I outline areas of media and health studies that have been quite thoroughly investigated and others that have been less well studied. For this, I draw on my recent survey of published literature (Seale 2003) and analysis of the content of the 96 abstracts submitted by researchers internationally who applied to write a paper for this monograph. In the course of this section, I show how each of the papers in this volume fits into the field and, in most cases, how these studies offer guidance for future directions of research. I begin with a brief introduction to the structure of the media studies field.

Structure of media studies

Media studies, as it is generally taught to students, is often understood to divide into three broad areas of inquiry: production, representation and reception. Studies of production (for example, Glasgow University Media Group 1976, Schudson 1989) may concern the manner in which media producers behave, or aim to deepen understanding of the commercial environment of media organisations, or involve a 'political economy' approach to media institutions. Such studies ask, for example, about the nature of the influence exerted by governments, professional organisations and business interests on those responsible for producing various media. How do cigarette companies influence magazine editors through paying for advertising? How do the public relations activities of, say, the food industry influence what we see in the media? How do journalists relate to their sources and decide on what counts as a good story? How do health pressure groups use the web? How do government agencies and the medical profession attempt to regulate health information available on the internet?

Studies of representation involve analysis of media messages themselves. Such studies may seek for ideological biases, or the discursive dominance of particular themes and constructions, or be concerned with whether messages are likely to promote or damage health. Or they may investigate the formal properties of media messages as linguistic, narrative or semiotic systems. How does a medical soap opera portray doctors as against nurses? What messages about personal versus societal responsibility for health are conveyed in the advice columns of magazines? Which political analyses of the problems of health care systems get most coverage? Is health information on the Internet at variance with medical advice?

Studies of reception involve investigations of media audiences. Once considered passive recipients (or forgetters) of information, audience 'theory' developed during the 1980s towards a conceptualisation of audiences as much more active in relating to mediated messages. A reconceptualisation of the 'mass' audience towards a view of fragmented 'audiences', with varying motivations and competencies, has also emerged. For example, politicians are important audience members: they are highly responsive to mass media reports. Media producers themselves are also members of the media audience. What they see in the media may influence what they produce. To what extent are health policies designed to assuage a potentially hostile media? To what extent do health professionals model their behaviour on what they see on the television? How do ordinary people respond to media messages about food scares, or safe sex, or exercise, or deadly diseases? How do people use health information on the Internet? These are examples of the questions that are of interest in reception, or audience studies.

Here, we can begin to see that distinctions between producers and consumers of media are not always easy to sustain. The concept of a feedback loop in which certain audience members are also involved in production is helpful here. In studies of the Internet the blurring of the boundary between audience and producer is particularly evident. The production of web sites and contributions to other Internet forums for the discussion of health matters and the promotion of particular health related messages is within the reach of many people, no longer being confined to specialist occupational groups of media producers. Action, pressure and patient groups may form around such Internet activities.

Understanding health and the media

The existing structure of this field of study is weighted towards analyses of health representations (this point will be made more evident in the survey of abstracts that follows this section). Any general account of media and health, if it is to be based on an adequate body of evidence, must therefore take this as the primary object of analysis. But in order to understand media health representations it is necessary to know a little more about the media health audience. In the discussion that follows, little reference will be made to media production issues[1] and, reflecting the balance of existing published work, the focus will be on traditional popular 'mass' media rather than the Internet or the more specialist media read by professional groups. They are nevertheless important areas and studies of the internet, as you will see, and are included in the papers in this volume because of their importance for the future of media health research.

Understanding the media health audience
This is necessarily brief, being the bare essentials of audience theory needed to understand the account of representations that follows (a fuller account that explains the underlying rationale for this selection is in Seale 2003: Chapter 1). In my view any general account of the media health audience

should take account of the following five points, which I list together with references to works in which the particular perspective is best expressed:

1. The audience may (or may not) seek health-promoting information as a part of rational risk profiling at fateful moments. The work of Giddens (1990, 1991, 1992) and to some extent Beck (1992) outlines this vision of the modern individual's relations to expertise, though not with particular reference to media audience theory.

2. The audience seeks emotional stimulation through dramatised contrasts that have an entertaining effect; fear and anxiety, for example, may be aroused so that they are experienced as a contrast to security and pleasure. Hill's (2000) studies of 'reality television' brings this out effectively, as does Langer's (1998) account of the 'other news'.

3. Audience readings are diverse, involving 'resistance' as well as alignment with dominant ideas. The notion of the 'active audience' was designed to replace earlier conceptions of audiences as passive recipients of information, a conception often embedded in early health education studies of 'effects'. The work of Hall (1980) and Morley (1986) has been influential here, although critical responses to over-enthusiastic depictions of audiences as always active and resistant have emerged to counter this (for example Philo 1999). This perspective is particularly important in any study of audiences where political issues are of concern.

4. The audience participates in an imagined conversation with mediated ideas, and in an imagined community of other viewers, people 'like me'. Anderson (1991) is responsible for this idea, relating it to the historical emergence of daily newspapers as the first such mass mediated conversation.

5. People draw on media in order to construct themselves – the media are mirrors for narcissistic (self-regarding) experimentation with different potential selves. Abercrombie and Longhurst (1998) outline this view.

Beyond these points there is a general one – perhaps the sixth in the list – that I feel has not yet been well recognised, which concerns the nature of audience experience. This is not structured in the same way as the neat divisions of research studies require. A media analyst, in general, picks a particular issue on which to focus: BSE, for example, or depression, or HIV/ AIDS, or the emergence of some new contested syndrome, and so on. Once chosen, data may be gathered about the way a range of media presents that particular issue. But audience experience is not like this – it is at once more fragmentary and in a sense more active. As we go about our lives we may at one point in the day hear a report about a health scare on a radio programme, then read about a health policy in the newspaper, then spend the evening channel hopping on the television, seeing a soap opera where characters eat a variety of health enhancing or damaging foods, a documentary where a medical breakthrough is described, finishing with reading a magazine where readers' letters about health issues are answered. Nowhere do we decide to spend the day focusing on the way a variety of media present the topic of depression. As the result of this fragmentary experience, we learn the conventions of an overall media health story, which has certain regular features. Media audiences generally are well schooled in recognising media conventions (the discipline of media studies only formalises a tendency to critique and analyse these which we all have to a greater or lesser extent). Members of media audiences, in fact, are able actively to 'fill in the gaps' when they experience a fragment of an overall story, as Benthall (1993) has argued in relation to audience experience of disaster relief stories:

> Even when only a part of a narrative relating to disaster is shown on television – for instance, pictures of starving babies, or an aeroplane setting off from a familiar airport bringing supplies, or an ambassador thanking the public for their generosity – viewers come to recognize it as part of the total narrative convention (Benthall 1993: 188–9).

It is in the context of this learned capacity of audiences to recognise narrative conventions (which media producers themselves may recognise and exploit) that we can understand media health representations.

Understanding media health representations
One of the many insights of narrative analysts (for example Propp 1968, Labov 1973) is that stories often work by creating and then exploiting oppositions. These are common in the overall story of media health. To list just a few classic oppositions, such stories contain heroes and villains, pleasure and pain, safety and danger, disaster and repair, the beautiful and the ugly, the normal and the freak, cleanliness and dirt, female and male, lay and professional, orthodox and alternative. Perhaps most importantly, media health stories often oppose life with the threat, or the actuality, of death. This last opposition explains, for Turow (1989), the enduring appeal of TV medical soaps, as well as the reason for the overriding focus on doctors rather than nurses or other health care workers in such dramas. Doctors can be more easily depicted making life or death decisions. This means that medical soaps – perhaps like all media health stories at some level – explore the most fundamental anxiety that we all face as embodied, finite beings.

A perennial complaint of scientists considering media reporting of scientific discoveries is that journalists sensationalise their findings, thus introducing inaccuracies (Nelkin 1995). For example, a new drug is either a miracle cure, or a potential Frankenstein's monster such as thalidomide. There is no room for a drug that is good in some respects but bad in others. This tendency to generate dramatic effect through extrematised oppositions is an aspect of what some have called 'tabloidisation' (Sparks and Tulloch 2000). Whether there exists an increasing tendency in Western media towards 'tabloidisation' or not (and there are those who will argue both sides of this), opinion is also divided on whether such tendencies should be regarded as desirable. One view (seen for example in Livingstone and Lunt's (1994) analysis of daytime TV talk shows) is that tabloidisation is a route to greater democratic participation in the public sphere. It constitutes the popularisation of otherwise complex areas, thus drawing in more participants than otherwise. Others (for example, Franklin 1997) claim that the tabloid format represents a regrettable dumbing down in standards of public debate.

Clearly, popular mass media would cease to be popular if complexity were represented in a way that a scientist would find acceptable in a scientific journal. Some degree of simplification must be necessary if the dramatic oppositions that are the core device of story telling are to be created. Above and beyond this, though, the complaint of inaccuracy, with which the critique of tabloidisation is associated, reflects an inadequate understanding of the conditions of media production. People do not make TV programmes or publish newspapers solely in order to provide the public with accurate health information. The entertainment agenda (and this applies to news and current affairs as much, probably, as it does to 'fictional' products) is more dominant, and scientists, medical care providers and health educators have increasingly come to recognise this (Naidoo and Wills 2000).

Because audiences are well educated, through repeated exposure, in the standard oppositions and other forms that go to make up the media health story, they have certain expectations. But entertainment cannot be based solely on meeting expectations, otherwise the appetite for novelty suffers. Media producers know this, and through the phenomenon of the 'twitch' or the 'reversal' (Langer 1998) they play with audience expectations. This is also seen in the phenomenon of the media 'template' (Kitzinger 2000). I shall consider each of these in turn.

Kitzinger (2000) developed her idea of media templates in relation to child abuse stories. A famous case in Cleveland, UK in the 1980s involved the media-orchestrated vilification of a doctor and some social workers for removing children from families suspected of child sexual abuse, thus constructing a powerful sense of opposition between innocence and incompetence (or, even, evil). Later, events occurred in the Orkney Islands that, in the media reporting of the new case, were said to be 'another Cleveland'. The imposition of the Cleveland template on the Orkneys case meant that a ready-made set of stereotypes, judgements and interpretations could be applied. The Cleveland case had set up a 'template' so that when new cases of removal of children from families occurred, they could be understood as further examples of the original story. This operated both at the level of production (how journalists researched, wrote and conceptualised the story) and carried through to audiences. Kitzinger's focus group work showed how people used their understandings of the Cleveland-Orkney association to help remember and interpret the more recent scandal.

Karpf (1988) explains how this used to happen in stories about heart transplants:

[Each one produces] perfect replicas of previous reports. They stress the desperation of those waiting for a heart, and the fear that time will run out. The fatal alternative is made plain. The operation is depicted as offering the chance of a new life or future, an opportunity to vanquish death. Grief and joy are voiced, and the press conference following the operation is an aria of hope (1988: 149).

We no longer see such heart transplant stories in Western media since the template that produced them has lost its currency with the proliferation and routinisation of the operation. A heart transplant story now needs an extra angle to become 'news' (for example, a dying Palestinian gives a heart to save the life of an Israeli). Templates, Kitzinger argues, can from time to time be reversed – indeed they must be when their currency begins to weaken. Thus stories of child abuse, in which adults were discovered to have committed abuse (a classic villain-victim opposition), became a tired format, the story being revived at one point by the reverse accusation of 'False Memory Syndrome', whereby the previously villainous father now became the victim, falsely accused by therapists and daughters (Kitzinger 1998).

Reversals of this sort, then, play on existing audience expectations to achieve a dramatic or entertaining effect. They confirm the existence of standard narrative conventions, their recognition by an 'active' audience, and the response to this by media producers. Langer (1998) presents some particularly subtle examples in his account of 'twitches'. Certain items become news because they disrupt expectations in an emotionally stimulating way. Langer suggests the following:

a safety barrier impales a car driver;
a schoolboy (rather than an engineer) builds a hovercraft;
the Queen and Prince Philip visit a theme park and take a ride in a 'tunnel of love'.

The first of these is a very common format in media health stories that involve risks to health. An everyday object turns out to be dangerous – in this case something that is supposed to promote safety. Food scares can work like this – food is an everyday object, necessary for life. Yet food can kill.

The other two twitches also work by disrupting expectations. Schoolboys are not supposed to be able to do the things that engineers do; royals are supposed to maintain their dignity by not engaging in popular pleasures. This last example reminds us that media celebrities can themselves set a media agenda by initiating twitches and reversals. Thus Princess Diana shook the hand of a person with HIV/AIDS in order to disrupt then-dominant negative stereotypes; the footballer Pele, a hero of masculinity, nevertheless advertises the benefits of Viagra; the royal family now sit uncomfortably through rock concerts trying to look as if they enjoy them, so that previous images of aloofness may be disrupted.

A meta-narrative that runs through contemporary mass media health representations, containing a series of opposed elements, arranged in a way that allows a range of sub-plots, templates, twitches and reversals to be placed, can now be described. Its five key elements are listed below, with explanations and examples of each following the list. They constitute a series of core oppositions:

1. the dangers of modern life;
2. villains and freaks;
3. victimhood;
4. professional heroes;
5. lay heroes.

The first of these is a collection of stories that generate fear, and a concomitant 'culture of safety' (Furedi 1997, Reinharz 1997) that is a marked feature of life in advanced industrialised societies with a highly developed mass media. In a variety of ways, popular mass media emphasise the dangers of modern life. Food scares (salmonella, BSE) are vehicles for such scares (as well as identifying potential villains – farmers, big business). Environmental dangers – nuclear power, acid rain, climate change, power lines and cancer – are also much emphasised in health-related scare stories, as are, from time to time, a variety of infections (for example, herpes) or 'killer bugs' (necrotising fasciitis, ebola fever). Images of medical and scientific activity gone wrong – GM foods, breast implants, tampon-induced toxic shock syndrome, contraceptive pill scares – are also important in generating a climate of insecurity.

The second of these (villains and freaks) also concerns things that can threaten health and the sense of normality with which health is nowadays associated (Petersen 1994). In this case though, the threats come from threatening kinds of people. A classic example of this, in some areas of the media, was the treatment of HIV carriers in the early stages of the emergence of this virus, whereby prostitutes, injecting drug users and gay communities were stigmatised and feared (Watney 1997). A similar level of stigmatisation can be found in the media treatment of mental illness (Philo 1996). From time to time, scientists or representatives of big business (for example, 'agribusiness', tobacco manufacturers, nuclear power station operators) may be vilified (though not often personally) if they can be associated with harmful developments. The history of depictions of people with disabilities in film is replete with negative stereotyping.

Unlike harmful objects, 'harmful' or threatening people can have their reputation defended or restored. Because of the overwhelming interest in subjectivity in media accounts, it is hard to present any person, or group of people, as irredeemably evil over a sustained period of time. Perhaps the only group whose subjectivity is largely deleted from media representations are those of child molesters, who appear to be a securely stigmatised category of person. Most other categories, in due course, attract stigma champions (as in the case of Princess Diana and HIV/AIDS), or they organise to resist media stereotyping (as in the case of the very successful disability movement).

With threats established and continually regenerated by a steady supply of stories, we can all imagine ourselves as potential victims. Yet, from time to time, media producers like to depict victimhood and for this they tend to choose people who represent ourselves at our most vulnerable. Thus the most effective victim portrayals in contemporary media are generally of children. Much concern with safety therefore focuses on child safety. Classically, stories of child abuse have served media producers well in this respect. A less common genre, but one that is more centrally located within the media health field, is the story of the sick child. The dimensions of this story and the way in which it compares with families' reported experiences of sick children (there are many disjunctures) have been analysed in a study by Dixon-Woods *et al.* (2003).

The fourth and fifth components of the media health meta-narrative are stories about professional and lay heroes. These, in their different ways, are set up to rescue the victims threatened by danger and villainy. Yet there are important tensions between these two kinds of hero, and understanding this helps us understand why villains cannot easily be securely stigmatised – their subjectivity comes through too often, as the elevation of the lay hero involves a quite pervasive media celebration of the subjectivity of the ordinary person that has gathered pace in recent years. This in turn generates an obligation to be tolerant and inclusive of difference, something which can test the ingenuity of media producers obliged to replace old hate figures with new ones, all the time risking the alienation of important media audience constituencies, should vilification be taken 'too far'.

Sociologists of health and illness are independently interested in the changing nature of professional-lay relations. For example, the 'proletarianisation' and the 'deprofessionalisation' theses (Elston 1991) assess the argument that there is a decline in the social and cultural authority of medicine. Karpf's (1988) study of media and health took this as its theme, concluding that in spite of some knocks, medical prestige was as strong as ever on the television. Perhaps if she was writing now, her view might have changed, as it is now quite routine for media health stories to appear announcing medical authority to be bankrupt (see also Bury and Gabe 1994). For example, in Britain in recent years individual doctors have been taken to task in a variety of scandals – the Cleveland child abuse scandal mentioned earlier, the case of the murderous family doctor Harold Shipman, a scandal concerning the storage of dead children's organs at Alder Hey hospital, another involving heart surgeons (again concerning children, significantly enough) in Bristol, whose mistakes were said to have cost lives. Entwistle and Sheldon (1999) list some typical headlines: 'Patients claim they woke during surgery', 'Therapy error in cancer cases', 'Surgeon is suspended over breast operations', 'Disease could be spread by surgical tools'. There are vestiges of the unassailable Dr Kildare in contemporary representations, though, and media health stories – particularly medical soaps – commonly contain images of doctors acting to rescue threatened victims. But in general this source of rescue is as likely to turn sour or dangerous as the villain is to turn good. Like the villain, the professional hero is no longer a secure category.

Instead, emerging in media health stories with particular force in recent years is the figure of the lay hero. Powers are often conferred on this figure that are at least as 'unrealistic' as those conferred on Dr Kildare in an earlier generation. The confessional narrative has become popular over a range of media genres. In relation to cancer and terminal illness, for example, personal accounts abound in which people recount their tribulations and successes in the face of life-threatening disease (McKay and Bonner 1999). These often contain a significant anti-medical component, in which orthodox medicine is cast as unhelpful or flawed. Additionally, lay heroism possesses a significant gendered component, as my own studies of cancer stories in the news have shown (Seale 2002). Women are generally portrayed as more skilful than men in managing their own health, confirming Giddens' observation that women have pioneered the transformation of intimacy that self-identity now involves, largely through the appropriation of emotional skills so that women are 'the emotional revolutionaries of modernity' while men experience a 'lapsed emotional narrative of self' (Giddens 1992: 130). Media health representations have played an important part in this shift, which is associated with a demagogic alliance of media organisations with the supposed interests of ordinary viewers and readers, championing Everyman or woman in the risky environment of modern life. Increasingly widespread involvement by lay people in producing Internet health sites seems likely to increase this tendency.

If sociological studies of health in the media were to become more oriented to understanding production and reception issues, it is likely that a pressing concern would be to understand the consequences of the increased emphasis on lay powers. Analysts might ask, for example, how institutional and governmental interests seek to exploit this apparent 'empowerment' of ordinary people. The development in the United States of 'direct to consumer' advertising by pharmaceutical companies is an example of such commercial exploitation of lay empowerment (Yamey 2001). No longer passively following medical advice, consumers are expected by pharmaceutical companies to respond to media advertisements by demanding particular products from their doctors. The paper by Kroll-Smith in this volume also shows an important way in which mass media, including the Internet, may bypass the influence of health care interests, showing how a new syndrome has been constructed in large part by lay activists with low levels of involvement by medical authorities. The papers in this volume that relate to the Internet show, too, how active consumers may behave, potentially placing the traditional advice of health care system representatives in a less dominant

position. In this changing power relation between professional and lay interests, it is important to understand how media producers and audiences relate
to health-related media messages. This is an important project for sociologists and media studies specialists alike.

Survey of abstracts and papers in this volume

In the light of this somewhat selective account of the media health studies
field it is instructive to survey the actual practice of researchers to examine
where current emphases lie, and where potential progress remains to be
made. To do this, I shall present a brief survey of the 96 abstracts submitted
by people who applied to write a paper for consideration for inclusion in the
current monograph. I shall also draw on my review of the field (Seale 2003)
and will show how the papers in this volume relate to the field as a whole.
In many cases, they were chosen because they point to new directions for
future media health research.

Media studies of health interest researchers internationally. Excluding five
abstracts that turned out not to involve media topics, and based on the
institutional location of the lead author, the most frequent originating country for proposals was the UK (33 abstracts), followed by Australia (19), the
USA (18), and Canada (7). Other countries (Israel, France, the Netherlands,
Spain, Taiwan, South Africa, Brazil, India, Singapore and Japan) produced
15 more abstracts. No doubt the bias towards English language authors and
the UK reflects in part the circulation of the journal, which is edited in the
UK and published in English only. In part, though, it reflects the geographical location of the relevant disciplines which is also reflected in the societies
that authors have studied. For example, we do not, on the whole, know very
much about how the Soviet media presented health matters and how this did
or did not change with the political changes of the last 15 years. Such an
omission might be considered important given the devastating impact on
population health of these upheavals (Seale 2000) and the subsequent slow
recovery (Shkolnikov *et al.* 1998). Nor do we know as much about African
media treatments of HIV/AIDS as we do about Western media depictions
(Watney 1997), there being only a few such studies (for example, Gibson 1994)
in spite of the relatively more devastating impact of this disease in Africa.

The abstracts also confirm the dominance of studies of representation
above those of production and reception. Of course, some studies are not
easy to categorise in this way but a crude categorisation revealed that 64 of
the 91 valid[2] abstracts (70%) involved analysis of representation (58 were
concerned with this alone). 23 (25%) involved analysis of reception and 11
(12%) involved analysis of production (percentages add up to more than
100% since several papers combined two or more dimensions). A large proportion of studies simply referred to 'the media' as a whole as their object
of study, or listed a large range of media types (23 abstracts). Of those with

a more specific focus, studies involving newspapers were most common (26), followed by magazines (15), television (12) the Internet (9), film (6) and health promotion literature (6). There was a tendency for studies focusing on magazines alone (rather than including them under the general 'print media' title) to involve investigation of gender-related issues. The division of magazines into 'men's' and 'women's' was useful for several analysts, with studies of women's magazines being more common than studies of men's. Other media studied included photographs, a theatre play, a piece of computer software, 'confessional' books in which authors told a personal story of illness, and advertisements in health professional journals.

The predominance of studies of representation and, to some extent, of written text (newspapers, magazines, etc.) over images (film, television, photos, etc.) is, in my view, related to the ease with which relevant data can be collected and analysed. Unsurprisingly, almost all of the studies employed a qualitative methodology which may be thought easier to apply to text rather than images. The material needed for studies of production and reception (transcripts of interviews and focus groups for example) are rather onerous to produce as these involve gaining access to settings, approaching and questioning or observing participants, and transcription of the talk that results. All of this is bypassed in studies of media representations, which are all around us and, in the case of many studies, are downloaded from electronic sources (for example, news archives) in electronic form amenable to analysis. The focus on representation is a notable feature in other areas of media studies, probably for the same reasons. As a result, not as much is known about issues of production and reception, with the former being particularly underdeveloped.

The biases evident in the abstracts were also true in my review of published literature. Exceptions in the health field are Karpf's (1988) British study of broadcast media, which provides an institutional analysis of media production of health stories by focusing on the history of the BBC, and Turow's (1989) account of American medical soaps in which relations between media producers and professional medical associations are charted. Miller *et al.* (1998) are notable in presenting a study investigating all three aspects, conceived as a 'circuit of mass communication', focusing on AIDS coverage. But the relative absence of media production studies means that political aspects of media health representations are inadequately understood.

Topics covered in the submitted abstracts were wide ranging, but revealed some more biases. Most notable was the relatively low number of studies investigating media and health policy issues, though this is probably the predominant focus of health news reporting. The lack of interest by media analysts in this area may parallel the rather thin level of interest shown by medical sociologists in the processes of policy making in health care (although there are some notable exceptions, for example, Strong and Robinson 1990). Although the published literature shows that there has been some interest in media coverage of health policy (for example, Entwistle and Sheldon 1999, Miller and Reilly 1995) it is an underdeveloped area. Only five abstracts fell firmly into this category and, in line with the aim of promoting work in hitherto neglected areas, the papers emerging from three of these (Davidson *et al.*, Hodgetts and Chamberlain, Hughes and Griffiths) are published in this monograph. One of these is a study of the news reporting of particular health policy initiatives (Davidson *et al.*); another (Hodgetts and Chamberlain) is a reception study in which links with the 'lay health beliefs' literature, a long-standing area of medical sociology, are made. These two papers also make important contributions to our understanding of media involvement in the health inequalities debate, another topic that has been of considerable interest to medical sociologists. The third paper (Hughes and Griffiths) concerns production and reception issues, being part of an ethnographic study of negotiations in health management organisations, focusing on the way these involve reference to media reporting.

As we have seen, Internet studies were somewhat rare in the submitted abstracts, partly reflecting the novelty of this medium. Such studies often depicted themselves as studies of 'information' rather than representation, sometimes focusing on the use people make of health information on the Internet, so that six of the nine studies of the Internet involved 'reception' analysis of this kind. Given the interest shown by some sociologists in the cultural construction of illness in medical textbooks (for example, Martin 1989) and in medical knowledge generally, as well as the orientation of other media health analysts towards critical social constructionist analyses of media representations, it is surprising that this approach appears not to be pursued by Internet health researchers. Such an approach, of course, is not to be equated with the concern often expressed by medical authorities (Kunst *et al.* 2002) over the issue of the 'accuracy' of health information that is available on-line. Three of the Internet abstracts led to papers that appear in this volume. Henwood *et al.* report on a 'reception' study, in which the focus is not solely on how Internet-based information is used, but on the consequences of having such information for approaches to patienthood. Gillett's is a study of 'production', charting the way in which web-based representations and discussions of HIV-related issues can be understood as a part of a broader social movement in which people with a health condition forge new identities. Kroll-Smith's concerns the cultural construction of a new condition (Excessive Daytime Sleepiness) across a variety of mass media, with the Internet playing an important role in disseminating information that allows people to self diagnose and treat without recourse to orthodox medical care.

The meanings of cyber-space for individuals seeking treatment for phobias are explored in the paper by Davidson and Smith in this volume. Though not about an Internet-based virtual reality, this study shows one possible way forward for Internet studies concerned to understand how this medium may construct health matters. The authors report on the cultural construction of 'nature' involved in such software based treatment programmes.

A significant, though quite small, group of abstracts concerned media representations of approaches to health care and health care workers. Of 13 such studies all but two were concerned with analysis of representations alone. Four of these concerned portrayals of alternative or complementary medicine; a further six concerned medical procedures or therapies that related to an interest in gender, and in particular the situation of women. These studies concerned reproductive technologies, cosmetic surgery and the oral contraceptive pill. The other three concerned medical soaps or dramas, a subject where portrayals of health professionals have been analysed in some detail (see for example, Turow 1989, Kalisch et al. 1983). The study by Davin in this volume is unusual in this literature in so far as it involves exploration of reception issues, comparing medical dramas with documentaries to produce a surprising result about the relative credibility accorded to these.

Health educators and promoters have a long-standing interest in the effects of health-promotion campaigns, including those mounted in the mass media. Health educators have also been at the forefront of concerns about potentially harmful effects of the incidental portrayal of health matters in mass media (for example, Gerbner et al. 1981, Signorielli 1993). Inevitably a proportion of abstracts (roughly 15) reflected these concerns, and these often involved reception studies. This genre of study also provided the few examples of quantitative work. Apart from studies specifically concerned with evaluating the effects of health education campaigns there were several studies that focused on the degree to which particular media forms portray healthy or unhealthy behaviour (for example, very thin female models; smoking; drinking; eating certain things). There were also some studies analysing health promotion literature, usually from a critical point of view. Critical analyses of materials involved in HIV-prevention campaigns were present in the submissions, and are very common in the published literature (for example, Watney 1997).

Another significant group of studies (roughly 12) concerned health risks, such as the media presentation of food scares or infectious disease of various sorts. Some of the published literature in this area concerns the underlying politics of news reporting (for example, Miller and Reilly 1995). However, perhaps the most common category of abstract (roughly 35) concerned studies of media treatments of personal health-related experiences, these often being illnesses. These included, for example, death, sleep, obesity, birth, cancer, suicide, Gulf War Syndrome, Excessive Daytime Sleepiness, old age, genetic disease, ADHD, organ donation, mental illness, accidents, herpes and depression. Selection of studies for this monograph has been guided by criteria of overall quality and originality, focusing in particular on areas that are relatively under-studied at present. But there is also an obligation to reflect the kind of work that is most commonly done in media and health studies. In selecting an example of a study of media representations of personal health experience we are fortunate in having the study by Kroll-Smith (mentioned earlier), which makes important new advances in understanding the medicalisation thesis (Zola 1972) and the analysis presented by Rowe *et al.* on the depiction of depression in Australian print media. This last study presents evidence that contrasts with the finding most usually reported in studies of mental health issues in the media – that these depictions overemphasise the violent and dangerous behaviour of those with mental health conditions (Philo 1996). Instead, depression is presented by media as a problem pervading the everyday lives of 'normal' people.

Evident in any review of the media and health field is the existence of some rather poor-quality studies of media representations. To paint a rather negative imaginary picture, consider the conduct of a study of the media representation of an illness condition that has attracted the attention of a researcher, perhaps through some personal experience that has generated strong feelings. The researcher decides 'the media' are responsible in some way for misinformation, and so a study is required. Rapidly, a great deal of information is collected in the form of news cuttings, tapes of broadcasts and downloaded files. What to do with this unwieldy mass of materials? The researcher is driven by the urge to discover the truth of his or her existing views rather than an interest in the theoretical problems of a parent discipline, or indeed the pragmatic concerns of health policy makers, providers and user groups. Thus the researcher bypasses the laborious business of turning such general considerations into a systematic coding scheme that will organise materials for analysis and facilitate a search for negative instances and analytic depth (Seale 1999). Instead, examples are selected anecdotally that support the analyst's views and a report emerges, that is usually strongly critical of the representations designated as 'dominant', sometimes also sprinkled with extracts from impressively worded social theory, brought in post-hoc as a kind of decoration.

In my selection of studies for this volume I have tried to avoid the publication of such material, so that the collection will serve as an example of studies that have been done to a good methodological standard, as well as showing how this important field of study may be developed in the future.

Acknowledgements

Thanks to Robert Dingwall, Jonathan Gabe, Jenny Kitzinger and Mary Dixon-Woods who all provided helpful comments on an earlier draft of this introduction. My thanks also to the many individuals who submitted abstracts and wrote papers for consideration. I was overwhelmed with the response to this special issue and am sure that many of the papers that could not be included will form excellent publications elsewhere. Numerous referees helped in assessing the papers and I am particularly grateful to referees who did this conscientiously and fairly even though their own abstracts were not accepted for the issue. Allison Pearson, the editorial board of the journal and, once again, Jonathan Gabe and Robert Dingwall provided valuable support throughout the process. My thanks to them all.

Notes

1   A fuller account of the media production processes underlying health stories is available in Seale (2003: Chapter 3) and is only touched on here.
2   Five abstracts turned out not to involve studies of media-related topics.

References

Abercrombie, N. and Longhurst, B. (1998) *Audiences: a Sociological Theory of Performance and Imagination*. London: Sage.
Anderson, B. (1991) *Imagined Communities: Reflections on the Origin and Spread of Nationalism*. London: Verso (2nd Edition).
Armstrong, D. (1983a) The fabrication of nurse-patient relationships, *Social Science and Medicine*, 17, 8, 457–60.
Armstrong, D. (1983b) *Political Anatomy of the Body: Medical Knowledge in Britain in the Twentieth Century*. Cambridge: Cambridge University Press.
Armstrong, D. (1984) The patients' view, *Social Science and Medicine*, 18, 9, 737–44.
Beck, U. (1992) *Risk Society: towards a New Modernity*. London: Sage.
Benthall, J. (1993) *Disasters, Relief and the Media*. London and New York: I.B. Tauris.
Bury, M. and Gabe, J. (1994) Television and medicine: medical dominance or trial by media? In Gabe, J., Kelleher, D. and Williams, G. (eds) *Challenging Medicine*. London: Routledge.
Castells, M. (1996) *The Rise of the Network Society*. Cambridge, MA: Blackwell Publishers.
Dines, G. and Humez, J.M. (eds) (2002) *Gender, Race, and Class in Media: a Text-reader* (2nd Edition). Thousand Oaks, California: Sage.
Dixon-Woods, M., Seale, C., Young, B., Findlay, M. and Heney, D. (2003) Representing childhood cancer: accounts from newspapers and parents, *Sociology of Health and Illness*, 25, 2, 143–64.
Elston, M-A. (1991) The politics of professional power: medicine in a changing health service. In Gabe, J., Calnan, M. and Bury, M. (eds) *The Sociology of the Health Service*. London: Routledge.
Entwistle, V. and Sheldon, T. (1999) The picture of health? Media coverage of the health service. In Franklin, B. (ed) *Social Policy, the Media and Misrepresentation*. London: Routledge.
Franklin, B. (1997) *Newszak and News Media*. London: Arnold.
Furedi, F. (1997) *Culture of Fear: Risk-taking and the Morality of Low Expectation*. London and New York: Cassell.
Gerbner, G., Gross, L., Morgan, M. and Signorielli, N. (1981) Health and medicine on television, *New England Journal of Medicine*, 305, 15, 901–4.
Gibson, M.D. (1994) AIDS and the African press, *Media Culture and Society*, 16, 349–56.
Giddens, A. (1990) *The Consequences of Modernity*. Cambridge: Polity Press.

18   Clive Seale

Giddens, A. (1991) *Modernity and Self-identity: Self and Society in the Late Modern Age*. Cambridge: Polity.

Giddens, A. (1992) *The Transformation of Intimacy*. Cambridge: Polity.

Glasgow University Media Group (1976) *More Bad News*. London: Routledge and Kegan Paul.

Hall, S. (1980) Encoding/decoding. In Hall, S. (ed) *Culture, Media, Language*. London: Hutchinson.

Hill, A. (2000) Fearful and safe: audience response to British reality programming, *Television and New Media*, 1, 2, 193–213.

Kalisch, P.A., Kalisch, B.J. and Scobey, M. (1983) *Images of Nurses on Television*. New York: Springer.

Karpf, A. (1988) *Doctoring the Media: the Reporting of Health and Medicine*. London: Routledge.

Kitzinger, J. (1998) The gender-politics of news production: silenced voices and false memories. In Carter, C., Branston, G. and Allan, G. (eds) *News, Gender and Power*. London: Routledge.

Kitzinger, J. (2000) Media templates: patterns of association and the (re)construction of meaning over time, *Media Culture and Society*, 22, 1, 61–84.

Kunst, H., Groot, D., Latthe, P.M., Latthe, M. and Khan, K.S. (2002) Accuracy of information on apparently credible websites: survey of five common health topics, *British Medical Journal*, 324, 581–2.

Labov, W. (1973) *Language in the Inner City*. Philadelphia: University of Pennysylvania Press.

Langer, J. (1998) *Tabloid Television: Popular Journalism and the 'Other News'*. London: Routledge.

Lawton, J. (2003) Lay experiences of health and illness: past research and future agendas, *Sociology of Health and Illness*, 25, Silver Anniversary Issue, 23–40.

Livingstone, S. and Lunt, P. (1994) *Talk on Television: Audience Participation and Public Debate*. London: Routledge.

Lupton, D. (1994) *Medicine as Culture: Illness, Disease and the Body in Western Societies*. London: Sage.

Martin, E. (1989) *The Woman in the Body: a Cultural Analysis of Reproduction*. Buckingham: Open University Press.

McKay, S. and Bonner, F. (1999) Telling stories: breast cancer pathographies in Australian women's magazines, *Women's Studies International Forum*, 22, 5, 563–71.

Miller, D. and Reilly, J. (1995) Making an issue of food safety: the media, pressure groups and the public sphere. In Maurer, D. and Sobal, J. (eds) *Eating Agendas: Food and Nutrition as Social Problems*. New York: Aldine de Gruyter.

Miller, D., Kitzinger, J., Williams, K. and Beharrell, P. (1998) *The Circuit of Mass Communication: Media Strategies, Representation and Audience Reception in the AIDS Crisis*. London: Sage.

Morley, D. (1986) *Family Television: Cultural Power and Domestic Leisure*. London: Routledge.

Naidoo, J. and Wills, J. (2000) *Health Promotion: Foundations for Practice*. London: Balliere Tindall.

Nelkin, D. (1995) *Selling Science: how the Press Covers Science and Technology*. New York: W.H. Freeman.

Petersen, A. (1994) Governing images: media constructions of the 'normal', 'healthy' subject, *Media Information Australia*, 72, 32–40.

Philo, G. (ed) (1996) *Media and Mental Distress*. London: Longman.

Philo, G. (ed) (1999) *Message Received: Glasgow Media Group Research 1993–1998*. Harlow: Addison Wesley Longman.

Pierret, J. (2003) The illness experience: state of knowledge and perspectives for research, *Sociology of Health and Illness*, 25, Silver Anniversary Issue, 4–22.

Propp, V.I. (1968) *Morphology of the Folk Tale*. Austen: University of Texas Press.

Reinharz, S. (1997) Enough already! The pervasiveness of warnings in everyday life. In Glassner, B. and Hertz, R. (eds) *Qualitative Sociology as Everyday Life*. Thousand Oaks: Sage.

Rose, N. (1999) *Governing the Soul: the Shaping of the Private Self* (2nd Edition), London: Free Association Books.

Schudson, M. (1989) The sociology of news production, *Media, Culture and Society*, 11, 3, 263–82.

Seale, C.F. (1999) *The Quality of Qualitative Research*. London: Sage.

Seale, C.F. (2000) Changing patterns of death and dying, *Social Science and Medicine*, 51, 917–30.

Seale, C.F. (2002) Cancer heroics: a study of news reports with particular reference to gender, *Sociology*, 36, 1, 107–26.

Seale, C.F. (2003) *Media and Health*. London: Sage.

Shkolnikov, L., McKee, M. and Leon, D.A. (2001) Changes in life expectancy in Russia in the mid-1990s, *Lancet*, 357, 9260, 917–21.

Showalter, E. (1987) *The Female Malady: Women, Madness, and English Culture, 1830–1980*. London: Virago.

Signorielli, N. (1993) *Mass Media Images and Impact on Health*. Westport Connecticut: Greenwood Press.

Sparks, C. and Tulloch, J. (eds) (2000) *Tabloid Tales: Global Debates over Media Standards*. London: Rowman and Littlefield.

Strong, P. and Robinson, J. (1990) *The NHS under New Management*. Buckingham: Open University Press.

Turow, J. (1989) *Playing Doctor: Television, Storytelling, and Medical Power*. Oxford and New York: Oxford University Press.

Watney, S. (1997) *Policing Desire: Pornography, AIDS and the Media*. London: Cassell. (3rd Edition).

Yamey, G. (2001) You can always pop a pill, *British Medical Journal*, 322, 804.

Zola, I.K. (1972) Medicine as an institution of social control, *Sociological Review*, 20, 407–504.

Chapter 2

'Radical blueprint for social change'? Media representations of New Labour's policies on public health

Rosemary Davidson, Kate Hunt and Jenny Kitzinger

Introduction

The policy/political background
There has been a long tradition of research on health inequalities in Britain, even predating the publication of the first decennial analysis of occupational mortality in 1855 (Macintyre in 2002). However, the centrality to the political agenda of inequalities and the elimination of poverty has waxed and waned, and the last quarter of the 20th century witnessed a period of marked contrasts in the balance of political priority afforded to the social environment as a cause of ill-health as compared with the 'choices' of individuals.

To understand the health inequalities debate in the UK a brief recent history is useful. In 1977 the Labour Government (of 1974 to 1979) commissioned an inquiry into inequalities in health, but was defeated before the Inquiry, the Black Report (Black *et al.* 1980), was published in 1980 in the early years of Margaret Thatcher's Conservative administration. Only limited copies were printed, in an apparent attempt to place the issues raised far down the political agenda. Although the Black Report did not 'discover' occupational social class gradients in health, it became a landmark in the inequalities debate (Davey Smith *et al.* 1990, Macintyre 1997), both because of the political context, and because the 'health gap' continued to increase in the three decades following its publication (Davey Smith *et al.* 2002). Although health inequalities were squeezed from the policy agenda, there followed a 'boom' of research and debate (with over 40 publications per year on health inequalities in Britain), often using different nomenclature as a form of 'tactical self-censorship . . . to get health inequalities back on the political agenda . . . without antagonising central government' (Macintyre 2002).

After four consecutive Conservative administrations between 1979 and 1997, a policy sea-change around health inequalities was heralded in 1997 when a Labour Government came to power in a landslide victory. An early initiative of the new government was the commissioning, on 10 July 1997, of Sir Donald Acheson to chair an independent inquiry into Inequalities in Health, thus signalling the new administration's concern to be seen to be tackling this issue (Coates 2000, Jones 1996). Ten months after their election, on 5 February 1998, New Labour's first public health Green Papers appeared. These consultative policy documents, *Our Healthier Nation: a Contract for Health* (Department of Health 1998) and its Scottish equivalent *Working Together for a Healthier Scotland* (Scottish Office Department of Health 1998), were published in tandem[1]. Both documents emphasised the link between deprivation and ill-health, accepted the role of wider social influences, and asserted an overriding aim to reduce health inequalities. These 'Green' Papers were transformed into White Papers (final policy documents) in February 1999 (for Scotland) and July 1999 (for England). These four official documents and their public profile in the media are the focus of our study.

The role of the mass media
The media are a key way in which policy enters the public domain. They serve as a major route through which people learn about government initiatives, and the nature of media coverage can inform, although not determine, public understandings (Kitzinger 1999). Over and above this the media are thoroughly integrated into policy making processes in multi-layered ways. Seeking media attention for a Green Paper can be an integral part of 'testing the water' and informing the transition to a White Paper. The media can be used to reach the 'general public', as an arena for playing out internal struggles between government departments or to provoke debates in specific networks of professional or interest groups. Media responses may also be used by policy-makers as a proxy for public reaction (Miller *et al.* 1998). Media coverage is thus not simply a *by-product* of policy initiatives. It can be an integral part of how policy is formed and re-formed as well as how it is packaged in reports and then framed by press releases.

In addition to this complex two-way relationship between the media and policy-making, many factors influence when and how a policy issue is represented in the media. Government can create a 'news event' (writing a policy document and launching a press conference) but they cannot control how this becomes a media 'story'. The nature of any media representation will be mediated through PR practices from competing sources (*e.g.* New Labour and Conservative spokespeople) and the operation of 'news values' (*e.g.* what counts as newsworthy) (Miller *et al.* 1998). Coverage is also influenced by everyday journalistic practices (including practical constraints such as deadlines and word limits) and how journalists envisage their audiences (Alasuutari 1999). These factors are cross cut by differences *between* media, such as the difference between newspapers operating from different political perspectives or addressing different audiences, *e.g.* within the UK the 'English' or 'Scottish' media. Another crucial dimension is the question of time and of context. It is vital to acknowledge that a story which might have attracted peak media interest one day may quickly be overshadowed by other world events. A PR strategy which works at one moment in time may back-fire at another and even the most sophisticated news management can founder on the rock of contemporary events.

Table 1 *Titles and publication dates of the four public health documents*

Document title	Date of publication
Our Healthier Nation: A Contract for Health' (English Green Paper)	5 February 1998
Working Together for a Healthier Scotland. *A Consultation Document* (Scottish Green Paper)	5 February 1998
Towards a Healthier Scotland. A White Paper on Health (Scottish White Paper)	17 February 1999
Saving Lives: Our Healthier Nation (English White Paper)	5 July 1999

Methods

Our study was designed to examine how New Labour policy entered the public domain via the mass media. In keeping with the policy background and the insights from media sociology referenced above this was explored at several levels. The study examined both the *English* and the *Scottish* policy documents and included the transition from *Green* to *White* Papers. The content of each of the four official reports and their associated press releases were reviewed in detail. Particular note was taken of all references to inequality, the language used to describe inequalities and the influence of social factors on health, and the extent to which government rhetoric surrounding inequalities related to the 'main goals' of policy.

We also examined the press coverage (in both the UK national (English-based) *and* the Scottish press) of each report for 28 days from the publication date. The analysis thus covered three periods across an 18-month time span (see Table 1). Lack of resources precluded a parallel analysis of the TV news.

The national daily 'UK' papers examined were the *Guardian, Independent, Times, Daily Telegraph* (all broadsheets[2]) and the *Sun, Mirror, Daily Mail, Daily Star, Daily Express* (all tabloids). We also examined their sister Sunday papers: *Observer, Independent on Sunday, Sunday Times, Sunday Telegraph, Sunday Mirror, Sunday Express,* and *Mail on Sunday*. The Scottish news-papers included in the study were the *Scotsman* and *Herald* (broadsheets) and their Sunday sister papers (*Scotland on Sunday* and *Sunday Herald*) as well as the Scottish daily tabloid: *The Daily Record*. A Glasgow-based tabloid, the *Evening Times*, was also included.

Each paper was scrutinised for coverage of the four documents. All such items (62 items in total) were subjected to detailed content analysis. The format, page number, headline of each item (see Tables 2 to 5) and journalist's specialism were recorded. Note was taken of images and captions used, and the space allocated to each item. We analysed which aspects of the official documents were reported, the tone of each item, which sources were quoted and the degree of emphasis placed on inequalities. Competing news stories and the broader news context were also noted.

Findings

The following discussion examines each official document in turn, in the chronological order in which they appeared, along with its associated press release and media coverage.

The 1998 English and Scottish Green Papers on public health

The Green Papers and their press releases
The main long-term targets outlined in the English Green Paper (Department of Health 1998) were to continue to reduce premature mortality from coronary heart disease (CHD), stroke and cancer, and to reduce accidents and suicide. The Scottish Green Paper (Scottish Office Department of Health 1998) did not explicitly propose targets, but outlined 'priority health topics' (CHD, stroke, cancer, mental health, sexual health, dental and oral health, and accidents and safety). As part of the move towards 'joined-up government', a number of initiatives were outlined including health impact assessments of key policies and Health Action Zones (in England) and Health Improvement Programmes (in Scotland).

Whilst many of these targets were similar to those identified by the previous Conservative government, New Labour sought to distance itself from the previous administration's 'victim blaming approach'. For example, the English Green Paper stated that past efforts to improve health had been 'too much about blame. Individuals were to blame for failing to listen to well-intentioned but misdirected health advice' (paragraph 3.1). The Scottish Green Paper described the Conservatives' prescription for improving health as 'limited, mainly because of its reluctance to acknowledge the social, economic and environmental causes of ill health' (paragraph 4.12), and as oscillating between two extremes '. . . individual victim blaming on the one hand and nanny state social engineering on the other' (Department of Health 1998: Summary and paragraph 3.2).

The Green Papers made extensive reference to inequalities both in terms of rhetoric used and initiatives proposed. The English Green Paper's summary stated that 'Health inequalities are widening. The poorest in our society are hit harder than the well off by most of the major causes of death . . . a key priority will be better health for those who are worst off' (DOH 1998: Summary p. 4). The Paper went on to refer explicitly to inequalities on more than 50 occasions, and several tables and figures presented data on inequalities by class, area and gender. The Scottish Green Paper described the 'root causes of our health problems' as 'poverty, unemployment and the environment' (Scottish Office Department of Health 1998: para. 1) and referred to health inequalities on 39 occasions. It emphasised the government's 'overall determination to tackle inequality and create opportunity' (Scottish Office Department of Health 1998: para. 2.35) and described health inequalities in Scotland as 'unacceptable', and their reduction as an 'overarching priority' in each of the Priority Health Topic areas.

The press release for the English Green Paper emphasised the need for a 'balance between Government action, local action and informed individual action in improving health: the third way for public health', and retained a focus on inequalities. The opening paragraph of the press release described the two principal aims of the English Green Paper as 'Extending years of fit and healthy life for us all and tackling inequalities in health'. The third paragraph stated that 'Tackling inequality sits at the heart of this Government's promise of a modern and fair Britain'.

The press release for the Scottish Green Paper, entitled 'Helping Scots to live a life less ordinary', opened with a vision of a 'self-confident Scot free from the spectre of poverty, unemployment, shabby housing and pollution. . . . [who will] choose life rather than being forced into ill-health'. Making a clear reference to national identity with the impending establishment of the Scottish parliament, the title and opening sentence borrowed phrasing from two recent films, 'A Life Less Ordinary' and 'Trainspotting', featuring Scottish actor Ewan McGregor. Findings from the Scottish Health Survey were included to demonstrate that 'people disadvantaged by poverty, unemployment, poor housing and poor environment live shorter lives in poorer health'. Two examples (variations in premature deaths in Lothian, and the stark contrast between mortality in 'prosperous Bearsden' and the contiguous 'struggling' Drumchapel) were given as 'compelling proof that deprivation is linked to ill health'.

The press coverage of the Green Papers
    a. Press coverage of the English Green Paper. Five newspapers covered the English Green Paper (EGP), involving 10 news reports and one editorial (Table 2). There were some diverse trends evident in the coverage depending on the paper's traditional political stance as outlined below.

The *Guardian*, a left-of-centre broadsheet, was most supportive of the proposed government initiatives. It strongly endorsed the Green Paper's acknowledgement of a link between poverty and ill health and its three news reports (EGP4, 5 and 6) constructed the document as a very positive step in the right direction. Its leading article highlighted the Government's intention to focus on 'the greatest inequality of them all', reproducing data and rhetoric from the English Green Paper itself. However, quotes from interviewees used in the article balanced this praise against criticisms over lack of target-setting and resources. The paper's editorial (EGP7) reinforced such criticisms and concluded that 'There must be a specific commitment to close the gap'.

The *Independent*, which presents itself as independent of the traditional left/right political divide, also communicated the inequalities debate clearly,

Table 2 *Details of items reporting on the English Green Paper*

no.	Date	Format	Paper	Page no.	Headline
EGP1	5/2/98	news report	Independent	5	Fluoride fear condemns children to tooth decay
EGP2	6/2/98	news report	Independent	6	Four goals for healthier Britain could save 15,000 lives
EGP3	6/2/98	news report	Independent	6	A shot in the arm for campaign trail
EGP4	6/2/98	news report	Guardian	10	Dobson pledges to cut illness gap
EGP5	6/2/98	news report	Guardian	10	Targets: four leading causes of early death
EGP6	6/2/98	news report	Guardian	10	There's a complex mesh of factors that cause poor health, but poverty is the key to it
EGP7	6/2/98	editorial	Guardian	18	Prevention is better than cure
EGP8	6/2/98	news report	Daily Telegraph	8	Labour 'ends the Nanny State' with new health targets
EGP9	6/2/98	news report	Daily Telegraph	8	Success 'is dependent on rationing resources'
EGP10	6/2/98	news report	The Times	3	Dobson starts a class war to improve health
EGP11	6/2/98	news report	Daily Express	19	Now nanny backs off in health war

but was more critical. The *Independent's* coverage drew less on the Government's rhetoric (as expressed in the Green Papers and press releases) than other newspapers (whether 'left' or 'right' wing). Rather than praising the shift in emphasis in Government policy, the *Independent* referred to the 'uncanny resemblance' to earlier policy (EGP3), and highlighted gaps in the new strategy, such as the failure to set targets to reduce the inequalities (EGP2) in other key areas (such as teenage pregnancy). Although acknowledging that Ministers were awaiting the results of the Acheson Inquiry, one item described discussion of inequalities in the Green Paper as 'confined to three paragraphs'.

Coverage in the traditionally right-wing newspapers was subtly different again. The three right-of-centre newspapers which covered the English Green Paper (*Telegraph, Times* and *Express*) all clearly outlined the Government's aims to narrow 'the health gap between rich and poor' but tended less often to explicitly use the term 'inequality'. They did, however, directly quote from Frank Dobson's statements at the press conference and acknowledged the main aims and underlying thesis. The *Telegraph*, for example, declared that the Government were now taking 'on board social problems, poor housing, unemployment and low pay which [are] linked to illness' (EGP8). Interestingly, however, even in presenting this initiative the *Express* described this as being the 'first time' ill health had been linked to social problems (a bizarre observation in the light of the long history of research outlined above).

The contrast between New Labour and the previous Conservative administration was also acknowledged in these reports. Indeed, two of the right-of-centre newspapers picked up on the English Green Paper's challenge to 'nannying'. The *Daily Telegraph* item 'Labour "ends the Nanny State" with new health targets' said that the document 'does not tell people what to eat or drink'. The news report in the *Daily Express* noted that the Government wished to distance itself from the Conservative's 'nanny state' alongside a large picture of a reproachful, finger-wagging nanny (EGP11). At the same time, however, some of the reporting seemed to reiterate the importance of individual behaviour. A sizeable proportion of an article in the *Times* was devoted to the views of the Conservative Shadow Health Secretary, who reasserted the importance of behavioural factors rather than life circumstances in causing ill health. The *Express* article concluded by placing the emphasis firmly back on lifestyle choices, noting that Britain was 'still a nation of junk food junkies who take little exercise' (EGP11).

Perhaps even more interesting is the subtle way in which readers were positioned by the *Times* and *Telegraph* (both right-of-centre and up-market publications). There was some implication in reporting in both these newspapers that readers might not wish to sympathise with proposed strategies to address the 'health gap'. The *Telegraph* featured comments from Mr Thornton of the NHS Confederation on the moral and ethical questions raised by plans to focus health care on the most needy, and declared that: 'Targeting resources in a cash-limited system means robbing Peter to pay

Paul. In this case Paul lives in a poor community and has no voice. Peter is middle class, vocal and articulate' (EGP9). The clear intent is that the paper's readership would identify themselves with someone more like 'Peter' and identify the threats inherent to them in this change in policy emphasis. This was echoed in the *Times'* headline, 'Dobson starts a class war to improve health' (EGP10), which intimated that their readers might be the victims, rather than recipients, of the proposed policies.

   b. Press coverage of the Scottish Green Paper. The publication of the Scottish Green Paper (SGP) was covered in four newspapers, involving eight news reports and two editorials (see Table 3), all in Scottish-based newspapers or Scottish editions of UK national newspapers. The coverage featured less comment-based or context-setting articles than the coverage of its English counterpart (where it has one) and was generally more positive in tone. Half of the items focused on Scotland's 'appalling health record' (*e.g.* SGP1, SGP5). The Government's recognition of a link between deprivation and ill health and their targeting of inequalities in health were communicated most strongly in the *Scotsman* and *Herald*, as were the Paper's key initiatives. These Scotland-based broadsheets embraced the complex linkage of both lifestyle and life circumstances to ill health. The *Scotsman* described the 'move away from the last administration's [victim-blaming] approach' (SGP1), whilst the *Herald* went further and firmly positioned the newspaper as a champion of the Government's cause. Their item 'United for a healthier future' (SGP4) stated how the Labour doctrine was epitomised in the Scottish Green Paper: 'Lecturing people on their lifestyles is futile while they are unemployed, illiterate and living in slums'. The Government's proposals were put into context with reference to the Black Report which was described as 'strangled at birth' by the Thatcher administration. This perspective was coupled with the sense of a radical shift of political direction, as the link between poverty and sickness gained recognition after '19 years of denial'.

   The Scottish edition of the right-of-centre tabloid, the *Daily Mail*, included just one item buried deep within the paper (SGP8). It communicated the Government's emphasis on inequalities by drawing on statistics in the press release and excerpts from the Scottish Health Minister's launch speech. It described the approach as a 'significant shift' from the Conservative Government's linkage of lifestyle to ill health. Much of its coverage, however, emphasised health behaviours, reinforced by an image of a man riding a bike and an insert entitled 'Habits that are killing us'.

   Surprisingly, given the pattern in the left-of-centre coverage of the English Green Paper, the *Mirror's* (a left-of-centre tabloid) coverage centred more clearly still on health behaviours (SGP9, 10). Even initiatives that were hailed by the Government as routes to reducing health inequalities, such as Healthy Living Centres, were framed in terms of health behaviours. As a consequence, the reduction of health inequalities was absent from the *Mirror's* coverage, although the Government's intention to tackle poverty was communicated.

Table 3 Details of items reporting on the Scottish Green Paper

no.	Date	Format	Paper	Page no.	Headline
SGP1	5/2/98	news report	Scotsman	2	Scottish health action plan to target poverty
SGP2	6/2/98	news report	Scotsman	1	Living in Glasgow takes 5 years off your life
SGP3	6/2/98	news report	Scotsman	12	War on root causes of ill health
SGP4	6/2/98	news report	Herald	7	United for a healthier future
SGP5	6/2/98	news report	Herald	7	Homes and jobs to build a better tomorrow
SGP6	6/2/98	news report	Herald	7	Network of centres funded by lottery windfall
SGP7	6/2/98	editorial	Herald	22	Far from a panacea
SGP8	6/2/98	news report	Daily Mail	28–29	Wealth is the key to health, says Dr Galbraith
SGP9	6/2/98	news report	Mirror	4	£300 m plan to help Scots live longer
SGP10	6/2/98	editorial	Mirror	6	A healthy future for the nation

Explicit criticism of the Green Paper in any newspaper was rather tame. The *Scotsman* made a muted observation about the absence of targets for reducing inequalities and the *Herald's* editorial expressed doubts about whether the Government was sufficiently committed in its allocation of resources to solving Scotland's health problems ('. . . we seriously wonder whether a combination of lottery funding, windfall taxation, and raiding a reduced Scottish block is the panacea') but that was all.

The Scottish White Paper: *'Towards a Healthier Scotland'*

The Scottish White Paper and its press release
The Scottish White Paper (SWP) was released a year after the Green Paper. Inequalities were referred to throughout, and were given prominence from the opening sentences: 'Being well is part of the pattern of opportunity and achievement we want for Scotland, as we start a new century. Being ill makes inequalities between people and groups in Scotland worse, and harder to bear' (SWP: v). The first Chapter described how the consultation process facilitated by the Scottish Green Paper 'revealed . . . agreement that we should no longer tolerate inequalities in health', and Chapter 2 stated that 'Inequality breeds despondency and pessimism, and health suffers'. The use of inclusive language ('we', 'our') in the document reflects its historical placing after the *Scotland Act 1998* providing for the establishment of a Scottish Parliament received Royal Assent in November 1998 and before the first elections to the new Parliament in May 1999.

The Scottish White Paper presented three Action Levels (life circumstances, lifestyles and health topics) and had an 'overarching aim' to tackle inequalities (SWP: 7). For each 'Headline Target' (reduction of CHD and stroke, smoking, alcohol misuse, teenage pregnancy and poor dental health), the White Paper described how the 'inequalities gap' would be 'regularly measured to assess progress in reducing the disparity in health status between different socio-economic groups' (SWP: 8). The third Chapter closed by stating that 'Together, pursued strongly, all these initiatives will reduce inequalities and help to change lives in ways that are conducive to good health' (SWP: 17). Inequalities were also mentioned in relation to smoking (SWP: 20) and child health (SWP: 26), the role of Government (SWP: 36), the NHS (SWP: 36, 38) and Local Government (SWP: 40), Health Demonstration Projects (SWP: 48), and 'Research, Evaluation, Targets and Monitoring (SWP: 54–5). By the conclusion, the document stated what was already clear:

> The White Paper refers repeatedly to the overriding importance of tackling health inequality and describes a comprehensive and co-ordinated use of health resources, relevant agencies and a raft of social and economic measures which will sustain the drive for better health for all our people.

Table 4 *Details of items reporting on the Scottish White Paper*

no.	Date	Format	Paper	Page no.	Headline
SWP1	18/2/99	news report	Herald	1 & 8	Fight to stub out ill health
SWP2	18/2/99	news report	Herald	8	Screen test a life saver
SWP3	18/2/99	news report	Herald	8	Curing the smoking habit on the NHS
SWP4	18/2/99	news report	Herald	8	Poverty
SWP5	18/2/99	news report	Herald	8	Young people
SWP6	18/2/99	news report	Herald	8	Alcohol
SWP7	18/2/99	editorial	Herald	18	Health of the nation
SWP8	18/2/99	news report	Scotsman	5	Government's cure for sick Scots
SWP9	18/2/99	news report	Daily Mail	6	A pinch of salt to put back sparkle in children's smiles
SWP10	18/2/99	news report	Daily Mail	6	More money on table for under-age sex clinics
SWP11	18/2/99	news report	Daily Record	9	We'll improve health from 'womb to grave'
SWP12	18/2/99	news report	Mirror	2	Labour takes on killers
SWP13	18/2/99	editorial	Mirror	6	Heartening attack on big killers
SWP14	18/2/99	news report	Sun	2	Milk to contain fluoride

Whereas inequalities were conspicuously absent in the press release for the Scottish *Green* Paper, they were clearly highlighted in the Scottish *White* Paper's press release. Although it gave prominence to the health of children and young people, cancer and CHD, the press release described how 'too many lives [are] scarred by the unmistakable stamp of poverty and deprivation', and focused on the Government's demonstration projects which, as 'cutting edge . . . beacons of best-practice and innovation', were described as all having a 'specific focus on tackling inequalities'. An 'all-encompassing attack on the health inequalities between Scotland's well-off and deprived communities' was also detailed as a 'key measure' of the new strategy.

Press coverage of the Scottish White Paper
The Scottish White Paper was covered by 12 news reports and two editorials (Table 4). Again coverage was confined to the Scottish-based broadsheets (*Herald* and *Scotsman*), a Scottish tabloid (*Daily Record*), and Scottish editions of UK national tabloids (*Daily Mail, Mirror, Sun*). The most extensive reporting (six news reports and an editorial) appeared in the *Herald*.

In contrast to the coverage of the Scottish *Green* Paper, no specific theme pervaded the coverage and there was less of an emphasis on Scotland's 'appalling' health record. Most items concentrated on specific policies, but there appeared to be little relationship between the political stance of the newspaper and the initiatives covered, perhaps because of a degree of anticipation pre-dating the first elections to the new Parliament. Political sources were given prominence in commentaries on the White Paper. The impending Scottish elections provoked passionate responses from political spokespersons, all critical of aspects of Government policy, and various health professionals and interest groups were cited as critical of the White Paper. These criticisms tended to be directed at specific initiatives rather than the document as a whole.

The strong stance taken by the Scottish White Paper (and its press release) on poverty and inequality did not transfer into the press reporting. The UK tabloids, the *Daily Mail, Mirror*, and *Sun*, made no reference to inequalities. Even newspapers which had previously highlighted this issue allowed it to slip down their agenda. The *Scotsman*, for example, which had referred to health inequalities frequently in its Green Paper coverage, did not mention the issue in its reporting of the White Paper. Indeed, the Government's intention to tackle health inequalities was communicated in only one item (in the *Daily Record*, SWP11).

The English White Paper, '*Saving Lives: Our Healthier Nation*'

The English White Paper and its press release
The UK Government published its long awaited White Paper on public health for England Wales 17 months after unveiling their initial proposals in the

Green Papers and seven months after the Scottish White Paper. The overriding aim of the English White Paper's (EWP) 'action plan' laid out in the policy document was to improve the health of everyone, and of the worst off in particular (Department of Health 1999: viii, Executive Summary). It highlighted 'tougher' targets aimed at preventing 300,000 'untimely and unnecessary deaths' from cancer, CHD, stroke, accidents, and suicide by 2010, and called for a 'new balance' in which people, communities and Government worked together in 'partnerships' to improve health. It noted the 'potency' of social, economic and environmental factors in the production of ill-health, but that people could 'make individual decisions about their own and their families' health which can make a difference'. The White Paper devoted a Chapter to each of its four principal health targets, and one on 'wider action' on sexual health, drugs, alcohol, the 'genetics revolution', and the health of minority ethnic groups.

Health inequalities were referred to on over 50 occasions. The Executive Summary described how 'widespread' inequalities resulted in the disadvantaged having 'suffered the most from poor health'. In the main body, health inequalities were addressed in Chapter four, 'Communities: tackling the wider causes of ill health'. Paragraph 4.4 stated that: 'The impact that could be made by an attack on inequality is clear. For example, if the death rates of all men of working age were the same as those in professional and managerial jobs, about 17,000 deaths would be avoided each year . . .'. A section on 'Evening up opportunity' described the Government's commitment to tackling social exclusion (EWP: 4.10). Another linked low income with ill health and outlined reforms to guarantee a minimum income (EWP: 4.13). Paragraph 4.16 stated that 'by improving education for all we will tackle one of the main causes of inequality in health'. Further initiatives for reducing health inequalities were featured under 'Housing and Health' (EWP: 4.28–4.31), 'Homelessness' (EWP: 4.32–4.33), 'Healthy Neighbourhoods' (EWP: 4.34–4.40), 'Environment and Health' (EWP: 4.41–4.44), and 'Health Impact Assessment' (EWP: 4.45–4.47).

However, although health inequalities were referred to in a number of policy areas, their subtle marginalisation could be inferred in the publication of an 'action plan', addressing the 'social, economic and environmental factors and the part they play in poor health', *separate* from the main body of public health policy. Details of this plan were confined to two sentences in the White Paper (EWP: 4.6). Thus, between publication of the English Green and White Papers, health inequalities had slipped down the policy agenda, and initiatives to reduce and monitor inequalities were somewhat overshadowed.

This downgrading of the health inequalities focus was also reflected in the press release, 'Biggest Ever Crusade for Health to Cut Preventable Deaths by 300,000 Within Ten Years', which detailed the proposals for improving health featured in the White Paper and the four 'significantly tougher' health targets. Reference to health inequalities was restricted to one statement about 'the most comprehensive plan to tackle smoking ever' which asserted that '. . . smoking is the single greatest cause of preventable death and health inequality'. The separate health inequality 'action plan' was mentioned only at the end of the press release in the 'Notes to Editors' which stated that media copies of *Reducing Health Inequality* were available from the Department of Health Press Office.

The press reporting of the English White Paper

Of the four documents studied, the English White Paper received most press attention. Seven different newspapers covered the story through 13 news reports, five editorials, four feature articles, four columns, and one letter (see Table 5). All the England-based UK national broadsheets ran stories on the English White Paper, as did one Scottish-based broadsheet, the *Scotsman*, and one Sunday newspaper, the *Sunday Times*. The *Daily Express* was the only tabloid to cover the report.

As with coverage of the English *Green* Paper, the most consistently reported area was the commitment to reduce mortality rates in the four target areas and save an estimated 300,000 lives. However, the trend observed in earlier reporting of the English Green Paper that left-of-centre newspapers highlighted initiatives targeted at the deprived, whereas those right of centre reported on more behaviour-based proposals, appeared to have all but disappeared. Instead, all newspapers reporting on the White Paper tended to concentrate their coverage on defibrillators, accident prevention and first-aid training, and Public Health Observatories. Initiatives designed to reduce inequalities received far less attention.

The coverage also conveyed a much more precarious political climate than had prevailed when the Green Papers were launched. The English White Paper was published in a week awash with medical and health-related controversies. Discussion of the English White Paper was inextricably linked with the NHS (a situation compounded by the timing of the British Medical Association's [BMA] annual conference). This included a controversy about organ donation when a hospital agreed to accept kidneys donated for use only in white patients, pleas for changes to the working conditions of junior doctors, and accusations that Blair was 'alienat[ing] the entire medical profession'. Comments were overwhelmingly critical in tone, as, for example, 'Labour, like the Tories in power before them, is on the rack over the NHS', and Labour's 'honeymoon' with the public sector unions and health profession was proclaimed to be 'over' (EWP26). Political and professional unrest was briefly touched upon in the *Guardian* and was the subject of a number of items in the *Daily Telegraph*. Frank Dobson, at that time Minister for Health, was described in the *Guardian* as an 'avowed populist who is keen to avoid charges of being a "food fascist" ', but the final draft of *Saving Lives* was described as the subject of 'protracted tussles' with Tessa Jowell, the Public Health Minister. The *Guardian* also described 'unrest' in the medical profession over the proposals for NHS Direct, a telephone helpline, and the English White Paper's policies were portrayed as crucial in their potential

Table 5 Details of items reporting on the English White Paper

no.	Date	Format	Paper	Page no.	Headline
EWP1	6/7/99	news report	Guardian	2	Public to operate heart machines
EWP2	6/7/99	news report	The Times	1	Children to have lessons in avoiding accidents
EWP3	6/7/99	news report	The Times	24	Safety lessons for children
EWP4	7/7/99	news report	Independent	1	Outrage as Blair attacks public sector
EWP5	7/7/99	column	Independent	8	An unhealthy dose of bile from ratty Frank Dobson
EWP6	7/7/99	editorial	Independent (Weds Review)	3	The people's road to hell is paved with government advice
EWP7	7/7/99	news report	Guardian	6	Children to assist in crusade to save lives
EWP8	7/7/99	column	Guardian	8	Dobson's throat-clearing raises blood pressures
EWP9	7/7/99	editorial	Guardian	19	Our national health
EWP10	7/7/99	news report	Daily Telegraph	1	Public may vote on putting fluoride in tap water
EWP11	7/7/99	news report	Daily Telegraph	2	Dobson reveals longer hospital waiting lists
EWP12	7/7/99	news report	Daily Telegraph	6	Big five killers targeted to save 300,000 lives
EWP13	7/7/99	editorial	Daily Telegraph	25	Rising temperatures
EWP14	7/7/99	column	The Times	2	Dobson sees his political life threatened by loss of health
EWP15	7/7/99	news report	The Times	8	Dobson's £96m crusade to help poor live longer
EWP16	7/7/99	news report	The Times	8	Going public to save heart-attack victims
EWP17	7/7/99	news report	The Times	8	Wartime diet is recipe for better national health
EWP18	7/7/99	editorial	The Times	21	Not Frank Enough
EWP19	7/7/99	news report	Daily Express	8	Dobson targets the four deadly scourges to save 300,000 lives
EWP20	8/7/99	column	Guardian	20	Corporate causes of cancer
EWP21	8/7/99	feature	Scotsman	17	Frankly, Dobbo, it's a fiasco
EWP22	9/7/99	news report	Editor (Guardian)	5	Doctors are sick of Labour
EWP23	10/7/99	feature	Daily Telegraph	21	Running for mayor may be bad for one's health
EWP24	11/7/99	feature	Sunday Times	12–13	The sickness at the heart of our NHS
EWP25	11/7/99	feature	Sunday Times	13	Resource gaps turn healthcare into a lottery
EWP26	11/7/99	editorial	Sunday Times	16	An unhealthy state
EWP27	12/7/99	letter	Independent (Monday Review)	2	Cold comfort

impact, 'with Tony Blair anxious to signal to Labour's wavering "core voters" that his team is delivering on their agenda'. The *Daily Telegraph* devoted significant column inches to the perceived backlash against Labour at the BMA's conference and an item on the English White Paper (EWP12) was overshadowed by two other health related stories on health reforms and hospital strikes. The *Daily Express* also reported on the English White Paper amidst three stories describing a health service in crisis, all placed under the banner 'SUICIDE, HEART DISEASE, ACCIDENTS AND CANCER TO BE TACKLED BUT HEALTH STAFF STILL SUFFER'. The headline to one adjacent item read 'Junior doctors could earn more at McDonald's'. The *Independent's* front page article (EWP1) framed the story in a similar way: 'As the Government launched a White Paper setting out targets for cutting deaths from cancer and heart disease, anger at the long hours and poor pay suffered by junior doctors spilled over again at the BMA's annual conference'.

In contrast to the previous sample periods, political uncertainty and cynicism were reflected in openly hostile headlines. Reference was drawn to the wider political context with the headlines 'Outrage as Blair attacks public sector' (EWP4) and 'Doctors are sick of Labour' (EWP22). Other headlines focused on Dobson's launch speech and included 'Dobson's throat-clearing raises blood pressures' (EWP8), 'An unhealthy dose of bile from ratty Frank Dobson' (EWP5), and 'Frankly, Dobbo, it's a fiasco' (EWP21).

The *Times, Guardian* and *Independent* all devoted political columns to the English White Paper. These placed heavy emphasis on Dobson's mood at the despatch box and his seemingly precarious job situation. Under the headline 'Dobson sees his political life threatened by loss of health' the writer asks 'Who rattled Frank Dobson's cage?' (EWP14). The 'normally jovial' Dobson was described as in a 'foul mood' as he delivered 'one of those lacklustre preventative healthcare statements that come around in every parliament and sink without trace'. Of Dobson's Commons statement, the columnist observed 'How well [Frank Dobson] knows the first law of Ministerial statements: the more frequent the occurrence of "action" or "tackle", the less is promised'. In the *Daily Telegraph* (EWP23) Dobson was described as 'griping and grumbling all week, snapping on the radio and sniping at the despatch box'. The *Guardian* (EWP8) noted how he had 'cleared his tubes in the morning by being nasty to Sue McGregor on the *Today* programme' (a daily news and current affairs radio programme) and 'disgorged the remainder of the bile-filled mucus in the chamber after lunch'. The furious exchanges between MPs were detailed as the columnist commented: 'There's nothing like a discussion on Our Healthier Nation to get everyone so fighting mad that, if the scenes had taken place in a pub near closing time, someone would have prudently called the ambulances before the glassing began'.

The mood of the Commons was reflected in the very critical pen of the columnist in the *Independent's* political sketch (EWP5). According to the columnist, Dobson opted for 'bile with a smile, the rictus in question being one of those tense grimaces with which ministers try to pretend that opposition attacks are risibly predictable' after a well publicised 'monstering' by the chairman of the BMA. Further negativity toward the Government was communicated with such headlines as 'The peoples' road to hell is paved with Government advice' (EWP6), 'An unhealthy state' (EWP26) and 'Resource gaps turn healthcare into a lottery' (EWP25). Serious doubt was expressed in such items about whether the rhetoric surrounding the Government's public health strategy would be translated into action, reflecting wider concerns about the rising dominance of political 'spin' (Franklin 1998, 2000, Esser *et al.* 2000). The *Scotsman* (EWP21) described the Government as 'so often . . . tough-minded in analysis but weak in delivery'. Policies such as those on the Health Action Zones were dismissed as 'guff, no extra money on public health and more guff'.

Amongst this negative focus on the Government's achievements and Dobson's own position and mood, some emphasis on the inequalities debate did permeate through. The Government's avowed intentions to tackle inequalities were communicated clearly, albeit against a much more openly critical and cynical backdrop. Running through all coverage, at the very least, was the reporting of Government rhetoric surrounding health inequalities (although only one headline (EWP15) referred to the Government's targeting of the 'health of the less well-off').

Different aspects of the reporting of health inequalities in previous periods came together in the English White Paper sample period. The Government's voice was heard thanks to Dobson's personal conviction surrounding the issue and reference to statistics demonstrating health inequalities. Furthermore, a political dialogue on the subject was prominent with the ensuing inequalities debates reported between the Health Minister and spokespersons from other major political parties.

Thus, in their coverage of the English White Paper, the UK national press entered more critically into the inequalities debate rather than merely relaying the Government line. This is in contrast to coverage in the earlier sample periods, particularly following the publication of the Green Papers, when journalists had a tendency either to ignore the Government's message or report it with a less critical eye. The notable absence of tabloid coverage, however, meant that a whole section of the print media, the section with the largest readership, went without reporting on inequalities at all.

Discussion

Although 'health' stories are seen as newsworthy and 'newspapers are an obvious constant source of information about health and medical issues' (Chapman and Lupton 1994: 28), little of the burgeoning interest in health and the media has focused on media presentations of health *policy*. The above analysis tracking four official documents discussing policy measures to improve health and reduce health inequalities, and their reception by the media, has charted a shifting discussion of health inequalities, both between official documents and as they have been represented in diverse press outlets. A clear trajectory is apparent across the 17-month time period under study, reflecting shifting relations between the Government and the press in the UK over this period.

By the time New Labour came to power, there was an impatience that much of the evidence on health inequalities accumulated since the publication of the Black Report should be translated into policy action. Immediately prior to New Labour's landslide victory in 1997, there had been much comment on the realignment of the support from various newspapers of the main political parties and New Labour's public wooing of sections of the tabloid press which had often had more right-wing allegiances (Franklin 2000). Some of this apparent enthusiasm (or at least expectant tolerance) for the new government was reflected in the relatively favourable coverage that the Green Papers on public health received when they were published in 1998. All the newspapers which covered the story included some acknowledgement of the Government's attention to the role of poverty in the aetiology of ill health and their move away from a 'victim-blaming' or 'nanny-state' approach. They all also, superficially at least, appeared to support elements of the initiative. However, the seeds of a more critical reception from the newsprint media were present in disquiet at the lack of targets for reducing health inequalities.

By the time the English White Paper was published, more criticism of New Labour was communicated. Although the government's targeting of premature mortality in key areas and its aim to reduce health inequalities were reported, this emphasis was overshadowed by a more hostile backdrop characterised by open scepticism about the government's willingness to see its policies through. Much of the coverage also focused on scathing personal comment on the composure and likely fate of the Health Minister as he launched the new policy on public health. By this stage, few vestiges of the expectations of a 'radical blueprint for social change' remained.

Time and shifting political and news story context is not the only variable here. There were also clear differences between different sections of the press. Diversity was evident between the 'English' and 'Scottish' presses with the latter more attuned to the issue of national identity. This may have been particularly relevant in this debate because of Scotland's particular position within the health inequalities hierarchy, and especially important at this time with the impending establishment of a new Scottish parliament. There were also differences between broadsheet and tabloid coverage, with the health inequalities debate gaining more prominence in the former. Perhaps the most interesting differences of all relate to the newspapers' diverse traditional political affiliations. Generally, across all the reporting, the (traditionally more left-wing) *Guardian* offered the clearest *support* for the Government initiatives, and the *Independent* offered the most thorough *challenge* (within the context of a belief in the importance of addressing inequality). By contrast, the traditionally more right-wing press, while apparently conceding that it was a 'good idea' to tackle health inequalities, subtly undercut the message. They achieved this through a tendency to re-emphasise the importance of individual health behaviour (*e.g.* by use of images and quotes) even while reporting health inequalities. They also sometimes addressed readers as if they were the potential victims of any such reforms, whilst the presumed beneficiaries were invisible or presented in abstract terms.

If tackling health inequalities was a flagship issue for New Labour then it has faced some rough seas. The alleged alliance between sections of the media and New Labour forged in the mid-1990s did not last long. The fate of reporting on the White Papers echoes a media disenchantment with the new Government which has become progressively evident across a whole ream of policy initiatives and press reporting whereby journalists proclaim against government 'spin' (Esser *et al.* 2000) and challenge New Labour's integrity and sincerity. Our analysis suggests, however, that this is not just about a media 'conspiracy' as seems to be implied by some Labour politicians. It reflects a complex mesh of the nature of the official documents and the form of the press releases as these interact with journalistic practices, news values and each newspaper's identity, market and projected relation with, and appeal to, their readers' class, nationality, income and politics.

Conclusion

This paper has examined the public discourse constructed around 'inequalities in health' through four government reports, their press releases and associated press coverage. It has shown how health inequalities are presented in different forms across the documents, re-presented in press releases and translated differently in different newspapers. Our analysis highlights how coverage is associated, but not always co-terminous, with newspapers' political affiliations and target audiences and 'national' identity/location. The analysis identified common themes across the press coverage – such as criticisms about lack of targets and, by the time the White Papers were released, a growing cynicism about the new Labour Government. It highlights too the crucial issue of political context and news timing, in particular illustrating how the English White Paper was overshadowed by other health stories which formed the basis for attacks on the Labour Government. The analysis demonstrates the difficulties of presenting stories centred on health *policy* and controlling which elements will render these less commonly covered health issues newsworthy.

Notes

1   Equivalent documents published in Wales and Northern Ireland are not covered in this analysis.

2   In the UK 'Broadsheets' are literally 'broader' newspapers which attract more educated and higher income readers compared with the smaller size and more popular 'Tabloids'.

References

Alasuutari, P. (ed) (1999) *Rethinking the media audience: the new agenda*. London: Sage.

Black, D., Morris, J., Smith, C. and Townsend, P. (1980) *Inequalities in Health: Report of a Working Party*. London: Department of Health and Social Security.

Chapman, S. and Lupton, D. (1994) *The Fight for Public Health. Principles and Practice of Media Advocacy*. London: BMJ Publishing Group.

Coates, D. (2000) The character of New Labour. In Coates, D. and Lawler, P. (eds) *New Labour in Government*. Manchester: Manchester University Press.

Davey Smith, G., Bartley, M. and Blane, D. (1990) The Black Report on socio-economic inequalities in health 10 years on, *British Medical Journal*, 301, 373–7.

Davey Smith, G., Dorling, D., Mitchell, R. and Shaw, M. (2002) Health inequalities in Britain: continuing increases up to the end of the 20ᵗʰ century, *Journal of Epidemiology and Community Health*, 56, 434–5.

Department of Health (1998) *Our Healthier Nation: a Contract for Health*. London: Department of Health.

Department of Health (1999) *Saving Lives: Our Healthier Nation*. London: HMSO.

Esser, F., Reinemann, C. and Fan, D. (2000) Spin doctoring in British and German election campaigns – how the press is being confronted with a new quality of political PR, *European Journal of Communication*, 15, 2, 209–39.

Franklin, B. (1998) Tough on soundbites, tough on the causes of soundbites: New Labour and news management, *Contemporary Political Studies*, vol 1–2.

Franklin, B. (2000) The hand of history: New Labour, news management and governance. In Ludlam, S. and Smith, M. (eds) *New Labour: Policy, Ideology and Government*. London: Macmillan.

Jones, T. (1996) *The remaking of the Labour Party*. London: Routledge.

Kitzinger, J. (1999) A sociology of media power. Key issues in audience reception research. In Philo, G. (ed) *Message Received*. Harlow: Longman.

Macintyre, S. (1997) The Black Report and beyond: what are the issues? *Social Science and Medicine*, 44, 723–45.

Macintyre, S. (2002) Before and after the Black Report: four fallacies, *Contemporary British History*, 19, 198–219.

Miller, D., Kitzinger, J., Williams, K. and Beharrell, P. (1998) *The Circuit of Mass Communication: Media Strategies, Representation and Audience Reception in the AIDS Crisis*. London: Sage.

Scottish Office Department of Health (1998) *Working Together for a Healthier Scotland. A Consultation Document*. Edinburgh: The Stationery Office.

Chapter 3

Narrativity and the mediation of health reform agendas

Darrin Hodgetts and Kerry Chamberlain

Introduction

During the 1980s and 1990s many developed countries experienced public-sector reforms intended to control expenditure and ensure the efficient use of resources during a global recession (Davis and Ashton 1995, Franklin 1999). These reforms reflected a general ideological shift in social policy towards decreasing state-funded services and the privatisation of public institutions such as hospitals. Central to these reforms was the introduction of competition between public and private providers in the delivery of services previously provided solely by state institutions. Alleged inefficiencies in state-sector management were invoked to justify the shifting of financial responsibility for health and welfare from the state to the individual. Following the 'trickle-down theories' of 'Reaganism' and 'Thatcherism', state-funded and managed health and welfare services were recast from basic entitlements to short-term privileges. These developments have been associated with the erosion of the ability of public health systems to provide universal and timely access to care, increased social fragmentation, public pessimism and increases in illness rates (Davis and Ashton 2001, Cullen and Hodgetts 2001, Golding 1999, Howell and Ingham 2001).

In New Zealand in the mid-1990s, when this research was conducted, debate surrounding the erosion of the welfare state, and the threats that social reforms pose for groups such as the elderly and economically disadvantaged, had been placed squarely on the public agenda. These reforms received increasingly critical media attention (Davis and Ashton 2001, Tully 1996). Our searches of the NEXIS LEXIS database and the TVNZ archives revealed over three thousand newspaper and television reports involving public opposition to the way in which public services were being rationed and rationalised. These reports covered specific failures in the health system and the dehumanising ramifications of a focus on cost containment rather than patient need. Reports often advocated for individuals who had been refused treatment, and criticised moves towards a two-tiered health system. The effect was to portray the health system as 'dangerous' for patients because of bureaucratic interference (Entwistle and Sheldon 1999, Gauld 2001, Hodgetts and Chamberlain 1999). Reflecting public anxiety over the health system, health became a 'political hot potato' and a major issue within media coverage.

This coverage tapped popular resentment of welfare bureaucracy and the virtues of market freedom in providing consumer choice. However, as Curran

(1998) pointed out in his discussion of public communication in Britain, '. . . there continued to be majority support for collectivist policies funded by taxation across a wide area of activity, as well as backing for extensive state action in support of welfare goals' (1998: 188). Media coverage constituted a sphere within which controversy surrounding the failure of the reforms to reduce expenditure and increase responsiveness to patient need was played out. It provided a cultural forum for working through the tension between the neo-liberal perception of the market as a self-regulating realm requiring limited government intervention and the neo-Keynesian view that state intervention is necessary to regulate the market and to assist those unable to look after themselves (Hodgetts and Chamberlain 1999, Meinhof and Richardson 1994).

Researchers have recently given increased attention to media representations of health and policy, focusing on both fictional and non-fictional print and broadcast media forms (Entwistle and Sheldon 1999, Franklin 1999, Tully 1996). These analyses provide valuable insights that can inform an analysis of public response to healthcare reform. Important questions, however, remain unanswered. For instance, how are tensions produced by health reforms construed by various interpretative communities? How do those dependent on communally funded healthcare navigate the increased emphasis on individual responsibility?

These questions are particularly pertinent for vulnerable groups, for whom the reforms pose a serious challenge. Recent research has emphasised the importance of lay beliefs for understanding the relationship between social inequality and illness (Blaxter 1997, Popay et al. 1998). Despite reference to the importance of media in the formation of lay beliefs in this research, little has been done to investigate the processes through which media representations contribute to the construction of these beliefs (Franklin 1999, Lupton 1999). This is surprising given that the process of mediation is central to how groups affected by health reforms make sense of change and its implications for their everyday lives. For instance, as an important daily ritual, television viewing provides people with access to ready-made stories that can be used to navigate the dilemmas of everyday life (Livingstone 1999, Silverstone 1999). Our objective is to illustrate storytelling processes through which lower SES groups can use such television coverage when constructing understandings of healthcare, their relationships to health services, and their place in the world.

Television viewing and the social negotiation of healthcare reform

Within contemporary society, people construct their understandings of events such as the health reforms from a multiplicity of interpersonal and mediated sources. Television has become an omnipresent storytelling institution, with adults in Western societies spending about 25 hours per week watching television (Desbarats 1994). Researchers have gone as far as to propose that:

Through mass television, society communes with itself, forms and revises collective opinion, and influences the public direction of society. Through the broadcasting system as a whole (including minority channels), people also explore their own group self-interest and relate this to the wider public interest. Thus, broadcasting is not only about individuals within society coming together but also about different groups within it constituting themselves, advancing their interests and negotiating with others within the wider totality (Curran 1998: 191).

Although we do not wish to be overly media-centric, Curran does capture the potential of television in communal sense-making processes. Viewers have become skilled at navigating amongst different channels and generic forms, and piecing together fragments of information from these to inform their own perspectives.

In providing the audience with information about wider social trends, television both reflects and reports on a social world and also shapes that world. The relationship between public sentiment and television coverage is reciprocal, although television is selective and subject to production conventions. The flickering box in the corner of the room provides an institutionally mediated cultural forum that draws upon, reframes and re-circulates ideas in order to construct stories about the issues of the day (Livingstone 1999, Silverstone 1999). In this way, coverage both draws upon and contributes to controversy surrounding issues such as health reform, and is influential in the development of our expectations for healthcare.

The audience is central to an understanding of the role of health coverage. Historically, audience researchers have invoked two different versions of viewers, as passive or active. Passive viewers are subject to the effects of an all-powerful medium; active viewers subject the media to interpretation according to their needs and expectations. More recently, research has emphasised the need to balance notions of media power with notions of viewer autonomy in the interpretation of coverage (Hodgetts and Chamberlain 2003, Livingstone 1999). These conceptualisations mirror assumptions underlying lay health beliefs research. In this case the contrast is between the colonisation of lay lifeworlds by medicine and the autonomy of self-reflexive agents or 'health consumers'. Again, contemporary research emphasises a dialectic of structure and agency in the construction of lay understandings (Popay et al. 1998, Radley and Billig 1996). Despite both domains having common trajectories, with few exceptions (see Hodgetts and Chamberlain 2003), little has been done to combine insights from both areas of research. Because television can be of fundamental importance in circulating explanations, combining contemporary insights from reception and lay beliefs research enables us to develop a more substantive understanding of the processes through which audiences make sense of health reforms.

The recent turn to narrative in social research (Bury 2001) provides a useful focal point for conceptualising the role of television in the construction of lay understandings of healthcare. Within television research, narrative theory has primarily been used to identify the underlying textual structures and stylistic conventions used to promote specific perspectives within coverage (Hodgetts and Chamberlain 1999, Kozloff 1992). Periodically, narrative theory has emerged in writing on the audience (Chisholm 1991, Thompson 1995), but has rarely been used for empirical research. Although narrative analysis is more common in lay beliefs research (Bury 2001, Popay *et al.* 1998), only passing reference is made to the role of storytelling institutions such as television. An emphasis on storytelling or narrativity as an ongoing and inherently communal process through which individuals and groups make sense of the world allows us to understand how stories told by coverage are appropriated by viewers and restoried within their lifeworlds. Narrative theory thus provides a basis for exploring how viewers actively fashion meaning while retaining a role for the media in framing shared understandings.

In presenting his social theory of media, Thompson (1995) argues that the self is an ongoing project constructed out of symbolic resources made available through interpersonal and mediated interactions. Viewers retell mediated stories from the perspective of their social and material positioning in society and according to their own views and life circumstances. By appropriating media stories, they link their own experiences and lives to wider social change. Reflecting the general stance adopted by Thompson, the lay beliefs literature often proposes that people make sense of their relationship to the wider social structures within which they live, and constitute their social identities, by telling stories or voicing accounts (Bury 2001, Radley and Billig 1996). Clearly there are various forms of narrative theory and analyses focusing on differing syntagmatic and paradigmatic dimensions, stylistic conventions, and character functions (see Bury 2001, Kozloff 1992, Sunwolf and Frey 2001). Rather than attempt to address all these dimensions we adopt the idea that people are 'storied beings' who are engaged in wider societal dialogues through which public narratives are articulated, enforced and refined (Bury 2001, Sennett 1998). Although people draw upon public narratives permeating everyday life, they do not simply reproduce them. They interpret and use fragments of these narratives in ways relevant to their own circumstances. As Benjamin (1968) notes, such storytelling '... does not aim to convey the pure essence of the thing, like information or a report. It sinks the thing into the life of the storyteller, in order to bring it out of him again. Thus traces of the storyteller cling to the story the way the handprints of a potter cling to the clay vessel . . .' (1968: 91–92).

Like any social group, people of lower socio-economic-status (SES) draw upon appropriate socio-cultural narratives to make sense of and respond to challenges posed by events such as illness and adversity within their own lives (Popay *et al.* 1998). As Bury writes:

Not only do language and narrative help sustain and create the fabric of everyday life, they feature prominently in the repair and restoring of meanings when they are threatened. Under conditions of adversity, individuals often feel a pressing need to re-examine and re-fashion their personal narratives in an attempt to maintain a sense of identity (2001: 264).

Because universal access to care has provided a means by which generations of New Zealanders have defined themselves as members of an egalitarian society, the challenge posed by the erosion of such initiatives requires the restorying of personal narratives. From this perspective the health reforms do not just present a barrier to lower SES people's access to care, but they also constrain their ability to present themselves as morally worthy members of society (c.f. Radley and Billig 1996, Cullen and Hodgetts 2001, Sennett 1998). Lower SES people in particular must strive to minimise the potential disruption to their sense of self and place. We will show how our research participants do this in part by appropriating television coverage and integrating it with their personal experiences in responding to the challenges posed by the reforms.

The present study

Previous lay health beliefs research has analysed stories produced primarily through interviews with individuals. Such work has provided useful insights into narrativity, but can only partially capture storytelling as a socially shared activity occurring through interpersonal and mediated interactions. Focus groups provide one means of generating accounts that reflect the ways in which people offer stories in response to others, stimulate others to tell their own stories, and appropriate aspects of television coverage. These groups can be used to reveal links between self-understandings, interpersonal relationships, mediation and important events in society. They can be used to investigate processes that:

> . . . involve sharing information, pooling experiences and comparing
> and contrasting them, negotiating divergent ideas and experiences,
> expressing agreement as well as disagreement with other participants,
> asking questions that challenge or which seek clarification, and
> providing answers that elaborate, justify or defend the speaker's views
> (Wilkinson 1998: 338).

Clearly there are limits in the extent to which any discussions constructed during a research project reflect 'everyday interactions'. Focus group discussions are generally longer and more formal engagements. However, focus groups do provide access to the linguistic resources and interpersonal dynamics evident in everyday discussions (Wilkinson 1998). The similarity to daily interactions was heightened by the first author facilitating the focus groups in a semi-directive manner, allowing participants to explore issues of

Table 1 *A description of participants in each focus group and the title and topic of the documentary viewed.*

Focus Group	Gender Male	Female	Age range (years)	Duration (minutes)	Programme title	Programme topic
One	3	2	43–60	90	The Great Kiwi Health Lottery	An investigation of problems in the health system
Two	2	3	42–53	100	Health and Wealth	An investigation of shifts from publicly to privately funded services
Three	–	5	20–40	80	Golden Oldies	An investigation of healthcare raised by aging population
Four	5	–	20–37	70	The Problem with Men	An investigation of men's healthcare needs

importance to themselves as well as prompting comment on issues identified by the research team.

Participants for this research were recruited in 1996 and 1997 through community organisations providing financial and social support to low income people in four provincial centres in New Zealand. We chose to elicit participation from people known to each other to facilitate more open discussions. Five persons from each location were interviewed individually about their general views on health and illness, and subsequently brought together to watch a television documentary followed by a focus group discussion (see Hodgetts and Chamberlain 2003). Documentary was chosen as an appropriate form because of its credibility as an information source and because the realist form it employs makes it particularly suitable for investigations of social change (Hodgetts and Chamberlain 1999). Four programmes, chosen to reflect different topics within healthcare, were selected from all available New Zealand health documentaries broadcast between 1995 and 1997. Table 1 provides specific information on each research group and the programmes watched.

Our analysis of these discussions follows what can be referred to as a 'text-and-context' approach (Meinhof and Richardson 1994). We move beyond the description of specific aspects of the discussions to broader observations about socio-cultural processes. Attention is given to the ways in which mediated stories are appropriated, reworked and situated within wider dialogues. Specifically, we explore how participants position themselves in relation to wider ideological debates surrounding individual and communal responsibility. More detailed analyses of the individual interviews, focus groups and their relation to the media texts can be found in previous publications (Hodgetts and Chamberlain 2000, 2003).

Narrativity and the negotiation of responsibility for healthcare

Each group watched a different documentary and engaged in contextually specific discussions of a range of health and illness issues. Talk related to health reform, however, occurred in all four groups, and invoked common concerns surrounding restrictions on health spending, equity in access to healthcare, tensions between bureaucrats and medical staff, and dilemmas concerning individual and communal responsibility for health. Not all groups emphasised every concern in the same detail. Focus groups one and two provided the most comprehensive illustrations of these concerns, whereas groups three and four, who watched programmes regarding more general health issues, made less elaborate references to these concerns. Differences arising from discussions of different programmes are not the focus here: rather we analyse the common concerns that emerge across groups at a general level. These concerns are not treated as isolated issues in participants' accounts, but are woven into the storytelling process we seek to investigate.

Navigating individual and communal responsibility for healthcare
State bureaucracy is commonly positioned as a barrier to efficiency in health and welfare provision within public discourse, and often unfavourably juxtaposed with private enterprise (Davis and Ashton 2001, Hodgetts and Chamberlain 1999, Meinhof and Richardson 1994). Reciprocating media coverage of health, our participants are highly critical of government mismanagement of the health system. They do not, however, accept that a shift to private care and managerialism is the answer to this problem. They challenge the government position asserting the benefits of competition and the use of private providers to bring efficiency, and present competition as leading to inefficiency and inequality. In this way, reforms emphasising the benefits of a quasi-market model for healthcare are positioned as the cause rather than the solution for inefficiencies in the health system.

This issue is brought to the fore when participants in focus group two discuss the privatisation of healthcare. They draw on the proposition from *Health and Wealth* that people are forced to shift to private services because the government has a hidden agenda to restrict public resourcing. Financial restraint and inequalities in access to care are presented as being indicative of the government's agenda to undermine the welfare state and increase emphasis on cost containment rather than patient need. Depictions of healthcare in the documentary prompt participants' discussion about specific healthcare services, but also a more general discussion of government services and policies. This wider framing of healthcare concerns locates them within everyday life. The shift to privatisation is presented as indicative of an increasingly unhealthy society in which private providers and the government are ignoring the needs of lower SES people:

Ed: They [government] started it and they had a secret agenda back then, that this was going to happen. But it's like anything, once a thing is in motion it takes a few years before it catches up and by then it's too late . . . And we have been chopped, channelled, kicked, demoralised, seven days a week. We've gone back to the 40s [. . .]

Don: If you have an operation privately you are certainly saving the Government money and I believe they know that.

Joy: But are they deliberately pushing for the private sector in healthcare because they want to save taxes? Or are they doing it because they want more people to get better healthcare quicker?

Don: Private doesn't necessarily mean better even if it seems to be quicker. If you put the same resources into the public it'd be just as flash. It's just the market thing again which we've got.

Mary: Another thing if they [government] want to push people into private insurance, then they are going to have to push the employers for the *Contracts Act* for a better standard of living for the ordinary people so they are can afford to buy it. And there's another one too, you go to a private hospital and you have the operation. If you get an infection or something goes wrong when you go home, you don't go back to the private hospital for them to . . . fix it . . . You then go to the public hospital where they clear up the mess.

Don: Yeah, they're [private providers] not accepting their responsibility.

Susan: Oh no, that's the thing. Was it guaranteed work? You go to a bloody panel beater or a mechanic, eh. You have got guaranteed work, eh.

Ed: . . . That TV clip in there, when I saw Roger Douglas and all them right early on in 1988, they first introduced a private system. The Labour Government. These people need to come up on criminal charges now because everybody here hasn't got . . . what they had then. And I actually really feel personally that from then on, this whole country is being sold down the tubes, health, education, jobs, the whole lot. It's all being sold down the tubes. The government is just avoiding the problem and putting it all back on us . . .

Don: Market driven makes it more costly. Wanganui and Palmerston North hospital they are competing with each other now, so what happens is one buys a flash piece of equipment which attracts patients which they get money for. The other has to have it and so then that pushes up the price . . .

This discussion reflects a renegotiation of the shift to consumerism and associated criticisms of the competence of state management of services. There is a tension between the proposed benefits of a free market and the uncertainty associated with reduced state intervention which must be managed by those with limited consumer power. The idea that the public system has to redress problems caused by private providers foreshadows the conclusion that the public system is superior to the private system. In order to do this, the public system needs to be adequately funded rather than purposefully undermined. The comparison of surgery to the motor trade functions to position healthcare as a commodity. As the health system has moved towards a commercial model, it is subjected to public evaluation along consumer lines. In the process, participants present themselves as health consumers whose needs are not being met. They draw on the very notions that have been used to justify the health reforms, accountability and responsiveness to consumer demands, to question the agenda for reform.

As potential health consumers, lower SES people must engage with a societal dialogue regarding individual and communal responsibility for healthcare. They are encouraged to take responsibility for their health and to be independent, but their lack of access to resources means they are forced to justify some dependency on state assistance. Our participants often manage this dilemma by accepting partial responsibility for their health while at the same time acknowledging limits to their ability to achieve this. In this way, they can negotiate a position that safeguards their identity as worthy members of society. The duty to be healthy (Blaxter 1997) is con- textualised by placing emphasis on people's right to access health-enhancing resources that are available to other, more affluent members of society. Participants renegotiate the proposition that health is an individual responsibility by shifting responsibility for their health to a lack of adequate government resourcing of healthcare. In this way, the government and private providers are presented as avoiding their responsibility. If institutions are not accepting their responsibility, why should society expect ordinary people to accept responsibility without adequate support?

Resourcing and access to healthcare services for lower SES people were central elements of the discussions in all focus groups, especially who should be responsible for ensuring access. The discussions in focus group four exemplify these issues. The documentary they viewed, *The Problem with Men*, emphasised the need for men to take responsibility for their health and to utilise health services more effectively. In discussion following this docu- mentary, participants went considerably beyond this by invoking previous experience. By situating the programme content within their own lives, these men contextualised influences which limited their access to care, particularly in relation to a lack of resources for lower SES people. This facilitated a shift in emphasis from personal to governmental responsibility for access to affordable quality care, and provided a challenge to the commercialisa- tion of healthcare:

Nigel: You'd probably find that a lot of the people who could get operations later on probably have health insurance and shit so their health insurance company is paying for it, not the government.

Ron: Working class Joe can't afford health insurance.

Nigel: It's a rip-off aye.

Ron: Not-care insurance, house insurance, bike insurance, kit insurance and all that sought of crap and bike insurance and health insurance, you know fuck.

Nigel: Insurance against over insurance. [. . .]

Ron: Well it [healthcare] should be free I mean you know we pay so much out in crap and our health is the last thing. I mean we don't have any cops . . . no fire brigade no fuck'n hospital or medical anymore. Just more speed cameras. The governments lost the plot with all these cuts.

Nigel: It's the same with skin cancer aye. Like if they had free things I bet we'd probably all go and get ya skin cancer things checked out.

Nick: Ah too right.

Nigel: But if you had to pay even . . . thirty bucks then ah she'll be right you'd just have a quick look at your arm, Na I'm probably sweet anyway. [. . .]

Nick: They brought in all these changes to make things run better and to make better use of the tax dollar. But its worse now. We get less but we've gotta pay more. We've gotta pay for everything these days. And if you can't pay then it's too bad for you mate, you miss out.

Mark: That's the problem with user pays isn't it? I mean it hurts the little people aye. You know and the people that can least afford it are the people that need it the most quite often.

Paul: There's lots being spent on health in the private and the public. But not everyone gets their fair shack of the stick. Healthcare should be for everyone and shouldn't be left to how much you can get it. That's pretty fucked.

Transcending the documentary, questions are raised about equity in the allocation of care according to social standing. Unlike the men in the documentary, who are portrayed as having immediate access to quality healthcare, our participants face constraints. By linking the quality of treatment to social standing, they restory the events depicted in the documentary into their own life situations. Voicing a distinction between the quality of care provided to different segments of the population reflects current reactions to the reform of healthcare. These men accomplish this by appealing to the same rhetoric that was used by government to justify reforms in terms of increased efficiency and rationalisation of care to demonstrate that the present system is inefficient and irrational.

To understand what is occurring in such interactions we need to move beyond the common preoccupation in reception research with establishing the extent to which specific programmes frame the stories of interpretive communities. As we see above, participants draw upon and extend aspects of coverage in order to navigate various dilemmas and manage the uncertainties and stigma posed by healthcare reform. This is appropriate because these participants are engaged in an ongoing societal dialogue within which aspects of specific programmes are constantly interwoven with personal experiences and ideas derived from their previous viewing.

Responsibility, personification and the dilemmas of healthcare
Debates about the health reforms raise complex issues beyond government inefficiency and problems of privatisation. Recognition of the increasing costs of public care involves consideration of eligibility for care, and has lead to public discussions of criteria for the allocation of care (Gauld 2001). Rationing care leads to moral dilemmas. Television documentaries often exemplify such dilemmas through the depiction of specific cases (Hodgetts and Chamberlain 1999, Kitzinger 2000). People mirror and extend this practice by relating such mediated cases to their own lifeworlds. In both television coverage and the lifeworld, this practice works to authenticate the consequences of inadequate access to healthcare. People use these cases rhetorically to negotiate their own situations and relationships within society.

Participants in all four groups discussed the dilemmas surrounding access to healthcare. This was frequently situated around calls to refocus the health system on serving people rather than profit. Criteria for allocating resources and the consequences of rationing decisions for those who cannot afford private care were particularly prominent in the discussions of group one, who watched *The Great Kiwi Health Lottery*, a documentary which provided a general commentary on the health reforms. These participants explored how resources might be allocated, and consequently engaged with moral dilemmas surrounding responsibility for the provision of care:

Warren: . . . Millions of dollars are spent on unhealthy living and it [documentary] didn't even touch upon that . . . It didn't mention the fact that our hospitals are full of people because of drinking, motor vehicle accidents that cost a billion dollars a year and other unhealthy things that can be altered. People can eat more healthy foods, cut down on the smoking, cut down on the alcohol . . .

Alan: . . . Maybe they should be spending more to encourage a healthy lifestyle so that people don't have to go into hospital.

Warren: . . . If I was the chief surgeon at Greenlane Hospital I'd be ruling below the line all those with cirrhosis of the liver for alcoholism, vascular surgery for feet going black because you're a heavy smoker . . . I'd make the list for those, I wouldn't give surgery to those who self cause the damage to their own bodies . . .

Jane: I agree we should take better care, but is that realistic for everyone. It wouldn't be fair to discriminate like that cos it's only part of the picture. And people who smoke and drink pay taxes. It's better to make sure that enough money is put in and we stop wasting it on these private fiascos. Businesspeople profiting off people's misery.

David: You have to have a safety net so people who need help get it. You can't just say 'bad luck to you'. You can't say no to one group just cos you change the criteria and then allow these others back in.

Jane: I went to an unveiling [funeral] last week of a young lady who was 24 years old and she was waiting for a heart operation and she was put off and put off. And she was happily married with four children husband working. An finally they give her a date after two years . . . and her little son goes in to wake her up in the morning to get ready for school and she couldn't make it to the operation because she was dead. An she was 24 years old. That movie just counted really on elderly people so its not really just affecting elderly people at all. To tell that girl to go out and get private insurance would just be impossible. Because people just, you know, he wasn't in a job that was paid enough money to have any form of insurance anyway. And the way I look at it now is everything that is happening within this government now, irrespective of whether its health or education or anything else, housing, its all from the view of privatisation and never mind you, if you don't have the money, too bad for you.

Designating criteria for access to care forms the basis for the group to deliberate whether treatment decisions should be made on the basis of health-related behaviours. A healthy lifestyle is viewed as a means of reducing demand for curative services and freeing resources to treat patients who are ill through no fault of their own. This deliberation is based in the programme's exploration of criteria, but the group introduces additional lifestyle considerations. Whereas the programme focused on biomedical and economic criteria, the participants introduce moralised notions of lifestyle. Deliberations over potential criteria are problematised by the framing of issues in terms of a dichotomy between the deserving and undeserving poor and associated tensions surrounding responsibility.

In such interactions, participants are not simply advocating specific strategies for resource allocation, but are trying out different potential solutions and imagining alternatives as they make sense of dilemmas faced in an under-resourced health system. Overall, participants advocate the rights of the deserving poor and chastise the undeserving poor, characterising needy public patients as the deserving poor. Warren and Alan emphasise how access to care might be restricted for those engaged in risky behaviour, and how this would free up resources for responsible people, such as themselves, who do not engage in risky activities. Jane and David, however, offer a different position for the deserving poor, pointing to the discrimination that can result from under-funding. Jane achieves this by personalising the plight of the young woman whose untimely death could have been prevented by equitable access to care. This argument is used by Jane to resist the emphasis being given to individual responsibility and to substantiate the proposition that responsibility for care should be attributed to the health system rather than to the deserving poor. Exemplifying the dilemmas of healthcare provision through cases in this way works to challenge current government practice and to justify the need for adequately resourced healthcare.

In these deliberations the significance of the health reforms is presented at two levels: general criteria for allocating resources and the personal consequences of resourcing decisions based on such criteria. The use of personalised examples documents how general discussions of criteria for allocating resources have specific implications for people's lives. These are stories that serve a number of rhetorical purposes in interpersonal discussion. For example, participants exchange horror stories about problems in the health system as one way of establishing the extent of the problem and assigning responsibility to government mismanagement. Stories enter into the flow of interpersonal discussions and are restoried as they are taken up and integrated within wider dialogues regarding reform. As Jane's use of the account of young women's death shows, stories are drawn from a wide context and are not limited to personal experience or taken solely from the documentary viewed.

It is notable that Jane's account of the case of the young women's death employs the same narrative structure as stories of cases presented regularly in the media. At the time of this research a prominent and contentious story in media coverage focused on the case of a needy patient (James McKewen) who was denied life-saving dialysis on account of his age and other health conditions. Although this case was depicted in *The Great Kiwi Health Lottery* and discussed within focus group one, it did not appear in any of the other documentaries. Its salience to society as a whole is reflected by reference to it in the discussions of two other focus groups. For instance, focus group three discussed this case to exemplify the implications of the reforms. This illustrates how cases live on within social discourse and are retold, reframed, and abstracted, as concerns are articulated and worked through. It is through the retelling of common examples that issues such as access to care are rendered coherent and assigned social significance. These cases become part of the folklore of contemporary culture and are taken up and used in subsequent reports to personify issues. The following extract is taken from a general exploration of funding health and welfare services for older people during focus group three:

Lisa: I think the government is fobbing off the issues . . . My mother and father saved for their retirement but they have come in behind to dwindle it down . . . People get caught up in this asset-testing bracket. Now they're constantly saying to . . . my generation save for your retirement and pay for your health needs. What for? . . . This user pays racket, you get sucked in. They take people's houses to pay for their care [. . .]

Jamie: They should show more about financial situations. What about the people who couldn't afford to get an operation or a healthy living.

Lisa: Now what about that guy who had to pay 30 thousand in hospital fees. There wasn't much on that and there . . . was there? Well not so much him, look at that guy. I think it was the 80-year-old. He had renal failure or something like that, within him anyway . . . Here's this poor guy [James McKewen] and he's denied the right of using the dialysis machine. But even though they swindled him out of money but the worse thing about it was what's-her-name? Jenny Shipley [Minister of Health], she brought it on TV. Now that is his own private life. And it's only relevant to his medical file. She decided to tell all of New Zealand . . . There's thousands of cases out there because they cannot fight the system. It's just wrong.

Jamie: James McKewen was his name. He was all set up to enjoy his retirement and they tried it on.

May: It's not just in the elderly though. There's thousands of cases out there in every age. There wasn't enough focus on negative side of things in that programme. They were showing people who could afford care and were doing things to preserve their health. What is going to happen to people who can't?

This illustrates how discussion can work to integrate general government policy with personal circumstance and specific cases. Lisa draws on her parents' situation and the McKewen case to illustrate how the needy should have access to care, and Jamie and May facilitate this by relating the McKewen case more broadly to uncertainties surrounding access to care. Invoking pressures faced by needy public patients, participants situate the seriousness and universality of problems faced by lower SES people. The McKewen case provides a way of meaningfully articulating one's anxieties about the implications of reforms.

It is in the process of retelling stories that personal experiences are transformed into illustrative examples of more general trends. In our research, such stories become cautionary tales that alert others to the implications of the health reforms. They provide a means for participants to claim commonality of experience and to construct a shared past, present and future. In providing accounts of the plight of others, participants are also making claims about themselves and the type of people they are (c.f. Radley and Billig 1996). Recourse to such cases has a performative function, and involves the presentation of a socially-sanctioned and moral self. These are moral stories that function to question issues such as the adequacy of healthcare resourcing. Such stories transcend the individual speaker and enter the social milieu as key elements in the reformulation of public under-standings of the reforms and their implications.

Life stories and the mediation of socio-cultural narratives

In exploring the attempts of these participants to make sense of and re-negotiate their relationship to the healthcare system, our analysis demonstrates how everyday interactions provide space for working through wider social change. Our project was conducted at a time of major reform in healthcare. These reforms were discussed widely and subjected to critical media coverage (Davis and Ashton, 2001, Hodgetts and Chamberlain 1999). By using television documentaries depicting healthcare, we could provoke discus-sions which elicited the complexities and contradictions surrounding these reforms for lower SES people. In discussing these issues, our participants were obliged to negotiate the dilemmas and tensions raised by the reforms and the threat these posed to their sense of self and place. Tension between individual and communal responsibility for healthcare was particularly salient in this context. Our participants acknowledged individual responsibility for health, but also deliberated upon the need for a communal 'safety net' to provide adequate resourcing of healthcare for those unable to provide fully for themselves. Reacting to assertions that the undeserving poor burden the health system, our participants worked to justify themselves as deserving poor who have legitimate needs. This enabled them to remain worthy members of society while responding to the potential stigma associated with an increased emphasis on individual responsibility (Cullen and Hodgetts 2001, Golding 1999, Howell and Ingham 2001).

In their attempts to justify and position themselves, our participants engaged in communal sense-making processes that enabled them to deal with the dilemmas and disruptions posed by the reforms. Narrativity enables participants to work through their relationships with the health system, to make sense of associated uncertainties, suggest reasons for events, and identify specific consequences (see Bury 2001, Sennett 1998). Like all good tales, participants' deliberations are played out through the actions of various colourful characters. These include health professionals, health consumers, needy patients, critics, concerned citizens, dishonest politicians and bureau-crats, who are all invoked to personalise abstract issues:

Everywhere the broader philosophical and policy issues of access, efficiency, equity, ethics and responsibility are constantly presented to us in highly personalised form, as individual stories of personal drama, heroism, emotional anguish, humour and triumph are rehearsed in public view (Davis and Ashton 2001: 1).

Our participants draw upon the ways in which unequal access to care is personalised within health coverage, but extend this framing to substantiate problems in 'the system' and to talk about more general social inequalities that place peoples' health at risk. Participants shift between criticism of and support for the public health system in order to make sense of uncertainties surrounding their personal access to care. They present cases of struggle for security through which the health reforms are interpreted. These viewers are very adept at making sense of abstract issues covered in health documentaries and grounding these within their own lifeworlds.

Such interactions between audience groups and documentaries are situated within a continuing dialogue between previous viewing, the programme perspective and viewer biographies (Livingstone 1999, Thompson 1995). New stories are framed in relation to older ones; people draw on stories circulated within personal, interpersonal and mediated spheres. Television viewing functions as a site for the reproduction of public narratives. The resulting narratives are never completed but always await the next instalment.

References

Benjamin, W. (1968) The storyteller: reflections on the works of Nikolai Leskov. In Arendt, H. (ed) *Illuminations*. New York: Schocken.

Blaxter, M. (1997) Whose fault is it? People's own conceptions of the reasons for health inequalities, *Social Science and Medicine*, 44, 6, 747–56.

Bury, M. (2001) Illness narratives: fact or fiction, *Sociology of Health and Illness*, 23, 3, 263–85.

Chisholm, B. (1991) Difficult viewing: the pleasure of complex screen narratives, *Critical Studies in Mass Communication*, 8, 4, 389–403.

Cullen, A.M. and Hodgetts, D.J. (2001) Unemployment as illness: an exploration of accounts voiced by the unemployed in Aotearoa/New Zealand, *Analysis of Social Issues and Public Policy*, 1, 1, 33–52.

Curran, J. (1998) Crisis of public communication: a reappraisal. In Liebes, T. and Curran, J. (eds) *Media, Ritual and Identity*. London: Routledge.

Davis, P. and Ashton, T. (2001) *Health and Public Policy in New Zealand*. Auckland, New Zealand: Oxford University Press.

Desbarats, P. (1994) The media and the dissemination of research. In Dunn, E.V., Norton, P.G., Stewart, M. and Indiver, F. (eds) *Disseminating Research: Changing Practice*. Thousand Oaks, CA: Sage.

Entwistle, V. and Sheldon, T. (1999) The picture of health? Media coverage of the health service. In Franklin, B. (ed) *Social Policy, the Media and Misrepresentation*. London: Routledge.

Franklin, B. (1999) (ed) *Social Policy, the Media and Misrepresentation*. London: Routledge.

Gauld, R. (2001) *Revolving Doors: New Zealand's Health Reforms*. Wellington: Victoria University.

Golding, P. (1999) Thinking the unthinkable. Welfare reform and the media. In Franklin, B. (ed) *Social Policy, the Media and Misrepresentation*. London: Routledge.

Hodgetts, D.J. and Chamberlain, K. (1999) Medicalization and the depiction of lay people in television health documentary, *Health: an Interdisciplinary Journal for the Social Study of Health, Illness and Medicine*, 3, 3, 319–35.

Hodgetts, D.J. and Chamberlain, K. (2000) The social negotiation of people's views on the cause of illness, *Journal of Health Psychology*, 5, 3, 325–36.

Hodgetts, D.J. and Chamberlain, K. (2003) Television documentary in New Zealand and the construction of doctors by lower socio-economic groups, *Social Science and Medicine*, 57, 113–24.

Howell, J. and Ingham, A. (2001) From social problem to personal issue: the language of lifestyle, *Cultural Studies*, 15, 2, 326–51.

Kitzinger, J. (2000) Media templates: Patterns of association and the (re) construction of meaning over time, *Media, Culture and Society*, 22, 1, 61–84.

Kozloff, S. (1992) Narrative theory and television. In Allan, R.C. (ed) *Channels of Discourse Reassembled*. London: Routledge.

Livingstone, S. (1999) Mediated knowledge: recognition of the familiar, discovery of the new. In Gripsrud, J. (ed) *Television and Common Knowledge*. London: Routledge.

Lupton, D. (1999) Editorial: Health, illness and medicine in the media, *Health: an Interdisciplinary Journal for the Social Study of Health, Illness and Medicine*, 3, 3, 259–62.

Meinhof, U.H. and Richardson, K. (eds) (1994) *Text, Discourse and Context: Representations of Poverty in Britain*. London: Longman.

Popay, J., Williams, G., Thomas, C. and Gatrell, A. (1998) Theorising inequalities in health: the place of lay knowledge. In Bartley, M., Blane, D. and Davey Smith, G. (eds) *The Sociology of Health Inequalities*. Oxford: Blackwell Publishers.

Radley, A. and Billig, M. (1996) Accounts of health and illness: Dilemmas and representations, *Sociology of Health and Illness*, 18, 2, 220–40.

Sennett, R. (1998) *The Corrosion of Character*. London: W.W. Norton and Company.

Silverstone, R. (1999) *Why Study the Media*. London: Sage.

Sunwolf and Frey, L.R. (2001) Storytelling: the power of narrative communication and interpretation. In Robinson, W.P. and Giles, H. (eds) *The New Handbook of Language and Social Psychology*. London: John Wiley and Sons Ltd.

Thompson, J.B. (1995) *The Media and Modernity: a Social Theory of the Media*. Cambridge: Polity Press.

Tully, J. (1996) Piercing the veil of health reporting. In McGregor, J. (ed) *Dangerous Democracy? News Media Politics in New Zealand*. Palmerston North, New Zealand: Dunmore Press.

Wilkinson, S. (1998) Focus groups in health research, *Journal of Health Psychology*, 3, 3, 329–48.

Chapter 4

Going public: references to the news media in NHS contract negotiations

David Hughes and Lesley Griffiths

Introduction

This chapter presents data from a study of contracting between British Health Authorities (HAs) and hospitals to examine how middle-level managers talked about media reportage and interacted with the local press and broadcast media. As one type of purchaser within the National Health Service, HAs contracted with a range of hospitals to buy clinical services for patients in their local area, and held regular meetings with providers to negotiate and monitor these agreements. The meetings were characterised by frequent disagreement about the cost of services, the volumes that should be purchased, and the need (or otherwise) to amend contracts to cope with additional service pressures. References to the media typically arose in the context of (a) HA attempts to manage the release of information to minimise unfavourable reportage and (b) hospital managers' implicit or explicit threats to 'go public' about alleged funding shortfalls. This chapter examines how managers presented the possibility of media involvement, and its consequences for purchaser/provider relationships.

Managers' interactions with the media were closely bound up with their attempts to grapple with the unintended consequences of a radical policy change. The introduction of the NHS internal market separated the functions of purchasing and providing health care, and thus defined the interests of managers charged with running hospital Trusts (and overseeing the delivery of care by health professionals) as fundamentally different from those of HA managers charged with purchasing services (and overseeing financial management and priority setting). Two parties, who under the previous system had been part of the same organisation, needed to adjust to a new environment in which they had greater scope for unilateral action. They had also to balance new policies about 'openness' with the need to keep contract negotiations confidential and fluid in a context where competition between trusts had been promoted. Earlier studies have documented the adversarial attitudes and difficult relationships that sometimes resulted (Flynn,Williams and Pickard 1996, Griffiths and Hughes 2000), and which was one factor behind the shift to the more co-operative framework introduced after 1997 (DoH 1997). This paper shows how such conflict could sometimes crystallize around media reportage.

We argue that conceptualisation of the relationship between the NHS and the media needs to take account of the complexity of policy implementation and to recognise that the 'policy community' is not a unitary entity. Some commentators have seen the news media as a channel used by élite actors to communicate policy issues in ways calculated to shape public opinion (Watney 1996, Huebner et al. 1997, Goldsteen et al. 2001). Thus Berridge (1991) has noted that many analyses of AIDS and the media take a 'Frankfurt School' position which portrays the press and broadcast media as servants of the powerful. This chapter suggests that the media are better seen as arenas for struggles over meaning in which competing discourses are expressed and negotiated (see also Lupton 1994). Such struggles involve a variety of interest groups and can pit one section of the 'policy community' against another.

Much of the existing media studies literature, especially that in the political economy tradition, sees no need for detailed empirical investigation of these fields of action. Media texts and programmes are analysed to show that they systematically favour the discourses promoted by political élites, but there is little attempt to document the mediating social processes. The observational studies that have been done centre on the newsroom, rather than the external interactional networks that connect news production to society. This research has shed considerable light on such issues as media ownership and bias, the recruitment and socialisation of journalists, the bureaucratic structuring of news, the role of 'gatekeepers', and the relative influence of journalists and sources (see Tumber 1999). However, the networks within which 'sources' operate away from the newsroom remain largely invisible (for an exception, see Schlesinger and Tumber 1994). The present study represents a small step towards filling that gap. It illustrates how 'sources' are themselves located in complex organisational environments, in which the primary relationships in news generation may be with other policy actors rather than journalists. NHS managers help to produce media representations but are also one of the key audiences. This applies to the overseeing central departments who may regard negative reportage as reflecting badly on local managers, and to local managers on both sides of the purchaser/provider split. Indeed media stories may be produced as 'moves' in the ongoing struggle between them. This means that negotiations take place in the 'shadow' of media reportage, in the sense that awareness of the consequences of good and bad publicity is a crucial element of the negotiation context in which NHS policy implementation proceeds. Although friction between health authorities and hospitals over media reportage also occurred in the 1970s and 80s, the internal market reforms brought the purchaser/provider relationship centre stage and changed the way in which the threat of 'going public' was used.

The paper focuses on middle-level NHS managers in a provincial city, and the media involved are local newspapers, and regional television and radio. The managers in the study almost always directed their press releases and interviews towards local specialist reporters, with whom they had had recurrent contact, rather than towards the national media. In the single case in our data where a story was reported at national level, it was doctors rather than managers who were the main news sources. Although we believe that the arguments advanced are transferable to national media coverage, we concede that we have little evidence on that point.

Methods

The research comprised an observational case study of a health authority (HA) and its main providers, and an interview study of all Welsh HAs and Trusts, both carried out in the mid-1990s. The study was conceived as a 'policy ethnography' (Strong and Robinson 1990) and takes a broadly naturalistic stance to data collection, influenced by interpretive sociology. Compared with earlier work, we focus more closely on the specifics of discourse to produce a version of policy ethnography that pays close attention to language and social interaction. This paper relies on data from the HA case study, including observations and tape recordings of over 80 contracting meetings over two annual cycles, and in-depth interviews with key participants. The majority of the meetings and interviews were transcribed, and represent a substantial corpus of data amounting to about 2800 sheets of typescript. Analysis took a broadly inductive form. We sought to identify themes emerging from the transcripts, which were then used to code and index relevant textual segments. Chronology was an important consideration, and analysis sometimes involved tracking issues through a series of meetings. Findings relating to the nature of the contracting process have been reported elsewhere, and here we concentrate on a subset of the data relating to the news media. Because of length constraints in this volume, we refer interested readers to other published papers for a fuller account of the methods used (see Hughes and Griffiths 1999a, 1999b, Griffiths and Hughes 2000).

Public and private domains

NHS managers' attitudes towards the media are conditioned by background understandings about work and work contexts, including notions about things that fall into the public domain and things that should remain private. The distinction between the public and private domains comes up repeatedly in everyday management work, and finds institutional expression in such forms as separate public and private agendas in HA meetings and the framework of law and official guidance governing the service.

The NHS is characterised by a particular juxtaposition of public funding, statutory duty and Parliamentary accountability, which places it in a different situation vis-a-vis the media from most other Western healthcare systems. The operation of the NHS is a matter of public policy rather than private corporate management, and is subject to a greater degree of political sensitivity to public opinion than would apply in a system based on independent providers. Something that elsewhere may be seen as a problem with a single provider, in the NHS takes on the appearance of systemic failure. The Government can be held responsible for the problems of the service, so that the channelling of information to the general public via the media can determine future electoral prospects. Because the Government is likely to take action to correct problems, media reportage can also affect the fate of those working in the system.

The issue of information disclosure and its limits in a public service has been a long-standing preoccupation. Since the early 1990s, Government has sought to refine policies on 'openness' and the 'right to know', which culminated in the *Freedom of Information Act* 2000 (Flinders 2000, Hughes *et al.* 2000). These policies attempted to strike a balance between increased transparency within public bodies and necessary confidentiality, both in respect of individual patients and quasi-commercial transactions. The perceived need for some limits on disclosure was reinforced by the introduction of the NHS internal market. Official policy recognised that contract negotiations should be private and only required disclosure of the content of NHS contracts after they had been signed. At the informal level many purchasers sought to delay the release of such information, so that the details of performance penalties and prices agreed with certain providers would not be available to others (Hughes and Griffiths 1999b). Many commentators have been disappointed that 'openness' has not gone further and by the many areas exempted from scrutiny (McKee 1999, Birkinshaw 2000, 2002).

Against this background, it is not difficult to find arguments both for and against disclosing information to the media. 'Going public', whether in terms of organisational policies promoting transparency, or individual 'whistle-blowing', can be constructed as the discharge of public duties. In other circumstances, however, it may be portrayed as strategically unsound or a betrayal of collegial trust, and out of step with responsible management behaviour. In our data there are many examples where HA managers complain about the 'unwise' or 'premature' disclosure of information by managers in NHS Trusts, who in turn seek to defend their actions. The flavour of such exchanges is illustrated by the following extract from a contract negotiation meeting between an HA and one of its main local acute hospitals. The two speakers are the HA finance director (HAFD) and the Trust finance director (TFD), who head their respective contracting teams. They are discussing the implications of a five per cent 'cost improvement' requirement, which the HA has said is likely to be imposed in the new contract, and which the Trust manager has said his board will discuss at its next meeting.

HAFD: They will talk about it in private probably.
TFD: No, it will be in the public section.
HAFD: Well I don't think that would be wise.
TFD: It is already in the public section.

HAFD: Well I don't think that would be wise at this stage, because it hasn't yet been through our Board and I wouldn't want it to go through your Board.

TFD: Well it depends on what I am going to say.

HAFD: Instructions from the health authority when we are still in a confidential negotiating stage. And I have to say this is not . . . we would not want any of these things said that have been said today to be raised in the public arena and that would be formal.

TFD: You don't know what I intended to say, I intended to say that five per cent admin and clerical cost saving is meant to be re-diverted back into patient savings and the health authority expect this in cash terms. What is your problem there?

HAFD: It isn't . . . Because we are interpreting a Welsh Office letter. Now if you are going to put that in the public arena then we need to get it in writing from the Welsh Office first, or tell the Welsh Office in writing that is what you are going to say in the public arena?

TFD: No, I will say the indications are . . .

HAFD: We are still in a negotiating stage and I would have thought the best way of dealing with that at the moment is in the confidential arena.

TFD: I don't want to negotiate about it. If the facts are that we are meant to do this and provide the money back then that is what is being said and that is what is confirmed and that is what has to happen. I mean I don't see it as negotiation about that, it is whatever the rules are. Okay?

HAFD: But why, I don't understand why you are public at this stage.

TFD: Well I have to say what our budget is for next year, I have to say what the problems for the unit are next year.

Here, several years after the introduction of the internal market, the tension between old relationships and the new order is still apparent in terms such as 'instructions' and 'unit', which applied to the time when hospitals were indeed under HA management control. The HAFD's request for private discussion and behind-the-scenes agreement might be seen as an attempt to project the old order into the new market context. Nevertheless the Trust takes up a strong negotiating position by saying it will make an early public statement of its projected financial position for the coming year, including the trimming of five per cent from administrative costs that has been foreshadowed. The granting of NHS Trust status in the 1990s created new and legitimate channels for the release of information by hospitals, which meant that they could interact with the media in new ways. In this exchange both parties avoid explicit reference to the significance of public disclosure, but they are well aware that funding cuts will attract media reportage. One effect of press reports is to give more solidity to events or bargaining positions than they typically have in the flux of ongoing contract negotiations. There is a risk that organisations will be locked into a particular stance, or that a provisional interpretation is overtaken by events, so that managers are seen to have provided wrong information. In this extract, the HAFD moves to try to keep his statement of the position (which he terms an 'interpretation') under wraps until later in the year, when the overall settlement will be known. Following this extract, he goes on to outline arrangements for additional funding, linked to a 'reconciliation' for lost general practitioner fundholder income, that will significantly benefit the Trust and which seems calculated to offset the cost improvements. One may suspect that this also serves to remind the Trust managers that the HA may withhold such incentives if co-operation is not forthcoming.

The new forms of interaction with the media touched on above arise partly because of the re-constitution of the roles of HA and hospital as purchaser and provider. The following interview with a senior HA contract team member makes an important point about the impact on public perceptions.

> It is very hard because the public (. . .) are not sympathetic to the reforms and therefore their first sympathy is going to be with somebody who's providing services. There's no way we can very effectively get into the media a purchaser perspective of what it means and sometimes we get blamed for the reforms. The reforms must mean . . . If there's competition, this old market idea must mean there is spare capacity within the system and you'll have seen recently, as we come towards the year end yet again, hospitals can say, we have spare capacity, we can treat another thousand patients but the purchasers won't give us money. Well, we're stuck. That, as I understand it, was the inevitable consequence and intention of the reforms. If there was no spare capacity, there'd be no competition and no ability to move. (. . .). But I think purchasers are, in public terms, in a lot of ways, losers. I think I said, maybe not to you, to someone before, a good purchaser is an unpopular purchaser, that's inevitable. A bad purchaser flows with the tide of what the providers are doing and tries, as far as possible, to fix any leaks that appear.

The case that each side can present is shaped by different expectations and different rhetorical resources. Providers can tell a story about unmet need and constraints placed on caring professionals, which has an immediate resonance for the public. Purchasers must construct an account about limited resources, the need for efficiency gains and difficult prioritisation decisions, which is much harder to communicate in the typical story formats used in the news media. Not surprisingly it is almost always the providers who turn to the threat of media reportage as a lever in contract negotiations.

Managing news

There was a pattern in many of the more 'difficult' contract negotiation meetings whereby requests from the HA for co-operation in managing publicity failed to elicit full agreement from Trust managers. In these exchanges HA managers made reference to the need to work together and present a united front. On occasion they asked for extra information that would 'help us to understand' the problems faced by the Trust, they pointed to Welsh Office demands placed on both parties, and they sometimes rehearsed the arguments that an agreed press statement might contain. However, against the background of Trust coolness towards such overtures, the discourse concerning 'publicity' tended to take on a more negative and limited form. Many exchanges centred on the 'adverse' results that would follow for the HA, the limited movement that the Trusts were willing to make, and the consequences for their relationship.

The following example centres on the perennial issue whereby Trusts were pressing for additional funding towards the end of the year to cover extra elective surgical cases, and the HA was arguing that the contracted treatments should be paced evenly through the year (with the extra cases going on the waiting list). The context is a routine contract monitoring meeting, and again the exchange is between the two persons heading the respective contracting teams – the HAFD and, in this case, the Trust chief executive (TCE). Following the refusal of extra funding, the TCE has just threatened to end Ear, Nose and Throat (ENT) work for the HA, once the funded numbers have been reached.

HAFD: It is in the contract.
TCE: Oh no it isn't. You will get your contract number, and if we choose to do ENT for Merryfield [fundholding practice] in the month of January we will do ENT work for Merryfield.
HAFD: Yes, but we have got to avoid the situation where there is publicity around the fact that South County patients are no longer being seen despite that you have got the capacity.
TCE: But that is the case Gerry[1], you can't avoid the facts of life.
HAFD: No, we have contracted with you for a level of activity to be phased over the year.
TCE: You will get your level of activity.
HAFD: Phased over the year.
TCE: Where does it say that, I will phase it. You can have 2,850 by the end of February and the month of March we will be doing work for somebody else. I mean what is wrong with that?
HAFD: Well what is wrong with that is that it would cause us adverse publicity, wouldn't it?
TCE: For you!

HAFD: Well obviously, I mean we are not going out of our way to try and be confrontational I didn't think.

TCE: Well I am not trying to be confrontational. I just want to get, I just want to get some income into the hospital. Okay, we will talk about it outside, perhaps we will switch two doctors away from your work.

In this extract it becomes clear that the Trust has recognised the difficulties that 'publicity' would cause for the HA and is using this as a bargaining tool. This is implicitly acknowledged in the HAFD's conciliatory comment that they were not intentionally being 'confrontational'. The conciliatory move elicits a like response. The TCE offers to talk outside the meeting and opens up the possibility of further negotiation in private before committing the Trust to a position which would be released to the media. As in many other meetings, the Trust steers a middle course where it avoids either a hard-line position or major concessions. However, the TCE is unwilling to concede the general points that the volume of patients awaiting treatments is above the level of funded activity, and that this should be a matter of public concern. In meetings over the following months this issue came up repeatedly, as it did with a second local Trust, and threats about possible approaches to the media began to surface more explicitly.

Going public

In our data there are many examples where Trust managers make subtle references to possible media involvement, but only a few instances where they make open threats to issue press statements. Even here the threat tends to emerge from a series of exchanges in which an argument develops, rather than being announced at the outset, as might occur with a planned negotiating tactic. The extract that follows comes from the next in the series of contract monitoring meetings [held on a Monday] between the same HA and the Trust. Discussion has already traversed several areas where the HA has refused extra funding. The HAFD has just said that no more money will be forthcoming for ENT work in the current year. The Trust managers have been pressing him to say that this will mean that ENT work for HA patients will now have to stop until April.

Quality Manager: I think, you know, that has to become a little bit more of a wider announcement than just that because we have to deal with all the phone calls from these people whose expectations are very high and handling parents who insist on their children not waiting is not the most enviable task that you can deal with. So if there is work stopping then it should be widely ahm . . .

TCE:	I will issue a press statement tomorrow morning.
Quality Manager:	And it has, this is not an exaggeration of the situation but it is not very pleasant for my staff downstairs to have to deal with the parents or any patients.
HAFD:	But I mean the question is clearly as to why these expectations have to be dealt with in the first place. We have a contract, there are contracts.

[17 lines involving a discussion of whether this breaches the Patients' Charter[2] omitted]

TFD:	But you are saying to slow down the work.
HAFD:	That we will only pay for work, emergencies aside because that is sort of addition, up to the level of contract in ENT.
TFD:	But I mean you know the politicians want to end waiting. At the end of the day you are telling us//
HAFD:	Well then it will heighten concentration in certain issues or around certain issues.
TCE:	I think it is also a little stage further in terms of us switching contracts from the health authority to fundholders where there will be potential money to pay for this work. If there is no money there, the upshot of that then is that you have to reduce your capacity in these areas and that is reducing the medical staffing levels within those specialities.
HAFD:	We have never given you, we have never given you an expectation of under our contract, we presume your price and everything else is based on our contract levels and that is what we are honouring. We are saying in some specialities we can't go above that.
TFD:	But in some specialities, like ophthalmology, we haven't got the capacity to deliver the numbers. In this one we have got the capacity to over-achieve the numbers it seems. So whereas we are short of medical staffing on ophthalmology we are over-provided with medical staff in ENT. So we have to get into line with that.
HAFD:	Well I mean I think it is an internal judgement at this stage as to whether or not you want to balance what you think will be an out-turn under-performance in ophthalmology inpatients with an over-performance in another one, what we are saying is that we are not prepared to off-set full cost adjustments in the shortfall in waiting list initiatives, sorry the waiting list specialities, by full cost of under-performance. We

	will off-set at the marginal cost if you under-perform on the marginal cost, the under-performance will count against you in full. But I am not sanctioning you to do that, because our first priority at this stage is to try to get ophthalmology up to contract level. It is your judgement if you can't do that, if you would save your loss of income by over-performing, and we are not saying don't do it in those circumstances.
TCE:	How is that looking now Gerry?
HAFD:	Tricky!
TCE:	Because this is obviously going to run its course and its course will include external examination of our individual and joint actions. So how is the issue to be presented?
Quality Manager:	I just need to talk about what we would say in a press statement.
TCE:	Can I help you draft it later?
HAFD:	I mean in terms of, in terms of press releases and I am not backing away from our advice, because that is what I suggest you do, but I would prefer you to wait a few days so if there is a view coming out of our contract meeting on Thursday as to how we might want to try and influence that press release then I would appreciate that.
TCE:	Yes, I will schedule to issue the press release next Monday.

In this extract an argument develops about whether it is enough to provide funding at a level that will ensure that urgent cases are treated within guaranteed times, or if there is a more general obligation not to slow down treatments (within this time envelope). The Trust managers press the HAFD on the question of whether he is explicitly requiring them to slow the work and cease operations in the closing months of the year, a move that might be expected to attract highly negative publicity. This is taken a step further by the TCE when he talks about switching work to fundholders' patients and says that the longer-term consequence may be a reduction in medical staffing, which again would be likely to be a highly visible and controversial matter. The HAFD must manage his response so as to avoid falling foul of a number of overlapping policy requirements – the need to achieve Patients' Charter guarantees, the avoidance of a two-tier service, and the requirement to avoid a significant budgetary deficit – and is aware that these are all highly reportable matters. This is highlighted by the TCE's statement that there will be external examination of their 'individual and joint actions'. The HAFD offers the conciliatory statement that all that he saying is that the HA cannot go above contracted activity in some specialties, and subsequently offers the limited concession that over-performance in ENT can be balanced against under-performance in ophthalmology, though at marginal rather than full-cost rates. The HAFD is well aware that this is an issue in need of careful representation to the media, and gets the TCE to agree to delay the press release until after the HA Board meeting.

The struggle over meaning

In the event the agreed timetable was not followed. Two days after the meeting (and five days before the press statement was due) two stories appeared in the local newspaper based respectively on interviews with the HA and Trust chief executives. The story under larger headlines, but on page 16, came from the Trust. It was entitled 'Surgery may have to be slowed down', but started with the positive news that plans to reduce emergency services had been shelved after extra money had been allocated, and only moved to the issue of ENT services later.

> Plans to close a ward at City's West Hospital to stem the tide of emergency patients have been halted. But the hospital may have to slow down waiting list operations for some women and children. West chief executive Derek White had warned of a possible closure of one of the hospital's four emergency wards because it had only enough cash to deal with 3200 emergency cases this year. But it has already dealt with an extra 1000. West hospital also deals with emergency cases from outlying areas dealt with by other hospitals such as Northtown and Steeltown. The announcement to stay open came from Mr White after a meeting with HA chiefs on Monday saw extra money being pumped into West's medical emergency service. Mr White said the HA had provided some extra funds for medical emergencies and therefore 'I am pleased to confirm that our policy of never closing to these emergencies is safe'. But he said talks were still going on with the HA over more money for waiting lists for ear, nose and throat and gynaecological surgery cases. 'We are ahead of contract numbers there and we are awaiting the HA decision', said Mr White. If the money is not forthcoming operations on women awaiting hysterectomies and D & Cs and children with tonsil and adenoid problems could be slowed down.

On page 14 there is a report by the same journalist entitled 'HA pays £123,000 to treat two patients'. This gives brief details of two high-cost patients treated in hospitals outside the county, and says that these examples highlight the financial pressures faced by the HA.

> The Welsh Office has given South County an extra £800,000 to deal with people waiting for operations. But with some hospital services being

contracted out, the money has had to be spread across 14 hospitals in the county [and three adjoining areas], said Mr Black. 'We are trying to provide the widest range of health care procedures that work for as many people as we can', he said. The HA has to decide priorities within the funds available and in some areas workloads in the first half of the year were well above the money available. The authority is also under pressure to see if it can increase the number of people dealt with in a year. 'We have to find additional money to fund emergency work – we can't turn it away – and that could mean that elective surgery has to be spread out', said Mr Black. 'But at the end of the day there is only so much cash in the system'.

We have no direct access to the subjective intentions that lie behind these stories. The Trust report, however, is put together in a way that avoids the damaging impact of a hostile press release, while communicating a message to the public and the HA about possible troubles ahead. The language of 'extra money being pumped into [services]' portrays the HA in positive light. But at the same time the story places an onus of expectation on the authority, by stating that the Trust is 'awaiting the HA decision' and foreshadowing the consequences if no extra money is allocated. One might say that it is the kind of statement a Trust manager might issue to apply pressure, while stopping short of a negative press release.

The journalist involved approached the HA chief executive for a response the day after the interview with his Trust counterpart. Interestingly he did not attempt to produce a composite report. Instead, he wrote two stories which were ostensibly about different issues, but can be read as a statement of a looming problem and an account of why no easy solution is possible. Both reports strike a sympathetic note, while distancing the writer from association with either side. This is achieved largely by using direct quotations or reported statements from the two managers. The HACE is given space to develop an argument in his own words about difficult prioritisation decisions made against the background of growing workload pressures and Welsh Office demands for increased activity. The pressure to slow elective treatments is dealt with by the measured formulation that 'surgery has to be spread out'. Amongst other things, the splitting of the stories no doubt served to preserve this reporter's good relationships with the two sides. It is evident that the two groups of managers were part of the readership of the articles, and it seems likely that the journalist oriented to this in his presentation of the facts.

Media reportage and purchaser-provider relationships

The stories were discussed by the HA contracting team the next day (Thursday), with their Chief Executive (HACE) present. The 'Derek' mentioned is the TCE.

HAFD: Derek has misinterpreted, I think, because I also said that if he was going to put this press release out, one, he ought not to do it so quickly because we might want to have some input in it to make sure it was a balanced press report. And he therefore agreed to wait until Monday. Now I think he has misinterpreted that as us reconsidering our position on the activity and certainly that is not the impression we gave him. As far as we are concerned he has to be within the contract and I think that is an issue we should pursue.

HACE: All I know is he spoke to [a reporter] some time before 10.20 on Tuesday morning because [the reporter] rang in the light of my discussions, quotes, with Derek White the day before, where we were going to stop and re-arrange the services. And I said I haven't got the foggiest idea what you are talking about, I haven't spoken to the man. So we then had a discussion about the generalities of how you place expenditure and how you cope with one-off ECRs[3] that cost upwards of £80,000 this year, that we have had//

HAFD: They managed to report that bit.

HACE: They managed to report that bit, yes. So I mean whether he issued a press release as opposed to speaking to the press is neither here nor there but he certainly talked with them.

HAFD: Derek's explanation is that they rang him because they knew from the Trust papers that a meeting was taking place.

HACE: He could easily have said that discussions were still going on.

HAFD: Couldn't he just.

HACE: But I mean if the City NHS Trust want to negotiate through the medium of the *Evening Mail* fine, I understand those rules.

The HAFD is suggesting that the TCE has misinterpreted the situation and talked with the press after the meeting, in order to increase pressure for HA concessions. The HACE says that the reporter subsequently telephoned him, and that he denied that cutbacks or service changes were involved and talked only in generalities. In this extract the press is presented as neutral. The local newspaper is not seen to have any systematic bias on issues affecting the health service, but rather as an arena in which different organisations can put forward competing versions of the news. In this instance the reporter has gone to both sides and indeed produced two stories. The reporting process is unpredictable but not inherently malign, and is presented as requiring management. The Finance Director's comment that 'we might want to have some input in it, to make sure it was a balanced press report', indexes the much-expressed HA view that purchaser and providers should co-operate to manage news reportage, rather than offering different versions.

Failure to co-operate is seen as unhelpful and opens up the possibility of attributions of blame, but actually the HAFD, in particular, works to limit the extent of the Trust's perceived culpability. The TCE had stated that he would issue a press statement on the Monday (almost a week later), but this is not used by the HA managers to allocate blame. The HACE says that it is 'neither here nor there' whether a press release or a conversation was involved. Rather than amplifying this concern, the HAFD replies by re-stating the explanation he has received and does not offer any detailed account of the earlier meeting. The two officers end up agreeing only that Derek was to blame for not holding back the information until later. The HACE's mention of the different 'rules' that will apply if the Trust wish to 'negotiate through the medium of the *Evening Mail*' points to the perception that the usual rules have been broken. While seen as illegitimate, however, the events are not constructed as relationship-threatening ones. The infer-ence that we draw is that the HAFD, as head of the contracting team, is not yet ready to concede that the chance of a co-operative relationship with the Trust is dead, and does not want this incident to worsen the climate irremediably.

Certainly this is the tone struck in an interview with another senior member of the contracting team:

I mean, I really do wonder (. . .) what our providers sometimes think they're doing. When some of the press releases and publicity that have come out of both (West and East Trusts) recently, how they think the things they're doing can help further the interest of the Trust, which is presumably getting them better services for patients. There seems to be . . . it's almost naive, this thing of closing the ward in [East Trust] and the way that was presented and in [West Trust] about cutting back on activity and things. If we were bitter people I suppose we would naturally sort of turn round and try and bite them back. But, I mean, it just doesn't help and it suggests that our relationship is worse even than I would think.

Issuing press statements to advance a bargaining position is a powerful lever, at least in the short term, but it is not one that the Trust managers in the study, who have all worked for many years in the NHS, readily used. As we have seen, subtle references to the risks of negative publicity are much more common than actual press releases. Even in the case above where a clear threat was made, the manager opted for a story which combined good and bad news, and was less destructive to relationships than a straight-forwardly negative story. No further press release was issued. It seems to us that managers in these situations are balancing short-term negotiating advant-age against the benefits of a good long-term relationship, and orienting to certain norms of management behaviour on which such relationships depend.

Managing an organisation through the turbulent seas of the reform process could depend more on the quality of relationships than the specifics of a single contract, and later in our study some local managers came to appreciate the dangers of excessive media coverage. In the following three years, relations between the HA and West Trust improved and the major problems centred on East Trust. Again there was a pattern where Trust managers made increasingly explicit threats to go public about inadequate funding, which this time did result in hostile press releases. The ongoing dispute escalated to the point where Welsh Office conciliation was required, which itself became a topic for further news reportage. This led to stern messages from the overseeing government officials about the need to improve relationships. However, bad relations between the HA and Trust continued, and resulted, *inter alia*, in the non-renewal of part of the contract in one area of clinical activity. The Trust responded by issuing medical staff in the affected specialty with redundancy notices, provoking a revolt by the medical staff, and eventually culminating in a nationally-publicised inquiry into management arrangements in the HA and Trust. The upshot was the resignation of the Trust chairman and the removal of the senior management team.

Conclusion

In this chapter we have argued that the creation of the purchaser/provider split resulted in new forms of interaction between NHS bodies and the media. Contracting between HA and Trust took place in the shadow of media reportage, and this had consequences for the quality of relationships. What a small-scale qualitative study cannot establish is whether media reportage simply reflected relationship problems emerging from the internal market and the resultant problems of service co-ordination, or if the use of the media by some Trust managers actually amplified these problems. Certainly this latter possibility exists. In any event, our study shows that managers involved in policy implementation were themselves part of the audience for media representations which were not wholly under their control. The paper has presented data on the local level, where the HA and NHS trusts comprising the policy community have different interests, and might attempt to use the media to advance competing representations of the reform process and its problems. It seems certain, however, that reportage of the problems of implementing health reforms feed back to the overseeing central department (in this case the Welsh Office) and to the policy formation process. Actors at that higher level are also located in contested fields of discourse and themselves interact with the local and national news media. Thus, future studies might develop the analysis further to examine the role media reportage plays in transmitting signals about policy implementation to those responsible for policy formation.

Although they are a powerful lever, most local NHS managers continue to feel uneasy about using the media in their battles for resources. In our data, references to possible media involvement often arose in statements that were ambiguous, less than fully explicit, or presented in ways that indicated some measure of ambivalence on the part of the speaker. Managers steered a delicate course between self-interest and the maintenance of particular conceptions of managerial/professional identity. Thus, the powerful, but potentially double-edged, weapon of public disclosure was usually broached in indirect terms, and might be presented as a last resort forced on managers who would rather behave differently. Arguably, these interactions reflect more general tensions that arise when managerial discourses, emphasising concepts such as adversarial contracting, markets and competition, are imported into professional organisations with a public service mission. The ways in which participants on both sides of the divide managed potential or actual media involvement illustrate how difficult many of the day-to-day negotiations, resulting from these policy changes, were for participants.

Notes

1   All proper names are pseudonyms.
2   The Patients' Charter was introduced by the UK Government to guarantee certain quality standards for patients, such as maximum waiting times for surgical operations. Achieving Charter standards came to be seen as a key test of the success of the internal market reforms, and the Government put considerable pressure on HAs and Trusts to meet the targets set.
3   ECRs (extra-contractual referrals) are cases not covered by NHS contracts for which one-off payments are made.

References

Berridge, V. (1991) Aids, the media and health policy, *Health Education Journal*, 50, 179–85.
Birkinshaw, P.J. (2000) Freedom of information in the UK: a progress report, *Government Information Quarterly*, 17, 419–24.
Birkinshaw, P.J. (2002) Freedom of information in the UK and Europe: further progress? *Government Information Quarterly*, 19, 77–86.
Department of Health (DoH) (1997) *The New NHS: Modern, Dependable*, Cm 3807, London: The Stationery Office.
Flinders, M. (2000) The politics of accountability: a case study of freedom of information legislation in the United Kingdom, *Political Quarterly*, 71, 422–35.
Flynn, R., Williams, G. and Pickard, S. (1996) *Markets and Networks: Contracting in Community Health Services*. Buckingham: Open University Press.
Goldsteen, R.L., Goldsteen, K, Swan, J.H. and Clemena, W. (2001) Harry and Louise and health care reform: romancing public opinion, *Journal of Health Politics, Policy and Law*, 26, 1325–52.
Griffiths, L. and Hughes, D. (2000) Talking contracts and taking care: managers and professionals in the NHS internal market, *Social Science and Medicine*, 51, 209–22.
Huebner, J., Fan, D.P. and Finnegan, J. (1997) 'Death by a thousand cuts': the impact of media coverage on public opinion about Clinton's Health Security Act, *Journal of Health Communication*, 2, 253–70.

Hughes, D. and Griffiths, L. (1999a) On penalties and the Patient's Charter: centralism v decentralised governance in the NHS, *Sociology of Health and Illness*, 21, 1, 71–94.

Hughes, D. and Griffiths, L. (1999b) Access to public documents in a study of the NHS internal market: openness v secrecy in contracting for clinical services, *International Journal of Social Research Methodology: Theory and Practice*, 2, 1, 1–16.

Hughes, D., Griffiths, L. and Lambert, S. (2000) Opening Pandora's box? Freedom of information and health services research, *Journal of Health Services Research and Policy*, 5, 59–61.

Lupton, D. (1994) The great debate about cholesterol: medical controversy and the news media, *Australian and New Zealand Journal of Sociology*, 30, 334–9.

McKee, M. (1999) Secret government revisited: draft *Freedom of Information Act* may be a step backwards, *British Medical Journal*, 318, 7200, 1712–13.

Schlesinger, P. and Tumber, H. (1994) *Reporting Crime: the Media Politics of Criminal Justice*. Oxford: Oxford University Press.

Strong, P.M. and Robinson, J. (1990) *The NHS: under New Management*. Buckingham: Open University Press.

Tumber, H.(ed) (1999) *News: a Reader*. Oxford: Oxford University Press.

Watney, S. (1996) *Policing Desire: Pornography, AIDS, and the Media, 3rd Edition*. Minneapolis, MN: University of Minnesota Press.

Chapter 5

'Ignorance is bliss sometimes': constraints on the emergence of the 'informed patient' in the changing landscapes of health information

Flis Henwood, Sally Wyatt, Angie Hart and Julie Smith

Introduction

Recent health policy documents in the UK (Department of Health 1998 and 2001a) suggest that the greater availability of health information via the Internet will lead to the emergence of more informed patients who are better able to assess the risks and benefits of different treatments for themselves. The now widely used notion of 'informed choice' is indicative of the greater agency and sense of empowerment said to be experienced by such patients. Such thinking exists within sociology, too, where, following Giddens' notion of the 'reflexive consumer' (Giddens 1991), there is some support for the idea that the overall expansion in medical knowledge via new media technologies such as the Internet will empower patients (see, for example, Hardey 1999 and 2001). The project upon which this paper is based started from a rather different premise. Rather than assuming that the Internet will necessarily and always empower patients, our own position was to remain alert to the important potential of the Internet without making too many prior assumptions about the extent and nature of its use and its relationship to patient empowerment. Our project investigated the ways in which individuals engaged with a range of different media and sources of health information in constructing their understandings about their health problems and treatments.

This chapter begins with a brief overview of the debates about the significance of the Internet for health information in the context of debates about the informed patient and the 'partnership' model of practitioner-patient relationships. This is followed by an outline of our methodology and an introduction to our research participants. In our results section, we first report on the 'information landscapes' currently inhabited by our participants. Here, we found that whilst the Internet does now feature in the information landscapes of half of our participants, it is just one of many different sources through which they currently access health information, with more traditional sources and media continuing to be very significant. We argue that there are still a number of serious constraints on the emergence of the 'informed patient' identity in our patient group. First, a significant minority of participants are reluctant to take on the responsibility implied by the 'informed patient' discourse. Second, there is a real problem with information literacy amongst our participants which has implications for the extent to which they are able to become more 'informed' about their health, whatever the media form involved. Third, participants' accounts of their expectations and experiences of information sharing in encounters with healthcare professionals suggests that there are serious constraints operating in the medical encounter itself which further inhibit this process of empowerment through information.

The Internet, health information and patient empowerment

Information and empowerment
Quality information, appropriately targeted, is seen as central to the empowerment of patients and is part of the UK government's agenda, as evidenced by policy documents such as *Information for Health* (Department of Health 1998) and *Building the Information Core* (Department of Health 2001a). In particular, information is understood to be a necessary precursor to the development of new 'partnership' relationships between healthcare practitioners and patients that the government is seeking to promote. The field of 'consumer health information' has become so important that one expert in this field has argued we are witnessing the growth of a new 'information specialism' (Gann 1991). The dominant discourse here is said to be one of 'rights', where patients have a right to information and are 'treated as individuals, not treatment opportunities' (Gann and Needham 1992).

Concern to provide more quality information to the public to help facilitate the emergence of this more informed patient has come from many quarters but particularly from those involved in assessing quality and providing tools for measuring the quality of health information offered to the public. One such UK organisation, the Centre for Health Information Quality (1999), has argued for healthcare practitioners to work in a partnership relationship with consumers to develop information materials and promote shared clinical decision-making. Information professionals, too, are calling for public empowerment through accessible health information (Calvano 1996).

There are many practical limitations on the extent to which this new partnership model can be realised. As one *British Medical Journal* (*BMJ*) editorial argued, there are two important questions to be asked here: how far do patients want to participate and how feasible is it in days of the eight minute consultation? (*BMJ* 1999). Research supports the notion that healthcare practitioners are experiencing new pressures which they associate with the growth of consumerism in healthcare. For example, Weiss and Fitzpatrick (1997), in a report on research into GP (general practitioner/family doctor) prescribing practices, found that GPs were prescribing 'irrationally' as a response to the growing demands and expectations of patients.

There is a much more fundamental problem with the informed patient discourse and with much of the consumer health information literature, however. As Dixon-Woods (2001) has argued in her analysis of publications about the use of patient information leaflets, the dominant discourse in this literature tends to privilege bio-medical over other forms of information and knowledge, and adopts a rather one-way model of communication. Dixon-Woods' analysis therefore points to a potential constraint on the patient empowerment process, where, in cases of conflict between bio-medical and 'lay' knowledges, for example, 'information for choice' might better be replaced with the more honest 'information for compliance'.

Recent work in medical sociology suggests that there continues to be a gap between the partnership and 'negotiation' models of practitioner-patient relations and the empirical reality of everyday practice. For example, Massé et al. (2001), in a qualitative analysis of clinical encounters between peri-menopausal women and women doctors, argue that there are very clear limitations on the enactment of the negotiation model proposed by Katon and Kleinman (1981). They conclude that viewing the clinical encounter as a transactional process between two rational actors is misleading and reductionist. Massé et al. identified two main 'strategies' used by doctors to convince women of the usefulness of hormone replacement therapy (HRT). First, they placed strong emphasis on the positive effects of HRT on the long-term quality of life and a low emphasis on the benefits of modification of lifestyle. Second, the information they provided was not 'neutral' but had itself to be considered as part of the strategy used to convince women to consider taking HRT.

Whilst Massé and colleagues tend to identify practitioner actions as particularly significant in constraining the emergence of more equitable practitioner-patient relations, Lupton (1997) has drawn attention to the fact that patients have agency here, too. Lupton argues that patients do not always act 'rationally' within the context of the medical encounter, in line with notions of the reflexive self of late modernity: 'a self who acts in a calculated manner to engage in self-improvement and who is sceptical about expert knowledges' (Lupton 1997: 373). Having analysed data from 60 in-depth interviews, she concludes that:

> in their interactions with doctors and other health care workers, lay people may pursue both the ideal type 'consumerist' and the 'passive patient' subject position simultaneously or variously, depending on the context (1997: 373).

For Lupton, 'late modernist notions of reflexivity . . . fail to recognise the complexity and changeable nature of the desires, emotions and needs that characterise the patient-doctor relationship' (1997: 373). As we demonstrate in a later section, our own empirical data support this view.

The Internet and patient empowerment

A powerful discourse around new media technologies such as the Internet and their potential for delivering and communicating health information has entered this debate about information and empowerment. Again, the UK government is putting massive resources into developing new media-based information services such as NHS Direct and NHS Direct Online[1], as well as promoting the use of these and other health information services via web kiosks, interactive television and other platforms (Nicholas, Huntington and Williams 2000, 2001). Huge efforts are also being made to encourage the use of new electronic media in the context of the patient-practitioner consultation (Department of Health 2001b, Watkins *et al.* 1999). Other countries are following similar strategies (see, for example, Health Canada 1999).

The potential of such new media in the development of new services and new practitioner-patient relationships is also widely discussed within the emerging field of 'consumer health informatics'. Ferguson (1997), in particular, has argued that, alongside technological developments, we are witnessing the emergence of a new health consumer identity which he terms the 'online self-helpers' (Ferguson 1997). He argues that the health care practitioners who participate in these online self-help networks are also experiencing an identity shift, moving from authority figure to facilitator.

Eysenbach (2000) also identifies a new and growing concern with the information needs of patients, and attributes a specific role to new interactive technologies such as the Internet in this shift of emphasis towards consumers' information needs:

> The increasing availability of interactive information that is accessible to consumers, most notably through the Internet and related technologies such as digital TV and web television, coincides *with the desires of most consumers to assume more responsibility for their health* . . . Information technology and consumerism are synergistic forces that promote an 'information age healthcare system' in which consumers can, ideally, *use information technology to gain access to information and control their own health care*, thereby utilising health care resources more efficiently (2000: 1714, our emphasis).

Eysenbach is very careful not to reify the Internet or see it as always the most appropriate means to deliver health information. For example, he argues that consumer health informatics is not restricted to the use of computers and telecommunications but also includes the delivery of information to patients through other media. Despite this conclusion, however, the overall tone of his work is very optimistic about the potential of the Internet, with a tendency for increased consumer control and self-reliance being attributed in some way to this particular information medium. He is also making the normative assumption, like Ferguson, that people want to operate as healthcare 'consumers', to take more responsibility for their own health through 'self-care'.

The arguments of Ferguson and Eysenbach are very persuasive and many critics of the paternalist model of practitioner-patient relations that has dominated state-provided healthcare systems for so long will have sympathy with these views. However, following the work of Lupton and others discussed earlier, we would argue that some of the assumptions underlying these arguments need further empirical testing. For example, are individuals really moving towards self-care in quite the way suggested by these arguments? Is there a direct link between information access and empowerment? And, most significantly, are Internet access and patient empowerment so inextricably linked?

Optimistic accounts of Internet use can be found in the sociological literature, too. Hardey (1999), for example, has claimed that, 'the Internet forms the site of a new struggle over expertise in health that *will transform* the relationship between health professionals and their clients' (1999: 820, our emphasis). In more recent work, Hardey (2001) re-affirms that the Internet has the potential to transform doctor-patient relationships by ending the medical monopoly over information. Drawing on a qualitative study of 10 households who do use the Internet and an online questionnaire sent to people who produced their own home pages about their illnesses, Hardey highlights the emergence of health service users as significant *providers,* as well as consumers of health information and advice.

Similar points have been made by Burrows *et al.* (2000) who explore the use of the Internet for online self-help and social support – what the authors term 'virtual community care'. Like Hardey, Burrows *et al.* draw attention to the rise of self-help groups; the privileging of lay knowledge and experience over the 'expert' knowledge of health and welfare professionals; the nature of professional-client relationships; the quality and legitimacy of advice, information and support; dis/empowerment; and social exclusion. They argue:

> Whether or not the large number of social actors who currently engage in online self-help and social support constitute themselves into virtual communities is a key area for debate. But whatever conceptualisation one favours, there is no doubt that growing numbers of people across the globe are using e-mail, the World Wide Web, mailing and discussion lists, news groups, MUDs, IRC, and other forms of computer mediated communication (CMC) to offer and receive information, advice and support across a massive range of health and social issues (Burrows *et al.* 2000: 101).

Such detailed empirical studies of Internet use can tell us much about the significance of this medium in the everyday lives of specific user groups and about the emergent relations and communities that may accompany such use. Thus, studies of online health communities tell us much about how the Internet can support community building which is valuable and interesting in its own right. They also demonstrate well the point made by science and technology studies (STS) that users of technologies 'shape' those technologies to fit their needs and that the context of use, in particular, is central to understanding the significance of such technologies (Bijker and Law 1992, MacKenzie and Wajcman 1999, Lie and Sørensen 1996, Silverstone and Hirsch 1992). There is, however, a danger that such work will be interpreted and/or used to imply that the Internet is, in itself, empowering of patients, and it is this type of technological determinism that we wanted to avoid in our own study. In the next section, we explain how we designed our study to do this.

The study and its participants

The study focused on a group of mid-life women in the context of their decision-making regarding taking hormone replacement therapy (HRT) for the relief of menopausal symptoms. However, rather than starting with the Internet as our focus and then trying to recruit users and non-users, we sought, instead, to identify a group of women who would have information needs and therefore be *potential* users of the Internet, and then to examine their information practices across a range of different media and sources.

Why mid-life women and HRT?
Following earlier work on technology and inequality (Wyatt *et al.* 2000), we were interested in examining some of the issues concerning the 'digital divide' and the inequalities surrounding Internet use, and we determined that the health information practices of mid-life and older women would be an appropriate focus. Whilst age and gender are factors that have been shown to affect Internet use, with older people and women being generally underrepresented amongst Internet users, women have been found to use the Internet more than men for accessing health information (Fox and Rainie 2000). We wanted to see, therefore, how far the Internet had begun to figure in the information landscapes of this particular group of women. HRT was thought to be an interesting focus here because almost all women in mid-life face some symptoms associated with the menopause, for which HRT is the most well-known conventional treatment, and were therefore likely to face a decision about its use. Thus, it would be possible to take this particular group and try to identify their information and decision-making practices regarding HRT. In particular, we aimed to map the information landscapes they inhabited and gain insight into the key information sources and media used to access health information as part of this decision-making process.

Hormone replacement therapy comprises a range of treatments that have been available since the 1960s. Such treatments are offered to women during menopause or following a full hysterectomy. At the time that most of our participants were prescribed HRT, it was the dominant conventional treatment for the relief of a range of menopausal symptoms as well as being used in the prevention of osteoporosis, heart disease and bowel cancer. Dangers identified at the time included increased risk of breast cancer and dementia.

Thus, the benefits of HRT are potentially huge but so are the associated dangers and uncertainties. More importantly, these risks and benefits are highly contested and always changing[2]. In addition, there are many alternative therapies available for alleviating menopausal symptoms and preventing the onset of osteoporosis, including herbal and homeopathic remedies as well as dietary adjustments; and so the range of information and advice available to women is both enormous and potentially conflicting.

HRT receives a great deal of coverage in the popular media in the UK and it may be argued that this would limit women's need to access information via the Internet. However, precisely because of this media coverage, including, at times, some very adverse reporting concerning prescribing practices and side effects, we thought it possible that women would turn to other sources to check and validate media accounts. It was this kind of 'cross-media' practice that we were keen to identify.

Recruitment and interview focus
Thirty-two women were recruited through a GP practice (family doctor) or gynaecological clinic in a city in the south east of England. Women who were taking, had considered taking, or had recently stopped taking HRT were all considered for inclusion in the study. Interviews, each lasting between one and two hours, were conducted between November 2001 and May 2002. All interviews were audio-recorded and fully transcribed. Our sample included participants from a range of socio-economic groups, with varied educational experience and qualifications. Of the 32 women interviewed, the average age was 55, with the youngest being 39 and the oldest 73. Six of these women did not have children. Eighteen were in a relationship. Twenty-six owned their own homes, although 15 had an annual income of less than £20,000. Thirteen had some form of post-secondary education. All were white.

The interview schedule included questions about health information practices in general before going on to ask about HRT-related health information practices. In the results section below, we present a very brief overview of the health information landscapes inhabited by our participants. We then discuss constraints on the emergence of the informed patient under three headings: taking responsibility; information literacy; and the medical encounter. The final section of the paper explores the implications of the study, as a whole, for both theory and policy in this field.

Results

Information landscapes
In order the better to understand how these women located themselves within the landscape of health information, the very first question we asked them was:

What, if anything, do you do when you first feel something isn't quite right with your health?

Not one woman, in reply to this question, stated that she sought information via the Internet as a first move. Results suggest that most women still rely heavily on their doctors as a first port of call for health advice and information. This was confirmed in responses to a subsequent question on other information sources used regularly, where GPs were confirmed as being *the* most important source of health information and advice for 31 of the 32 participants. Family members, usually women, were the second most often cited source, by 23 of the women. Friends, pharmacists and alternative healthcare practitioners were mentioned by 22 participants.

Again, as a result of prompting, the following information 'media' (in order of importance) were cited as having been used by participants to access health information at some point in the past: the Internet; women's and health magazines; television; self-help books; newspapers; radio; NHS Direct; and 'other' such as leaflets from pharmacists or those that come with drugs.

Of the 32 women interviewed, 19 had access to the Internet. Of these, 16 had actually used the Internet at some point, some more regularly than others. Nearly all users (15 out of 16) had used the Internet to access health information at some time, which appeared to be one of the most popular uses of the Internet outside work, with leisure/hobbies, holiday and travel information and finances also being important. Twelve Internet users accessed the Net at home and three accessed it elsewhere (one only had work access, one preferred work access as her son dominated the home PC, and one had regular access through her daughter's friend at her daughter's friend's home). Of these 15 users, three had sought information about the health of others, but not about themselves.

Thus, results suggest that our participants access a range of different information sources and media, but the interesting questions remain. How keen are they to become more informed about their health? Does access to information necessarily lead to feelings of empowerment? Does access to the Internet enhance information-related empowerment? Below, we explore the constraints on the emergence of the 'informed patient' under three headings: taking responsibility; information literacy; and the medical encounter.

Taking responsibility

The informed patient discourse and its sociological equivalent – the 'reflexive consumer' – assumes that individuals want to take more and more responsibility for their own health and that this involves active information searching, above and beyond the traditional visit to the doctor. In order to assess how far our participants engaged in such active information searching, we therefore asked:

Have you ever looked something up for yourself before going to see a doctor, nurse or other health care practitioner?

Eighteen of the 32 participants had never looked anything up for themselves before a visit to a doctor or other healthcare practitioner. Eleven of these offered no explanation for this and many seemed surprised by the question. Two kinds of explanation were offered by the seven other participants. The first suggested a reluctance to take the kind of responsibility for self-care suggested by the 'informed patient' discourse. The feeling here was that it was the doctor's job to know about such matters. This view was evidenced by comments such as: 'that's what they're trained for' (Helen); 'I would just trust a doctor' (Betty); and 'I wouldn't look in anything, I'd just go by what the doctors tell me. For myself I wouldn't look anything up. Ignorance is bliss sometimes!' (Christine). The second kind of explanation suggested a different kind of constraint on the emergence of the 'informed patient' identity. Here, there appeared to be a fear of being seen to challenge the doctor: 'it might be like telling your granny how to suck eggs really, he might not want to know' (Annie); and 'They don't like to be told you've got X. They like to tell you that you've got X' (Caroline).

Thus, we cannot assume that everyone sees the importance of taking on more responsibility for their health, especially where that involves 'becoming informed' outside of the traditional medical encounter. This particular group of mid-life women felt either that it was a doctor's job to inform patients about their health or that there would be problems in trying to work in partnership with doctors in the way suggested by the informed patient discourse. We return to this discussion later when we discuss womens' accounts of information exchange in the medical encounter.

Information literacy
Becoming informed involves skills and competencies that relate both to the information itself and to the medium used to access that information. Amongst our participants we found women who had very few information literacy skills and others who lacked general computer literacy skills and/or web searching skills. Below, we discuss how lack of competency in these areas can inhibit the emergence of the informed patient identity. To illustrate this point, we compare more and less 'literate' participants, some of whom have access only to the more traditional media, others who have access to the Internet as well.

Annie is interesting to us because, whilst she claimed never to have looked something up before a visit to her doctor, she is clearly an avid information seeker and literate in relation to the health information she accesses through traditional media and sources. At the time of the interview, Annie did not own a computer and had never accessed the Internet herself.

Annie told us how she clipped and saved articles from both tabloid and quality newspapers and magazines, sent off for additional information and collected leaflets from her doctor's practice, from hospital waiting rooms, from the pharmacist, from health food shops and from prescriptions. She regularly bought health books, and used bookshops as a sort of reference library (looking things up in books in shops rather than going to a library). She watched things on television if they caught her eye. She bought popular health magazines every couple of months. Annie talked with friends, colleagues and family, especially her sister, about health matters. She was discerning in her use of information, explaining that when she received unsolicited 'junk mail' on health matters, she tended to ignore it, thinking they were trying to sell her something.

Annie had accessed a range of traditional information media to inform herself about the pros and cons of HRT and the use of alternative herbal remedies to treat menopausal symptoms. In addition, when very concerned about a specific treatment she had been prescribed, she had enlisted a friend with access to the web to help her find the precise information she needed. She represents our more information-literate participants.

In contrast to Annie, Marge appeared to be far less information literate and really rather uninterested and disengaged from debates about HRT and related health matters. Marge was in her early 50s at the time of the interview. She lived alone in state-subsidised housing, had four children and two grandchildren. She had trained and worked as a nurse but was retired on health grounds. She was registered disabled. She had been taking HRT for about four years since being diagnosed with osteoporosis. She had had a hysterectomy in 1981 but was not offered HRT at the time and was uninterested in why that might have been. She was unaware of any alternative treatments for osteoporosis and had not looked for any.

All Marge's information and knowledge about HRT came either from specialists or her GP. Her first port of call when concerned about her health was always her GP, whom she trusted absolutely. She did not look up health issues in self-help books which she thought can be 'frightening'. She did not actively look for health information in traditional media but might read/watch something if she noticed it. She has had home Internet access, via Sky, for three to four years but rarely used it for health-related matters. Her main use was for accessing digital photos of her granddaughter who lived in another part of the country. She reported using the Internet for health information when she was first diagnosed with osteoporosis but could remember little about this search other than that her son-in-law, who worked 'in computers', had given her a specific web site to go to. Marge showed little awareness of the sources of information (publisher, organisation, etc.) she found on the web and expressed no interest in issues of information validity or quality, tending to trust whatever she found there, regardless of source. She identified no particular advantage to finding information online and complained about getting 'too much information' with no possibility of asking anyone any questions.

Information literacy skills are crucial when searching on the web. Awareness of sources (individual or organisation publishing the information) is one means by which one can begin to assess the validity of the information found on the web. While Marge is our least information-literate Internet user, many others were similarly uninterested in information source and validity issues, displaying low levels of information literacy.

When asked about source, some clearly felt that the Internet was itself the source, and a trustworthy one at that. Others, whilst recognising that the web, in particular, offered access to many different sources of information, still seemed relatively unaware of the importance of checking the source. For one woman, repetition was a sufficient indicator of information validity:

> . . . there are so many different sources that you can go to, so many different sites and you are able to compare them with and you find, 'oh yes it said that on the last site so that must be right' (Sharon).

Perhaps surprisingly, there was little awareness of commercial interests on the Internet with only two participants being overtly critical of commercial sites. Jane was one of them. However, Jane demonstrated a rather low level of information literacy being apparently unaware that she was, herself, making use of what others would consider commercially-biased information. As a vegetarian, she was interested in using the web to find alternatives to dairy products as a source of calcium. She explained her search strategy:

> I mean you could put in there 'dairy products' or something, or you could go the opposite way like I do . . . I could look up 'soya'.

Jane explained how this search strategy took her to the site of a well-known soya products company and that here she found out about 'the benefits of soya in your diet'. She continued:

> . . . so you go backwards actually, you find out the benefits, or not the benefits of dairy produce, by looking up something that's actually opposite. . . . I mean you could put in 'dairy products' but it might not tell you what you want to know, so you think there might be another way, so I go round the back door and go to 'soya milk' and then it tells you about that.

Clearly, Jane is unwilling to trust the information about dairy products from producers of dairy products but is, at the same time, more than happy to accept what producers of soya products say about the benefits of soya. As she says herself at one point, a particular site 'might not tell you what you want to know'. For her, this was confirmation that many humans are not able to tolerate cow's milk and that soya is a good substitute.

Perhaps surprisingly, only four participants thought medical sites more trustworthy than other sites. Two women who worked in the health sector specifically mentioned using medical sites as their preferred sources of health information but both seemed relatively lacking in confidence about their use of the web. Carol had access to the Internet both at home and at work. She spoke about looking for something on abortion with a colleague at work and looking for information about a specific health problem of her own. When asked about specific sources she accessed, she described herself as 'quite discerning' in her use but was unable to name any sites she particularly trusted. Barbara, who worked in health administration, mentioned using *Medline*, the medical database, but disliked computers and had few computer or web-related skills and always worked through an intermediary – a health librarian.

Another woman who claimed that she trusted medical sites above others also failed to name any specific sites she used, and seemed unaware of the existence of NHS online information services:

> If there was, probably, an NHS site or something like that on there, that's probably the one I'd go to first, because you trust the NHS. I don't know why, but you do! Because that's what they're there for (Phoebe).

These Internet users contrast well with our most information-literate user – Janet, who worked in the information profession. Janet had been prescribed HRT following a hysterectomy but had reacted badly to it and had ceased taking it. She used the Internet to find out about alternatives to HRT, among other things. She described her web search strategy:

> I go straight to a search engine and put in some terms and in that way then you get the mix of sources that you might want to go for. You're not just targeting medical journals for example and that's not what I want to do. I want to find more of a serendipity kind of approach really and see what comes up and then skim through it because there's usually thousands and thousands but just do it that way.

Janet understood that most people would probably be more trusting of medical sites but explained that she was more sceptical, as she was aware of medical links with the pharmaceutical industry:

> I know what the conventional thinking is which is that something in the *British Medical Journal* or something is meant to be reliable – its backed up by conventional research. Then the other me says 'that's funded by pharmaceutical companies, they've got an axe to grind, they know what they want and there are other natural things that you can do' and so I don't consider either more reliable. I consider all of it.

Clearly, whilst medical sites are a signpost to trustworthiness for some, this is not a universal experience. The same sign will be 'read' or interpreted quite differently by different people. In particular, those with an interest in alternative or complementary therapies may well find conventional medical sites restrict and circumscribe their 'informed choice', just as some health-care practitioners were reported to have done in the context of the medical encounter, discussed next.

The medical encounter

When discussing the first constraint on the emergence of the informed patient – 'taking responsibility' – we found that 14 of the 32 women had, at some point, actively searched for information about their health prior to a visit to the doctor. These women were asked whether they disclosed what they already knew. As with those who did not look up information for themselves, there was, amongst the more informed participants, still a great concern about appearing to over-step the boundary between 'expert' and 'patient' here. The following examples illustrate this point well:

> I wait . . . I'm old-fashioned. I go in for them to tell me what's wrong with me . . . I wouldn't teach them how to do their job, I would defer to their greater knowledge on whatever subject (Peggy).

> No, because I think he's got to make his own diagnosis. It's not very helpful if I go in there and say, 'Look, I feel that I have –' I think that's very inappropriate (Carol).

> You have to be very careful because they come back with – and I don't blame them at all – they say, 'don't believe what you read in the paper, you're here with me now and I'm telling you this'. I don't blame them, because it must be very hard, when you go and say, 'Oh, I read this in the paper'. It's not easy for them . . . (Pat).

The last example is particularly interesting for the way in which the patient, here, feels the need to protect the doctor from the 'informed patient' who she sees as exerting extra pressures on an already busy professional. Clearly, there is a distinction to be made between informing oneself about one's specific health conditions and treatments and being prepared, or feeling able, to disclose what one has found out to one's doctor. This point is supported by our analysis of participants' accounts of medical encounters during their HRT decision-making.

First, we return to Annie whom we have described as information literate and highly engaged and motivated to take responsibility for her health. However, when it came to her relationship with doctors she appeared not to perform the informed patient identity at all. In the interview, she mentioned, many times, her concern about the weight gain which, according to women's 'lay knowledge', is widely thought to be caused by HRT. She claimed, however, to have been 'reassured' by her doctor when told that menopausal women on HRT gain less weight, on average, than those not on HRT. Despite being very active in relation to information, Annie was very reluctant to engage with her doctor about this. She is clearly slightly intimidated by doctors and claims she would be more likely to disclose what she knows to an alternative/complementary practitioner because 'they are not on such a high level' as medical professionals. Annie shows us that it is perfectly possible to be very engaged with one's own health and informed about treatment options through traditional information media and sources but, at the same time constrained in the full development of an informed patient identity because of a reluctance to challenge the doctor.

Barbara is a good example of participants who seem to have been denied their right to make an 'informed choice' about HRT. She describes being given an implant following a hysterectomy. She told us that she understood that she had no choice – if she did not take it, her doctor told her, she would develop osteoporosis. She suffered many ill effects, including migraines, from the HRT and yet claims she was told nothing about the possible negative side effects, only later discovering that oestrogen is linked to migraines. After trying many different HRT preparations, Barbara eventually came off it altogether, citing migraines and weight gain as the main reasons. Barbara described her experiences of trying to share information with doctors:

I kind of researched it a little bit myself, looked it up, came up with suggestions and they don't like it or they'll say 'well, you might have heard that, you might have looked that up but that's not the case.
The case is this'. And you can see them getting uptight, shoulders going up, arms crossing . . . I mean they might be right sometimes, I'm not saying they're wrong, they might well be right but they're not open. It's a closed door all the time, It's closed. It's black and white and you have got to be out of that [place] as quick as possible . . . there is no negotiation.

Other women described feeling similarly dismissed when seeking to become more actively engaged in decision-making. Liza was concerned about being prescribed HRT after only a 10-minute consultation, particularly as her sister had died of breast cancer. She took the prescription and had it filled but never took the pills. She subsequently consulted a colleague at work (a nurse) about alternative ways of taking HRT. She had been offered only pills or patches but wanted to explore nasal spray and cream options so suggested this to the doctor:

I asked if I could have the creams and he just said, 'no' because nobody else had asked for them, so they'd never prescribed them, so they weren't sure of their efficacy.

She continued:

I decided not to use anything . . . In the end [I] came away with a prescription which I didn't use.

In Liza's story, it appears no-one was empowered. Liza felt that she was denied her right to an 'informed choice' and her doctors failed to get the compliance they sought when prescribing HRT.

Another woman, Sharon, described how she was concerned that taking HRT might well be making her fibroid grow. She had found this information in a book she had obtained from her local library and took this knowledge to her GP, who dismissed her concerns. She never did find out if there was any relationship between HRT and fibroid growth but believes that prevarication and uncertainty on the part of her doctor resulted in an eventual hysterectomy to remove the fibroid growth. Sharon was frustrated about her attempts to engage more fully with her GP.

Despite nearly half the women in our sample being willing and able to look things up for themselves prior to visits to healthcare professionals, in no instance did it seem to be the case that disclosing what was already known about their particular health problems and their treatments was a completely straightforward process for these women. Exceptions might be the one woman who stated that she would feel confident disclosing to a complementary therapist (though not to her GP), and another who felt that 'a lot of doctors now know that some people know their bodies better than what [the doctors] do' and that things were, therefore, getting better over time. In general, however, for this particular group of mid-life women, it seems that the boundary between the expert healthcare professional and the patient is still fairly robust.

Conclusions

The research we have reported on here sought to locate the Internet in the overall information landscapes of a specific group of health service users – mid-life women – and to analyse the significance of different information media in the development of the 'informed patient' or 'reflexive consumer' identity. In the ideal types of patient and practitioner, patients take it upon themselves to become informed about their own health conditions and the treatment options available, and doctors agree to listen to patients and negotiate regarding treatments, taking patients' interests and values into account. We conclude that there appear to be very real constraints on the emergence of the informed patient identity for this group of patients, at least.

First, many patients do not want to take responsibility or seek out information for themselves – they are more than happy to trust their GPs and leave decisions to them. There may be many different reasons for this as Lupton (1997) has suggested but it is important that the patient perspective is acknowledged nevertheless. This finding is particularly interesting in terms of the 'rights' agenda inherent within the consumer health-information literature discussed at the start of this paper. 'Rights' carry 'responsibilities' and, whilst many commentators in the consumer health-information and consumer health-informatics fields may believe that increased consumer/ patient responsibility for health is the way forward, some patients are clearly not yet convinced. The arguments of consumer health-informatics experts such as Ferguson (1997) and Eysenbach (2000), discussed earlier, might need to be revised to accommodate such findings.

A second constraint on the emergence and enactment of the informed patient identity has to do with skills and competencies in what we might call 'information literacy'. These skills involve general awareness of where to find information, information retrieval, understanding the context of the information being provided, and interpretation and communication of that information in the context of health-care decision-making. This point becomes all the more pertinent when we come to look at Internet use. Although almost half of our participants had used the Internet for accessing health information, we found that the search strategies used were very unsystematic. In addition, we found, as did Eysenbach and Köhler (2002) in their qualitative study of health information searching on the Web, there was almost no awareness of who or what organisation was publishing the information being accessed. Indeed, for some, the information 'media' and 'source' were collapsed and the Internet was itself considered a source of health information and, for many, a good one at that.

The third constraint in the emergence of informed patients and partner-ship relations comes from the apparent reluctance of practitioners to take on this new role. Our analysis found plenty of examples of women who *had* informed themselves regarding their particular health condition and its treatments but who, on trying to negotiate with their GPs, had had their views and opinions quite decisively rejected or dismissed. This seems to be particularly the case where 'lay' knowledge does not coincide with expert/ medical knowledge and where a certain level of compliance with medical opinion is required. These findings reflect the arguments made by Dixon-Woods (2001) and Massé *et al.* (2001) and suggest that there are real limits to the 'information for choice' agenda, embedded within the notion of the informed patient.

What is clear is that the informed patient will not emerge naturally or easily within existing structures and relationships. Constraints exist within both practitioner and patient communities and within the space occupied by both in the medical encounter. Analysis from data collected during a later stage of this project will explore practitioner views and experiences of work-ing with informed patients and will be reported upon in due course. More research is needed into how this encounter can be re-designed to enable a more equitable exchange of lay and expert knowledges. Further, more time and resources need to be allocated for reflection on the necessary changes that are needed in both consumer health and medical education to facilitate such fundamental shifts in the balance of power implied in the informed patient discourse.

Acknowledgements

The research on which this paper is based is jointly funded by the UK Economic and Social Research Council and the Medical Research Council under the 'Innovative Health Technologies' programme (Project No. L218252039).

Notes

1   These are National Health Service initiatives. NHS Direct is a telephone-based service, NHS Direct Online is an Internet-based service, both offering health information and advice direct to patients and the public.
2   Indeed, the abandonment of a US HRT trial in July 2002, which received extensive media coverage, changed the balance of risk factors. A planned publication will report on how our participants reacted to this new information in the context of their own HRT decision-making.

References

Bijker, W.E. and Law, J. (eds) (1992) *Shaping Technology/Building Society, Studies in Sociotechnical Change*. Cambridge, MA: MIT Press.
British Medical Journal (1999) Editorial Paternalism or partnership? *BMJ*, 319, 719–20.
Burrows, R., Nettleton, S., Pleace, N. *et al.* (2000) Virtual community care? Social policy and the emergence of computer mediated social support, *Information, Communication and Society*, 3, 1, 95–121.
Calvano, M. (1996) Public empowerment through accessible health information, *Bulletin of the Medical Library Association*, 84, 2, 253–56.
Centre for Health Information Quality (1999) Involving consumers in the development and evaluation of health information, *Topic Bulletin 4*, Centre for Health Information Quality.
Department of Health (1998) *Information for Health: an Information Strategy for the Modern NHS, 1998–2005*. London: Department of Health.
Department of Health (2001a) *Building the Information Core: Implementing the NHS Plan*. London: Department of Health.
Department of Health (2001b) First patients get on-line access to their own medical records: pilot trials begin at two GP practices, Press release 21 January.
Dixon-Woods, M. (2001) Writing wrongs? An analysis of published discourses about the use of patient information leaflets, *Social Science and Medicine*, 52, 1417–32.
Eysenbach, G. (2000) Consumer health informatics, *British Medical Journal*, 320, 7251, 1713.
Eysenbach, G. and Köhler, C. (2002) How do consumers search for and appraise health information on the world wide web? Qualitative studies using focus groups, usability tests and in-depth interviews, *British Medical Journal*, 324, 573–7.

Ferguson, T. (1997) Health online and the empowered medical consumer, *Journal of Quality Improvement*, 23, 5, 251–57.

Fox, S. and Rainie, L. (2000) The online health care revolution: how the web helps Americans take better care of themselves, *The Pew Internet and American Life Project*, 26 November.

Gann, R. (1991) Consumer health information: the growth of an information specialism, *Journal of Documentation*, 47, 3, 284–308.

Gann, R. and Needham, G. (1992) *Promoting Choice: Consumer Health Information in the 1990s*. London: Consumer Health Information Consortium.

Giddens, A. (1991) *Modernity and Self-Identity*. Oxford: Polity.

Hardey, M. (1999) Doctor in the house: the Internet as a source of lay health knowledge and the challenge of expertise, *Sociology of Health and Illness*, 21, 6, 820–35.

Hardey, M. (2001) 'E-health': the Internet and the transformation of patients into consumers and producers of health knowledge, *Information, Communication and Society*, 4, 3, 388–405.

Health Canada, Office of Health and the Information Highway (OHIH) (1999) *Canada Health Infoway: Paths to Better Health, Final Report of the Advisory Council on Health Infostructure*. Ottawa: Health Canada.

Katon, W. and Kleinman, A. (1981) Doctor-patient negotiation and other social science strategies in patient care. In Eisenberg, L. and Kleinman, A. (eds) *The Relevance of Social Science for Medicine*. Dordrecht-Holland: D. Reidel Publishing Co.

Lie, M. and Sorensen, K. (eds) (1996) *Making Technology our Own? Domesticating Technology into Everyday Life*. Oslo: Scandinavian University Press.

Lupton, D. (1997) Consumerism, reflexivity and the medical encounter, *Social Science and Medicine*, 45, 3, 373–81.

Mackenzie, D. and Wajcman, J. (eds) (1999) *The Social Shaping of Technology*. Buckingham: Open University Press.

Massé, R., Legare, F., Cote, L. and Dodin, S. (2001) The limitations of a negotiation model for perimenopausal women, *Sociology of Health and Illness*, 23, 1, 44–64.

Nicholas, D., Huntington, P. and Williams, P. (2000) Digital information health information provision for the consumer: analysis of the use of web kiosks as a means of delivering health information, *He@lth on the Net*, 17, 9–11.

Nicholas, D., Huntington, P. and Williams, P. (2001) Determinants of health kiosk use and usefulness: case study of a kiosk which serves a multi-cultural population, *Libri*, 51, 1, 102–13.

Silverstone, R. and Hirsch, E. (eds) (1992) *Consuming Technologies: Media and Information in Domestic Spaces*. London: Routledge.

Watkins, C. and Harvey, I. (1999) General practitioners' use of computers during the consultation, *British Journal of General Practice*, 49, 442, 381–3.

Weiss, M. and Fitzpatrick, R. (1997) Challenges to medicine: the case of prescribing, *Sociology of Health and Illness*, 19, 3, 297–327.

Wyatt, S., Henwood, F., Miller, N. and Senker, P. (eds) (2000) *Technology and In/equality: Questioning the Information Society*. London: Routledge.

Chapter 6

Media activism and Internet use by people with HIV/AIDS

James Gillett

Media activism and Internet use by people with HIV/AIDS

There is an increasing number of studies in the sociology of health and illness that focus directly on the media. This work has begun to foster a critical and theoretically-informed body of knowledge about the representations of health and illness in the mass media (Lupton 1999a). Most of this research has sought critically to examine mass-mediated messages on a range of subjects, including television's portrayal of health and healthcare (Turow 1989, Bury and Gabe 1994), the depiction of lay people in televised documentaries (Hodgetts and Chamberlain 1999), and the representations of moral panic regarding health (Dew 1999). This literature has been influential in developing a foundation for the critique of institutional discourses regarding health and illness.

Research on HIV/AIDS and the mass media provides a good example of the emphasis that has been placed on providing a critique of social institutions by scholars in the social sciences. In the mid-1980s, after several years of ignoring HIV/AIDS, the epidemic became a 'newsworthy' topic of consideration in the mass media. At this time, social scientists began to argue that the mass media were misrepresenting those directly affected by the epidemic and hence fuelling a growing moral panic regarding HIV/AIDS (Albert 1986, Bayer 1991, Lester 1992). This analysis was made most convincingly in relation to messages conveyed in the media about gay men and HIV/AIDS (Gronfors and Stalstrom 1987, Watney 1987). The moral rhetoric regarding gay men as deviant became a dominant motif in the way in which people with HIV/AIDS were portrayed in the media – homophobia became the foundation for a more generalised AIDS phobia (Sontag 1989, Patton 1990, Lupton 1994). The policing of gay sexuality through the media was extended to include other marginalised groups (Sacks 1996, Lester 1992). This critical research indicated that the representation of HIV/AIDS in the late 1980s and mid-1990s prevented mass media institutions from performing a democratic or informative role during a serious health crisis (Lupton 1994, Reardon and Richardson 1991).

Since the early 1990s the HIV/AIDS epidemic in most industrialised democracies has changed dramatically. This transformation has been characterised by Berridge (1992: 45) as a period of normalisation 'in which the rate of growth of the epidemic has slowed and public interest and panic has markedly decreased'. Advances in the area of treatments, brought about by the efforts of activists and through the development of more effective medications, have contributed to this process of normalisation (Flowers 2001). A significant impact of this trend has been that during the 1990s HIV/AIDS increasingly became defined and understood as a chronic rather than terminal disease. Griffin (2001) has noted a decreasing visibility of HIV/AIDS in the media during this period of normalisation as the disease has become less stigmatised and perceived to be less of a public health threat. The impact of this decreasing visibility, Griffin argues, has been to obscure and ignore the expanding global HIV/AIDS crisis that continued during the 1990s in developing nations. The mass media failed to draw attention to the situation of those affected by the disease on a global level who have been, and continue to be, denied access to treatments and other resources for survival.

Research on HIV/AIDS and the media over the course of the epidemic has provided a strong critique of institutional representations of the disease and their social and political impact. What has been largely overlooked has been the wealth of critical cultural representations of HIV/AIDS that has been produced outside the mass media (Crimp 1988, Miller 1992, Juhasz 1995). In the context of the contemporary AIDS movement in North America, people with HIV/AIDS have collectively developed and sustained their own media projects since the early 1980s. Publications, telephone hotlines, posters, fax, video, television, and radio: all are media that have been used to mobilise those infected and affected, challenge misconceptions regarding the disease, provide practical and useful information, and transform power structures which inhibit an effective response to the HIV/AIDS epidemic (Juhasz 1995). Media projects have created public forums through which people with HIV/AIDS can share their stories and knowledge and seek out mutual support, education and advocacy.

The use of media to create cultural spaces as a forum for those with marginalised or stigmatised identities has become a common feature of contemporary social movements. Literature on the role of contemporary social movements in revitalising the public sphere in post-industrial societies provides insight into the trend toward media activism. The foundation for this literature has been Habermas' (1989) writing on the bourgeois public sphere. Feminist scholars, while critical of Habermas, have used his work to understand the process by which social movements create their own public forums as a means of bringing about social change. It is argued that organised social networks provide the foundation for the formation of alternative public spheres (Fraser 1992, Felski 1989). This literature on activism and the public sphere has been taken up by scholars in the area of media and communication studies. They argue that media activism, in its various forms, can be understood as a response to the failure of social institutions, particularly the mass media, to provide a forum for citizens to address problems and issues of common concern (Downing 2001, Atton 2000). Media activism in all its various forms contributes to the constitution of alternative public spheres.

Media activism by people with HIV/AIDS has developed in relation to the institutional response to the epidemic and to political organising in the context of the AIDS movement by those infected. The initial years of the epidemic were characterised by a lack of response by public institutions and a growth of community mobilisation and political organising (Kirp and Bayor 1992). By the mid 1980s, groups of people with HIV/AIDS in most large urban centres in Canada and the United States had developed coalitions and formulated political ideologies (Altman 1986, Patton 1985, Treichler 1999). In terms of media, those involved in coalitions started newsletters to provide health information, to counter the stigmatisation of people with HIV/AIDS, and to facilitate communication among activists. At this point only a minority of people with HIV/AIDS with a knowledge of computers were making use of electronic mail and electronic bulletin boards to share information and connect with one another.

In the late 1980s and into the early 1990s organising among people with HIV/AIDS grew dramatically. Attention was directed towards addressing the health needs of those infected and calling for a more concerted societal response to the epidemic by public institutions, particularly the state (Ariss 1996, Patton 1990, Padgug and Oppenheimer 1992, Whittaker 1992). This expansion in community organising fuelled a flourish of media activism: organisation newsletters expanded and began to take on a magazine format; media collectives of people with HIV/AIDS formed to start their own treatment and health information publications; zines and magazines were started to highlight the cultural and political activities of people with HIV/AIDS. Media projects by people with HIV/AIDS began to experiment with publishing an electronic version of their publications on the Internet.

From the mid-1990s to the present there has been a gradual institutionalisation of activism by people with HIV/AIDS in industrialised democracies (Altman 1994). A more comprehensive and concerted institutional response to HIV/AIDS has contributed to a more formalised and professionalised AIDS movement. The result has been that political organising and activism among people with HIV/AIDS has declined, with the exception of mobilising among AIDS dissidents and mobilising among people with HIV/AIDS in developing nations. This institutionalisation has meant that many grassroots media collectives that emerged in the 1990s have disbanded or become incorporated into AIDS service organisations. Existing media projects have become more mainstream, professionalised and less political because of their closer alignment with dominant power structures. Use of the Internet during this period has flourished as access to technology has increased and as organisations have received greater institutional support for infrastructure and outreach initiatives.

A significant trend that has emerged during this period of institutionalisation has been the rise of Internet sites produced not by AIDS organisations but by HIV positive individuals. This paper examines Internet sites that have been created by people with HIV/AIDS as their own individual media projects. The analysis focuses on two main questions: Are there common themes among Internet sites by people with HIV/AIDS? And, is there a lineage between media activism within the contemporary AIDS movement and Internet sites that have been created by people with HIV/AIDS?

Methods

The methodology used in this research builds on the work of Hine (2000) who has developed an ethnographic approach to studying the Internet. This approach takes the position that it is possible to apply conventional qualitative methodologies to Internet research. Along this line, the methodology for this study followed an inductive grounded theory approach (Glaser and Strauss 1967, Strauss and Corbin 1990). The data collection and analysis occurred in three phases.

The first phase involved searching the Internet for sites that were created by people with HIV/AIDS. This search included sites by individuals with HIV/AIDS and organisations by people with HIV/AIDS. The starting point for this search was a webring entitled 'People Living with HIV/AIDS Ring – One World, One Hope' or the PLWA Ring. A webring is a series of Internet sites that are linked by subject and monitored by a 'ringmaster'. The PLWA Ring was started in 1996 and is located at: *http://e.webring.com/hub?ring=plwa*. Internet sites by people with HIV/AIDS that are a part of the PLWA Ring provide a means of 'linking' to a broader range of Internet sites by people with HIV/AIDS. The purpose of this initial phase of the research was akin to doing ethnographic fieldwork. I visited and explored the range of Internet sites that people with HIV/AIDS were involved in producing. This first phase was completed when I no longer encountered Internet sites with new themes and when I had an overall understanding of Internet sites that I had visited (approximately 150 sites). This first phase began in July 2000 and finished in December 2000.

In the second phase of the research I sent an e-mail survey to 63 Internet sites that were homepages produced by people with HIV/AIDS. The survey asked producers: (1) to describe their site; (2) why they created their site; (3) about the central purpose of the site; (4) the impact of the site on them and on visitors to the site; and (5) their involvement, if any, in local AIDS organising. The sites were primarily located in the United States and Canada, though several were in Australia, England, and Europe. There was a diverse range of people with HIV/AIDS who produced their own site (women, people of colour, heterosexual and gay), though more than half were gay men. Twenty one producers received and responded to the e-mail survey. Of the 42 produers who did not respond, 24 had inactive e-mail addresses. The data collected from fieldwork and from the survey was used to identify a set of basic characteristics or organising themes across Internet sites. The four themes were autobiography, expertise, self promotion, and dissent. The themes

Table 1 *Internet sites by organising theme*

Organising theme	Internet sites
Autobiography (8)	http://trekkingwithAIDS.com http://www.xs4all.nl/~w8705438/diversen/survival.htm http://www.westom.com/coolsite http://CowboyFrank.net http://www.geocities.com/SouthBeach/Tidepool/1718 http://www.geocities.com/HotSprings/Bath/8648 http://queensknob.therapids.net/speakingout/speaking.html http://www.home.earthlink.net/~richard2sf
Expertise (7)	http://homepage.interaccess.com/~bbarnes http://www.geocities.com/WestHollywood/3390 http://members.aol.com/walterm432/index.html http://www.angelfire.com/tx2/Caresurvivinghiv1 http://members.aol.com/BLawre5385/index.htm#top http://www.smartlink.net/~martinjh http://www.chestnutmare2001.com/mares_pages.html
Self Promotion (5)	http://www.bonusround.com http://www.riverhuston.com http://www.onetoughpirate.com http://www.openyourheart.org/thomcollins http://www.sod.net/shawn
Dissent (3)	http://www.ed-sherbeyn.com http://www.riverpages.com/hivmyth1.html http://www.blancmange.net/tmh/articles/clinicalbias.shtml

were not equally prevalent or mutually exclusive. For instance, almost all of the sites contained elements of the first two themes, autobiography and expertise. Only a minority of sites had elements of self promotion and very few sites by people with HIV/AIDS had dissent as a central organising theme. The second phase began in January 2001 and was completed in July 2001.

In the third phase of the methodology, 23 sites that were representative of the four organising themes were selected for a more in-depth analysis. Table 1 lists the Internet sites that were selected according to each organising theme. This third phase began in August 2001 and ended in December 2001.

The 23 sites were analysed as a strategy for self representation. This analysis considered: the intended use of the web page; the meanings that were encoded in the content of the web pages; and the relationship, if any, between each site and the organised AIDS movement. While focusing on the Internet sites selected for the third phase, the following analysis and discussion draws on data from all three phases of the research.

Internet sites by people with HIV/AIDS

The indeterminacy of the Internet, the diversity of its applications and users, and struggles over its regulation, have been recurring themes in the development of this communication technology (Poster 2001, Slevin 2000). The fragmentation and openness of the Internet has led scholars to explore relations of commonality and divergence as well as interconnection and disconnection among users of the Internet. Castells (1996: 199), for instance, has argued that networks across the Internet resist any single unifying culture or structure and comprise 'many cultures, many values, many projects, that cross through the minds and inform the strategies of the various participants'. This pluralism of 'cultures, values and projects' raises the question of whether there are structural elements that Internet users draw on in seeking self representation (Hardey 2002).

The Internet sites in this study were all unique; they were an expression of the distinctive experiences, interests and life circumstances of the individuals who created them. A number of sites were quite elaborate, using advanced software and featuring chat rooms, webcams, and audio files. There were also sites that were very rudimentary, consisting of only a few pages of text. Most sites had been produced for two to three years, yet some had been in existence for over seven years and others had only been online a few weeks or months. There was a range of activity, some sites were updated regularly while many seemed to be dormant or inactive.

Despite these variations several recurrent themes were evident across Internet sites. The organising themes identified in this research provided a structure or framework for self representation for people with HIV/AIDS. All the sites incorporated several of the themes, though in many cases one or two predominated. It is in this use of cyberspace that the producers of Internet sites engaged activist and institutional discourses regarding HIV/AIDS.

Autobiography
The first theme was the most commonly used in Internet sites by people with HIV/AIDS. Almost all of the sites in the study incorporated some aspect of a personal story or autobiographical narrative. There were many sites for which autobiography was the central purpose. An interesting example of this type of site is 'Trekking with AIDS' (*http://trekkingwithAIDS.com*), a website by Dawn Averitt who hiked the Appalachian trail. In her website the trail is carefully reconstructed through text and pictures so that you can follow her from state to state throughout the trail. The personal reflections are a way of documenting and archiving her experiences.

A more typical use of autobiography was a designated section of the site that recounts the producer's story of living with HIV/AIDS. Most stories were relatively short, lasting only a few pages though they did vary in length from site to site, in many cases depending on the level of dedication to the Internet site and the number of years living with HIV/AIDS. A typical example is the site by Wolf (*http://www.xs4all.nl/~w8705438/diversen/survival.htm*) entitled simply, 'my life with AIDS'. The site comprises Wolf's story of living with HIV/AIDS with particular emphasis on his experiences with an AIDS diagnosis and treatments:

> My story is short. Maybe one day I'll write a book about it, including the nice things that do continue to happen. In August 1997 I was admitted to hospital for the first time, I was very sick. . . . I have been HIV+ since at least the end of 1984 so I was really surprised to hear that I had AIDS. At the hospital I had lengthy discussions with doctors and other people about this new therapy that I had heard about but had no confidence in: I remembered the euphoria about AZT and other drugs that proved not to work, I was not prepared to be some test lab rat and die a horrible death, but then one day I looked at my skinny self and decided that if I wanted to give myself another chance I had to decide right there and now otherwise it would be too late.

The story told by Wolf is presented simply as an account of his experiences, and his reflections on the challenges of an AIDS diagnosis. At the same time, though, implicit in his writing is the message that visitors can learn from his experiences. The use of autobiography for the purposes of assisting and inspiring people with HIV/AIDS, and people who are oppressed in general, was a strong and recurrent motif among the Internet sites in this study. Returning to 'Trekking with AIDS', Dawn writes about the intent of her story and its impact:

> I hope to portray my Appalachian Trail trek as a metaphor for the potential each and every one of us has, whether or not we are HIV positive. I want to demonstrate that it is possible for anyone – whether you are battling a life threatening disease, a difficult spouse or an untenable employment situation, or simply feel powerless in the face of everyday difficulties – to experience life's bounty simply by taking charge of your own life, whatever its parameters may be. Particularly for people who have AIDS, taking control of your life is vitally important. Live life to its fullest. Without a doubt that's the single most important lesson I have learned.

The use of autobiography enabled individuals to engage directly with discourses that have become frequent in activist and institutional representations of HIV/AIDS. You are not a victim, people survive; do not give up; take control of your health; HIV/AIDS is not a death sentence; you are not alone: these are but some of the messages of empowerment that people with HIV/AIDS are trying to convey through example by representing their autobiographies on the Internet. Such 'heroic' uses of autobiography are not exclusive to the experience of people with HIV/AIDS; they have also been identified in studies of media portrayals of women with breast cancer (Seale 2001, 2002).

Expertise
The expertise of people with HIV/AIDS was the second theme. Sites organised around the idea of expertise were dedicated to informing and educating visitors, particularly people with HIV/AIDS. Such sites contained a broad range of useful information: a basic overview of HIV/AIDS, a history of the epidemic, advice about what to expect after being diagnosed, health problems associated with HIV/AIDS, the pros and cons of treatments, explanations about how treatments work, including complementary therapies, advice about dealing with health care professionals and social services, and so on. Another common feature is a compilation of links to online and offline resources for people with HIV/AIDS.

The site by Bruce Barnes, entitled 'A Long Time Survivor, Living with AIDS' (*http://homepage.interaccess.com/~bbarnes*) features extensive information about HIV/AIDS and strategies for survival. Bruce's disclaimer reflects both the breadth of the material and also the tension between professional and lay knowledge when making health and healthcare decisions:

The information posted on these pages is taken from medical journals, drug package inserts, manufacturers technical bulletins, continuing education study guides and my own personal life experience. It is intended only to give you some basic information to use in conjunction with your doctor, pharmacist and other health care practitioners when making the decision about which drugs to use or not use in your own therapy. Do not make changes to any drug therapies yourself – always consult a medical professional – if you can find one who knows more than you about AIDS and HIV!

'The HIV Zone' (*http://www.geocities.com/WestHollywood/3390*) by Tony Gardner is another good example of an Internet site that emphasises the expertise of people with HIV/AIDS. The purpose of 'The HIV Zone' is 'to help bring information to people living with HIV/AIDS, and to hopefully bring knowledge to those people seeking such information, from an objective yet sometimes personal view'. In addition to providing extensive information, advice and links to resources, Tony also produces his own newsletter, comprising links to articles and webcasts about the realities and practicalities of living with HIV/AIDS, that begins:

Since the human immunodeficiency virus was discovered in the early '80s, the letters 'HIV' have become a familiar – and often frightening – expression to most people. But what do you really know about the virus and its effects? Join us as we discuss what everyone should know about HIV, and how to separate fact from fiction.

Typically, the authors or producers of 'expertise' web pages, like Bruce Barnes and Tony Gardner, are usually long-term survivors and have closer ties to local AIDS service and advocacy organisations. Many consider themselves public educators and take great pride in the knowledge represented on their site and their efforts at outreach. Tony's 'The HIV Zone', for instance, has a letter from Bill Clinton acknowledging his efforts and a section devoted to visitors' comments like 'I checked out your web page, you are quite a guy! I think its great that you are so forthcoming with your story – it makes it so much more real to people that are learning more about AIDS'.

Like autobiography, expertise is a theme through which producers of Internet sites engage and challenge established discourses regarding HIV/AIDS. Sites like those by Bruce Barnes and Tony Gardner build on activist discourses that assert the legitimacy and the authority of lay knowledge among people with HIV/AIDS. While not ever advocating rejecting professional knowledge, they challenge the assumption that people with HIV/AIDS, and people with health problems in general, cannot or should not be experts in their own care or in the area of HIV/AIDS. In addition, expertise sites also promote the value of people with HIV/AIDS using knowledge gained from their lived experiences to educate one another and the general public.

Self promotion
Among the Internet sites in this study there were a number devoted to self promotion. In this case self promotion refers to individuals with HIV/AIDS who have created their own website in order to publicise specific activities or projects that they are involved in. One of the more established Internet sites with this theme is 'Living in the Bonus Round – The Online Diary of Steve Schalchin, the Life of a Somewhat Famous Songwriter Living with AIDS' (*http://www.bonusround.com*). This site is about the career and life of HIV positive singer and songwriter, Steve Schalchin. To describe the beginning of his Internet site, Steve writes,

> I began this diary in March 1996 as a sort of a goodbye letter to the world. In 1997 *The Last Session* opened off Broadway. It was the diary that grabbed the attention of the NY Times. At that time very few musicals had web sites and no musical had come in with the Internet site as a major part of its story. . . . We have been featured in the NY Times, People Magazine, the LA Times, NY Newsday, and AIDS publications such as POZ and ARTS & UNDERSTANDING. I even spoke at HARVARD UNIVERSITY in 1997 and played two sold out concerts in Harvard Square.

Internet sites like 'Living in the Bonus Round' often incorporate personal reflections, similar to the use of narrative in autobiographical web sites, but the attention to autobiography in self promotion is linked specifically to advancing a particular activity, career, or event.

Another example of a site in which self representation is tied to self promotion is by River Huston (*http://www.riverhuston.com*), a woman with HIV/AIDS who is 'a writer, comedian, poet, activist and performance educator'. This Internet site provides information about the projects and activities that River Huston is involved in, which include lectures and workshops, poetry, and a book about women living with HIV/AIDS:

> My name is River Huston and I am the author of *A Positive Life, Portraits of Women Living With HIV*. *A Positive Life* is a photo documentary book about Women and HIV in America. I have been living with HIV since 1990. In 1992 I went public because I felt that there were very few images of women living with HIV/AIDS in our society and I had nothing to lose. I am so proud of this book and I want to share it with you.

The tone of self-promotional Internet sites is not one of personal gain or profit from the activities or projects that are being publicised. Such sites do offer products like books, CDs or artwork; in most cases, however, the proceeds are donated to an organisation that provides services to those affected by HIV/AIDS. Rather than profit, the sentiment behind Internet sites like 'Living in the Bonus Round' and 'RiverHuston.com' is making use of a vocation, skill or art to provide public education and outreach. In this way self-promotion sites also engage HIV/AIDS discourses in very similar ways to sites that emphasise autobiography and expertise. However, the representation of life experiences and lay knowledge is situated in the context of a consumerist or entrepreneurial discourse rather than a lay-activist discourse, as was the case with Internet sites organising around the theme of autobiography and expertise.

Dissent

A minority of Internet sites in this study were created by people with HIV/AIDS who considered themselves AIDS dissidents. The web page produced by Ed Sherbeyn (*http://www.ed-sherbeyn.com*) is an example of a site that is organised around the theme of dissent. The introduction to Ed's site describes his perspective as an AIDS dissident:

> Dissidents are unorganized groups and individuals challenging and questioning the veracity of what we have been told over and over again for the past 20-something years as being 'The Truth'. Dissidents come in many different varieties. The Far Left Dissidents are those who believe that neither HIV nor AIDS exist. The Far Right can be described as those people who adhere to the concept that both HIV and AIDS exist but seriously question the effectiveness of the drugs currently being given as treatment. I fall into the group on the Far Left.

There are several common features of dissident Internet sites: personal experiences with medications (using them or avoiding them) and with HIV/AIDS; alternative explanations for HIV/AIDS; testimonials from other dissidents; links to similar sites, resources, and appeals for support.

Dissident discourses lie outside mainstream and activist orthodoxies regarding HIV/AIDS. Consequently, they are often silenced or the subject of critique by health professionals, activists, and people with HIV/AIDS. As a result, use of the Internet is seen to be an important source of information and self-expression. This sentiment is expressed by Ed in his website:

> There are many people who believe that HIV and AIDS actually exist. The information abounds in the media, government proclamations and drug company advertising. Every doctor you consult who treats people with HIV or AIDS can give you the perspective of the AIDS Advocates. What is most difficult to find is information disseminated by those people who call themselves AIDS Dissidents. The main sources of information are pretty much limited to the Internet where at least SO FAR there is very little if any censorship.

The Internet is one of the few forums through which dissidents can represent themselves and challenge existing AIDS discourses. There is a sense of urgency and injustice among dissidents that is similar to the political and cultural activism of people with HIV/AIDS in the 1980s. Internet sites by AIDS dissidents are the most politically explicit among the web pages included in this study. While explicit, there is careful consideration not to be prescriptive with views regarding the relationship between HIV/AIDS. The purpose of the Internet sites is to provide information and research so that individuals can make their own decisions regarding the nature of HIV/AIDS.

Discussion

Taken collectively, the Internet sites examined in this study can be under-stood as having an elective affinity with media activism as it has evolved in the context of the AIDS movement in North America. All of the Inter-net sites have an activist orientation that is consistent with prior forms of media activism; they seek to redress forms of inequality and oppression, they challenge institutional discourses, and they reach out to people with HIV/AIDS in need of support, education, and advocacy. Internet sites that emphasise autobiography, expertise, and self promotion build on and continue activist discourses that emerged through organising among people with HIV/AIDS since the early 1980s. HIV/AIDS is not a death sentence, long term survival is possible, the stigmatisation of those infected on the basis of sexuality, health status, race, gender or lifestyle is harmful and unjust, people with HIV are not victims, people with HIV/AIDS need to be involved in any decisions that affect their lives: this is only a partial list of activist discourses that creators of web sites have drawn on and advanced through representing their own experiences and life circumstances.

And yet, it is evident that Internet sites by people with HIV/AIDS are not a direct extension of AIDS media activism. People with HIV/AIDS who create their own web sites do so as individuals, and the overarching purpose is self representation. HIV/AIDS is usually only one aspect of an Internet site that represents the person's broader identity, experiences, interests, and life circumstances. Despite having a history of involvement in AIDS organising, many people with HIV/AIDS who have their own Internet sites do not make explicit reference to political organising or to an organised community of people living with HIV/AIDS. Most of the Internet sites in this study do not make reference to existing AIDS media. Nor do many of the producers of Internet sites mention having been involved in AIDS media activism, with the exception of several self-promotional Internet sites in which the producers had previously written for AIDS media, as in the case of River Huston who has written for *POZ*, an activist magazine for people with HIV/AIDs.

Activism among those infected at this historical moment has become contained within existing institutional structures. Media projects by people with HIV/AIDS that emerged through community mobilisation in the 1980s and 1990s, while still critical, have tempered their critique in part because of partnerships that have been established between activists and public and corporate institutions. The exception are AIDS dissident groups who have through their renegade scepticism remained on the very political margins of both activist and institutional responses to HIV/AIDS.

The pressure of institutionalisation has led many forms of AIDS media activism to become more formal and professionalised. The Internet, in contrast, has provided a more open and democratic venue for people with HIV/AIDS who are seeking self representation and social change. Yet, the Internet creates a more isolated and individualised public forum. Hence, the relationship between use of the Internet and prior forms of AIDS media activism reflects the current state of political organising among people with HIV/AIDS. The gap between involvement in the Internet and a lack of involvement in activist AIDS media cannot be explained by a lack of interest among those infected. Instead, the lack of involvement may be more the result of fewer opportunities for a diverse range of people with HIV/AIDS in organised forms of media activism like magazines and organisation publications.

Conclusion

Paula Treichler (1999: 316) has observed that 'the AIDS epidemic compels us to make sense of it – hence its enormous power to generate meanings'. People with HIV/AIDS have been compelled to make sense of their relationship with the epidemic and have done so through the use of media technologies like the Internet. The meanings represented through the Internet sites in this study are far ranging, from expressions of dissent and expertise to autobiography and self promotion. Research on the media practices of people with health problems represents for sociologists an important component in the development of a critical body of knowledge on health illness and the media. A research agenda for the sociology of health and illness that focuses exclusively on the mainstream or mass media is no longer acceptable, given the breadth of involvement in generating meanings among people with health problems. Attention to the meanings generated through the use of media like the Internet, however, only tells part of the sociological story. As Treichler continues, scholars must,

> ask more precise questions about the conditions under which meanings proliferate. What are the key cultural and structural characteristics that promote the generation of meanings? What are the processes and mechanisms through which individual meanings originate? Whose discourses speak through particular understandings of the AIDS epidemic? Whose are obscured? And what are we to make of them? (1999: 316).

It is important that research in the area of health and the media takes a critical and broad approach to understanding the way meanings are produced, reproduced and contested.

In the case of Internet sites by people with HIV/AIDS, the meanings generated have been produced in the broader social context of activist and institutional responses to the epidemic over the past 20 years. Over the course of the epidemic, activists have countered the mass media's response as an institution of social control. Early in the epidemic, media by and for people with HIV/AIDS filled the gap left by the refusal of media organisations to cover what was perceived to be a gay disease. Media activism helped to create an alternative public sphere for the exchange of experiences, knowledge and opinions when the mass media failed to do so. Once it was evident that HIV/AIDS posed a threat to the general public, the media did respond; however, the fear and panic associated with prior epidemics served as a frame of reference for representing the HIV/AIDS epidemic. The dominant view of HIV/AIDS that emerged emphasised how the disease was highly contagious, not well understood, terminal and potentially more devastating than any prior epidemic (Lupton 1994). As Crawford (1994) has argued, such representations twinned HIV/AIDS with death and thus reinforced divisions in our culture between the healthy and the diseased.

This portrayal of HIV/AIDS in the mass media, however, has not remained static. As Lupton (1999b) has noted, while the images and stories in the media about people with HIV/AIDS continue to deal with issues of contagion and death, current representations of those who are HIV positive have begun to emphasise more positive themes such as the possibility of long-term survival. By contesting the meanings generated by the mass media, activists can challenge and transform the representation of what it means to be a person with HIV/AIDS. One of the key successes of AIDS media activists in their efforts to 'give the disease a human face' has been promoting and legitimating an understanding of HIV/AIDS as chronic and manageable as opposed to terminal. The Internet sites in this study drew on and advanced activist representations of what it means to live with HIV/AIDS.

In recent years, as the institutional response to HIV/AIDS has expanded, there have been fewer areas of contention between activist and mainstream media. Many of the initiatives that emerged through community mobilisation in the late 1980s and early 1990s, including media projects, have been incorporated into or contained by institutional structures. In this context, it becomes increasingly difficult for the alternative public sphere created through the AIDS movement to remain connected to the lives of many people with HIV/AIDS. Critics of current AIDS media argue that they are overlooking many of the pressing issues facing those infected, such as poverty, the dangers and difficulties of side effects, and the global dimensions of the epidemic.

Given the current state of AIDS media, with activists struggling to find a place within institutional structures, the Internet represents a public forum that has a closer proximity to issues and concerns that are facing people with HIV/AIDS. The Internet provides a forum for self representation by individuals who are excluded from the public sphere and from activist public spheres. For Bauman (1999), the unavailability of means through which citizens can collectively make the link between private troubles and public issues is one of the central problems that faces post-industrial democracies. There is potential, as can be seen in the web pages by people with HIV/AIDS, for the Internet to be used as a bridge between private troubles and public issues, what Bauman (1999: 3) refers to as the agora, 'the space neither private nor public . . . where private problems meet in a meaningful way . . . where ideas may be born and take shape as the "public good"'. There are, however, many uncertainties regarding this more idealistic view of the potential for social change through the Internet: affordable access to the Internet on a local and global level continues to be a problem; while the Internet is a public forum it also tends to isolate and fragment individuals, may limit the possibilities of offline collective mobilisation (Jordan 1999); and increasingly, as Bauman notes, the Internet is subject to the control of regulatory institutional forces, and forces of the marketplace, which threaten its potential to bring citizens together in collective efforts towards social change.

References

Albert, A. (1986) Acquired immune deficiency syndrome: the victim and the press, *Studies in Communication*, 3, 135–58.

Altman, D. (1986) *AIDS in the Mind of America*. New York: Double Day Press.

Altman, D. (1994) *Power and Community: Organizational and Cultural Responses to AIDS*. London: Taylor and Francis.

Atton, C. (2000) *Alternative Media*. London: Sage.

Ariss, R. (1996) *Against Death: the Practice of Living with AIDS. Australia*. Amsterdam: Gordon and Breach Publishers.

Bauman, Z. (1999) *In Search of Politics*. Cambridge: Polity Press.

Bayer, R. (1991) Covering the plague: AIDS and the American media, *AIDS Education and Prevention*, 3, 1, 74–86.

Berridge, V. (1992) AIDS: History and contemporary history. In Herdt, G. and Lindenbaum, S. (eds) *The Time of AIDS: Social Analysis, Theory and Method*. London: Sage.

Bury, M. and Gabe, J. (1994) Television and medicine: medical dominance or trial by media? In Gabe, J., Kelleher, D. and Williams, G. (eds) *Challenging Medicine*. London: Routledge.

Castells, M. (1996) *The Rise of Network Society*. Oxford: Blackwell.

Crawford, R. (1994) The boundaries of the self and the unhealthy other: reflections on health, culture and AIDS, *Social Science and Medicine*, 38, 10, 1347–65.

Crimp, D. (1988) *AIDS: Cultural Analysis, Cultural Activism*. Boston: MIT Press.

Dew, K. (1999) Epidemics, panic and power: representations of measles and measles vaccines, *Health*, 3, 4, 379–98.

Downing, J. (2001) *Radical Media: Rebellious Communication and Social Movements*. London: Sage.

Felski, R. (1989) Feminism, postmodernism an the critique of modernity, *Cultural Critique*, 13, 33–56.

Flowers, P. (2001) Gay men and HIV/AIDS risk management, *Health*, 5, 1, 50–75.

Fraser, N. (1992) Rethinking the public sphere: a contribution to the critique of actually existing democracy. In Calhoun, C. (ed) *Habermas and the Public Sphere*. Cambridge: MIT Press.

Glaser, B. and Strauss, A. (1967) *The Discovery of Grounded Theory*. Chicago: Aldine.

Griffin, G. (2001) *Representations of HIV and AIDS*. Manchester: Manchester University Press.

Gronfors, M. and Stalstrom, O. (1987) Power, prestige, profit: AIDS and the oppression of homosexual people, *Acta Sociologica*, 30, 1, 53–66.

Habermas, J. (1989) *The Structural Transformation of the Public Sphere*. Cambridge: MIT Press.

Hardey, M. (2002) 'The story of my illness': personal accounts of illness on the Internet, *Health*, 6, 1, 31–46.

Hine, C. (2000) *Virtual Ethnographies*. London: Sage.

Hodgetts, D. and Chamberlain, K. (1999) Medicalization and the depiction of lay people in television health documentary, *Health*, 3, 3, 317–33.

Jordan, T. (1999) *Cyberpower*. New York: Routledge.

Juhasz, A. (1995) *AIDS TV*. London: Duke University Press.

Kirp, D. and Bayor, R. (1992) *AIDS in Industrial Democracies*. Montreal: McGill-Queens University Press.

Lester, E. (1992) The AIDS story and moral panic: how the Euro-African press constructs AIDS, *Howard Journal of Communications*, 3, 3–4, 230–41.

Lupton, D. (1994) *Moral threats and Dangerous Desires*. London: Taylor and Francis.

Lupton, D. (1999a) Editorial: Health, illness, medicine and the media, *Health*, 3, 3, 259–62.

Lupton, D. (1999b) Archetypes of infection: people with HIV/AIDS in the Australian press, *Sociology of Health and Illness*, 21, 1, 37–53.

Miller, J. (1992) *Fluid Exchanges: Artists and Critics in the AIDS Crisis*. Toronto: University of Toronto Press.

Padgug, R. and Oppenheimer, G. (1992) Riding the tiger: AIDS and the gay community. In Fee, E. and Fox, D. (eds) *AIDS: The Making of a Chronic Disease*. Los Angeles: University of California Press.

Patton, C. (1985) *Sex and Germs: the Politics of AIDS*. Boston: South End Press.

Patton, C. (1990) *Inventing AIDS*. New York: Routledge, Chapman and Hall.

Poster, M. (2001) *What is the Matter with the Internet?* Minneapolis: University of Minnesota Press.

Reardon, K. and Richardson, J. (1991) The important role of mass media in the diffusion of accurate information about AIDS, *Journal of Homosexuality*, 21, 1–2, 63–75.

Sacks, V. (1996) Women and AIDS: an analysis of media misrepresentations, *Social Science and Medicine*, 42, 1, 59–73.

Seale, C. (2001) Sporting cancer: struggle language in news reports of people with cancer, *Sociology of Health and Illness*, 23, 3, 308–29.

Seale, C. (2002) Cancer heroics: a study of news reports with particular reference to gender, *Sociology*, 36, 1, 107–26.

Slevin, J. (2000) *The Internet Society*. Cambridge: Polity Press.

Sontag, S. (1989) *AIDS and Its Metaphors*. London: Anchor Books.

Strauss, A. and Corbin, J. (1990) *Basics of Qualitative Research: Grounded Theory Procedures and Techniques*. Newbury Park, California: Sage.

Treichler, P. (1999) *How to Have Theory in an Epidemic*. Durham: Duke University Press.

Turow, J. (1989) *Playing Doctor: Television, Storytelling, and Medical Power*. New York: Oxford University Press.

Watney, S. (1987) *Policing Desire: AIDS, Pornography, and the Media*. London: Methuen.

Whittaker, A. (1992) Living with HIV: resistance by positive people, *Medical Anthropology Quarterly*, 6, 4, 385–90.

Chapter 7

Popular media and 'excessive daytime sleepiness': a study of rhetorical authority in medical sociology
Steve Kroll-Smith

Introduction

The National Sleep Foundation (NSF) recently disclosed that 69 per cent of Americans report experiencing sleep problems, though only four per cent have sought advice or treatment from a doctor or healthcare provider. Nearly 100 million Americans complain of insomnia symptoms, but only six per cent are diagnosed with insomnia by doctors, and only half of those receive treatment for the disorder. Moreover, 40 per cent of adult Americans experience intense sleepiness at least once during the course of the day. Slightly more than half of the US adult population report driving while drowsy; one in five (19%) admit to dozing off behind the wheel (NSF 2001)[1].

Importantly, nearly 80 per cent of adults surveyed by the NSF think their sleep troubles are not serious enough to report to doctors, or think there is little their doctors can do for them (NSF 2001). Fewer than 14 per cent of medical interns in the US question patients about their sleep patterns (Haponik, Frye and Richards 1996). In a study of 222 patients' charts in one Veterans' Administration clinic, no sleep disorder symptoms were recorded, though 47 per cent of the patients reported sleep-related problems during doctor consultations (Meissner *et al.* 1998). Problems with sleep and sleepiness, it appears, are occurring with considerable frequency outside institutionalised encounters between patients and doctors.

The apparent chasm between self-reported sleep troubles and the routine medical gaze is a point of departure for this inquiry. Practicing physicians rarely identify and name people's sleep troubles or co-ordinate their behaviours in response to them. Clinical medicine, for all practical purposes, is currently not part of what Dorothy Smith would call the 'relations of ruling' (1993: 6–8 and passim) in shaping and controlling the contemporary problem with sleep. This observation begs the question, what indeed are the patterns of discipline and regulation that direct thinking, control emotion, and govern conduct around the somatic goal of good or sufficient sleep? This question, in turn, invites consideration of how a sociology of medicine might look in an historical era marked by the decreasing salience of the medical gaze, an era Bauman refers to, with a hint of hyperbole, as 'post-Panoptical' (2000: 11).

The evidence will suggest that popular media are key resources in shaping public perceptions of sleepiness without the direct intervention of clinical medicine. The evidence itself is an amalgam of theorising and data that builds a plausible case for a public increasingly advised and informed by extra-local, textualised forms of knowledge. Two closely related levels of analysis are implied in this inquiry. At one level is a substantive discussion of the popular representation of sleepiness as a peculiarly modern somatic trouble. At the other is a modest theoretical deliberation on a contemporary social order increasingly reliant on 'textually mediated forms of ruling' (Smith 1993: 212). The discussion begins with a succinct deliberation on texts, readers, and relations of ruling followed by a word on methods. A lengthy discussion examines several popular media and their varied messages on the problem of sleep and sleepiness. A final section recalls Alain Touraine's (1998) appeal to sociologists to amend their idea of society and concede the historical rift between social actors and social systems. To close, I introduce and modestly critique his entreaty, link it to related work, and suggest the relevance of this new literature to a broader, possibly more interesting, sociology of medicine, one that assumes the increasing salience of popular media. Inspired by this contemporary history, two key ideas in medical sociology are revisited: naming diseases and the classic distinction between illness and disease.

Texts, readers and relations of ruling: a strategy for reading popular media

Substantial work exists on how individuals use stories or narratives to make sense of their illnesses and fashion a corresponding identity (a short list includes Ezzy 2000, Kroll-Smith and Floyd 1997, and Frank 1995). Missing from this work, however, is a consideration of how popular media fashion these stories. Recent work from an eclectic group of social and cultural theorists is converging on a new way of talking about media, personal stories and the government of the person that beckons inquiry into key quarters of medical sociology.

Representatives of several intellectual traditions converged in the past 15 years on a single, evocative idea: the institutional arrangements organising and regulating people's lives are increasingly mediated by ways of knowing inscribed in texts (Rorty 1989, Appadurai 1996, Smith 1993). Texts, or what Rorty (1989) might call vocabularies, are words and images conveyed in digital, electronic and print media that inform and shape the 'quotidian mental work of ordinary people' in global societies (Appadurai 1996: 5). Giddens (1991) sees this mental work as a cardinal feature of a late modern world. Here, lay people are continually accessing expert ways of knowing, tinkering with them sufficiently to answer a question or make sense of their misery, and fashioning stories that reflect a correspondence between situated biography and abstract, disembodied texts (1991: 138). Tellingly, he illustrates this lay appropriation of expert knowledge by describing in some detail a person suffering from chronic back pain who searches popular media for therapies, medications and theories of back troubles. 'Many non-technical books about the back', Giddens observes, 'are available on the popular market' (1999: 140). Apropos Giddens, Fairclough observes, 'The media are full of expert advice' (2001: 3), or, perhaps more realistically, messages embedded in the rhetorics of expertise.

Faced with decisions, questions and dilemmas, people are increasingly apt to turn to magazines, books, newspapers, newsletters, and the Internet to acquire new perspectives, facts, explanations and prescriptions for acting. Personal reasoning and sense-making are increasingly tied to clusters of words and images that are 'detached from local contexts' and 'occur simult-aneously in a multiplicity of socially and temporally disjointed settings' (Smith 1993: 211). Texts, in short, are public fragments of social conscious-ness that work (albeit loosely) in concert, encouraging people to reason, know and fashion their worlds in particular ways.

Dorothy Smith concludes her study of texts and relations of ruling with the following summation: 'Advanced . . . societies are pervasively organized by textually mediated forms of ruling' (1993: 211). Giddens (1991) suggests a theoretical angle on this novel state of affairs. If expert knowledge, from making a nuclear bomb to theorising spinal disorders, is procurable by virtually anyone living in 'conditions of high modernity', authority is unavoidably democratised: '(forms) of traditional authority become only "authorities" among others, part of an indefinite pluralism of expertise' (1991: 195). Institutional authority with its hierarchical procedures of obser-vation, categorisation and judgment is increasingly complemented, and at times challenged, by at least one new species of authority; one that no longer occurs in an institutional, territorially fixed encounter between, for example, elected officials and citizens, teachers and students or doctors and patients.

This new species of authority is exercised (at least in part) through a congeries of often weakly related popular media. It is an extra-territorial authority, existing more in time than in space. For want of a better term, we call this novel form of authority *rhetorical* and search for its existence in the remarkably varied media on the contemporary problem of sleepiness.

The salience of popular media in personal knowledge of health and disease

There are more than good theoretical reasons to examine the role of popular media in shaping people's interpretations and behaviours around the issues of health and disease. The US National Cancer Institute (NCI), for example, recently announced, 'health news has become a part of everyday life' (NCI 2001: 1). The American Council on Science and Health (ACSH) concluded its survey of magazine use from 1990 through to 1992 among people inter-ested in nutrition and dieting with this observation: 'Magazines are the principal source of diet and nutrition information in the American home' (Woznicki and Case 1994: 6). The ACSH also reports that most American women learn about hormone replacement therapy from the media

(Lukachko 1999). Similarly, most people who suffer from arthritis use popular media to learn about its pathology and possible treatment regimens
(Pisetsky 1995). A paper in the *Journal of the American Medical Association
(JAMA)* acknowledges the porous boundaries between medical research
and popular media, noting the growing significance of the 'lay press' in
transmitting medical knowledge to the public (Phillips *et al.* 1991: 1180).

The Internet, not surprisingly, is now a primary source of popular knowledge about health and disease (Cotten 2001). A recent study estimates that
more than 60 million US residents search for health and disease information
yearly on the World Wide Web (Fox and Rainie 2000). Moreover, and of
some importance, 70 per cent report using the knowledge they acquire from
the Internet to change personal habits and learn about diseases and treatments (Fox and Rainie 2000). The prevalence of web-based information in
shaping personal awareness of health and disease prompted a key article in
JAMA on the quality of health-related information on the Internet and
education levels appropriate for accessing it (Gretchen *et al.* 2001).

In short, it appears likely that popular media are a salient source of
knowledge about health and disease among non-experts in an historical
era increasingly organised around the authority of texts. Coalescing into a
pattern of rhetorical authority, popular media inform and shape people's
thinking about themselves, their bodies, and their wellbeing. Recalling
the apparent disconnect between clinical medicine and the growing number of Americans who self-identify as suffering from some type of sleep
trouble, magazines, newspapers, radio, and the WWW are even more likely
sources of personal knowledge in the identification and management of
sleepiness.

A word on methods

Data for this paper are taken from print and electronic media and represent the plurality of messages and texts that inform and advise people on
the problems of sleepiness in contemporary American society. *The Reader's
Guide to Periodical Literature* was used to track and identify popular print
coverage of sleep and sleepiness. The first time-period examined is 1982,
the year 'excessive daytime sleepiness' is first mentioned in non-technical
media. While the occasional article and story on problem sleepiness follows
throughout the 1980s, it is not until 1990 that sleepiness emerges in popular
media as a public and personal health concern, and continues unabated
today.

Literature from *The Guide* was subdivided according to whether or not
it was *targeted* at a singular audience or intended for a more *general* audience. The magazine *Working Woman,* for example, targets a particular
demographic group, while *Newsweek* aims at a far broader, more general
public. Drawing a distinction between targeted and general audiences is an

opportunity to comment on both the more sweeping, inclusive messages shaping sleepiness as a medical problem and the more specific messages written to appeal to discrete life-styles or life-stages. Circulation rates for periodicals are noted throughout the discussion. In addition to *The Reader's Guide*, the *New York Times* and the *Washington Post*, the papers of record in the US, were surveyed from 1980 to 2000. Like their counterparts, the popular magazines, before 1990 these signal papers reported only occasionally on the medical and social risks of sleepiness. From 1990, however, each paper printed a steady stream of news about drowsiness and chronic sleep problems.

Finally, sleep and sleepiness begin to appear on the Internet with predictable frequency in 1997 with the posting of the National Sleep Foundation website. Prior to this time, Internet messages on sleep and sleepiness were limited primarily to postings by researchers. Three popular search engines were examined for their sites on sleep: Ask Jeeves, Dogpile and Yahoo. Sampling from the WWW falls far short of a textbook exercise in a reliable selection strategy. Moreover, and as with print media, we do not know who, in fact, is accessing a website. What we do know is that this new medium is increasingly important in informing and shaping lay knowledge about health, illness, and treatments (see below). A total of 32 sites were examined for their various messages to general visitors. These sites appear on all three search engines.

Redescribing sleepiness: a new language game emerges

To redescribe a thing is to create new and opposing adjectives, adverbs and, occasionally, nouns that coalesce into a qualitatively different picture of it. Redescription becomes sociologically interesting when it changes the way people routinely see, think and behave towards themselves, others and the world. To redescribe buildings as sick, for example, as in sick-building syndrome, is a recent illustration of redescription (Bain *et al.* 1999). Sleepiness too is currently being redescribed. We can glimpse this change by juxtaposing the popular, common grammar of sleepy as an endearing bucolic and peaceful somatic state with the nascent grammar of sleepiness as an object of scientific and medical investigation.

The common vocabulary of sleepiness, the one most of us know and use, portrays it as a benign, wholesome, and welcomed somatic state. We routinely encounter this vocabulary in verse. Robert Frost brings a day of picking apples to a close. Tired, he is 'done with apple-picking now. Essence of winter sleep is on the night, the scent of apples; I am drowsing off' (2001: 76). Shakespeare also knew the poetic in sleepy. It was 'The death of each day's life, sore labour's bath, Balm of hurt minds, great nature's second course' (Muir 1996: 189). Complementing literature and verse is the more popular genre of fairytales and contemporary children's books. Recall, for example, the lovable character Sleepy, one of seven dwarfs in Snow White, a fairytale originating in the 17th century.

A discernable change, however, is now occurring in the way sleepy and sleepiness are described in popular media. Alongside the time-honoured description of this somatic state as innocent and unaffected is an increasing chorus of voices redescribing it as a treacherous, perilous condition. These contemporary redescriptions are not apt to replace the historical meanings of these terms, but they will likely secure a place alongside them, creating a new language game for making sense of these temporal rhythms of the body.

A prelude: the print period from 1982 to 1983

The earliest examples of this emergent vocabulary in the US occur in 1982. Arguably, the point of departure for the redescription of sleep and sleepiness is the February 1982 issue of *JAMA*. The study found that 51 per cent of 3,900 patients surveyed reported suffering from 'excessive daytime sleepiness' (Coleman *et al.* 1982: 997). At the end of February, the popular magazine *Science News* (1983 circulation 173,156) ran a one-page story on the *JAMA* article entitled 'A nation of sleepyheads' (Weld 1983). Its lead paragraph is instructive:

> If you only listened to television commercials, you might think Americans' number one sleep problem was difficulty in falling asleep at night. But that isn't true, a study reported by . . . the *Journal of the American Medical Association* reveals. The major difficulty is excessive daytime sleepiness, not insomnia (1983: 138).

The article continues, alerting readers to the study's major conclusion: 'Fifty-one percent of the patients surveyed experienced excessive daytime sleepiness' (1983: 138).

The language here is important for what it conveys about how popularising is accomplished. The figures cited in the *JAMA* article refer to people who present to doctors with sleep troubles. The title of the *Science News* article, however, is 'A nation of sleepy heads', suggesting sleepiness is a pandemic problem, not something the *JAMA* article necessarily intended to convey. Nevertheless, by the mid-1990s, as we see below, national surveys of non-patients reveal a remarkable number of people reporting sleep troubles, particularly problems with sleepiness.

In August of 1982, six months after 'Sleep-wake disorders based on polysomnographic diagnosis: a national comparative study' appeared in the *JAMA*, *Psychology Today* (1983 circulation 85,000) published 'The drowsy crowd' further popularising and extending Coleman *et al.*'s research. The authors (Browman *et al.* 1982) acknowledged their debt to the *JAMA* article by introducing an alternative grammar that transforms sleepiness from benign repose to 'hypersomnia,' 'excessive sleepiness,' and 'excessive daytime sleepiness'. This latter term is also referred to as 'Pickwickian syndrome', named after Dickens's character Joe who slept a good deal of each day at the most inappropriate times (Browman *et al.* 1982: 35). Drawing from the article in *JAMA* and their own clinical work, the authors note that excessive sleepiness as a medical problem is more prevalent than insomnia. Indeed, 'We estimate that perhaps as much as 15 percent of the adult population suffers from excessive sleepiness' (1982: 36), a condition that is 'not only disabling but dangerous' (1982: 35).

In October of 1982, eight months after the appearance of the *JAMA* study and two months after the article in *Psychology Today*, *Business Week* (1982 circulation 776,565) carried its first article on sleep problems (11 October). The article 'Dealing with troubled sleep' (Cochet 1982) uses short vignettes of business owners, Chief Executive Officers (CEOs) and managers who suffer from a host of sleep troubles. Featured in this article is the problem of 'daytime sleepiness'. The majority of people who complain of sleep troubles report that their most significant problem is 'excessive daytime sleepiness' (Cochet 1982: 132).

In 1983, the *US News and World Report* (1983 circulation 2,050,000) ran a six-column story on sleep (Steinberg 1983) reminding readers that 'daytime sleepiness' might result in 'loss of attention, frequent lapses in performance, (and) accidents . . .' (1983: 68). *Forbes* magazine (1983 circulation 70,000) linked daytime sleepiness to car accidents in 1983, noting that sleepy executives might suffer from 'Pickwickian syndrome' (Love 1986: 156). *The Washington Post* ran its first article (Rovner 1984) on sleepiness in March of 1984, alerting adults to a faulty notion that should be put to rest, to wit, they require less sleep than children. Sleepiness, the article notes, is a growing 'health problem' in the US (30 March 1984). In short, popular print media were redescribing sleepiness, creating an alternative understanding of this cyclic somatic condition.

We might expect a substantial increase in the coverage on problem sleepiness immediately following the clutch of articles appearing in 1982 and 1983; the facts are otherwise. From 1984 through to 1990, only 12 articles listed in *The Reader's Guide* examine this particular issue, though sleep as a human interest topic, or the subject of verse or story, occasionally appear. *The Washington Post* did not print another article on sleepiness until 1990. *The New York Times* ran its first series of articles (totaling five) on problem sleepiness in 1990. Typical of these articles is the assessment that chronic sleepiness leads to 'gravely impaired judgment and an increase in accidents' (Wise 1990: 15 May Section C: 1). Why some health issues incubate longer than others before (if ever) achieving national attention is a question worth exploring, but we must leave it unanswered at this time and continue. The issue at hand is the marked increase in national coverage of problem sleepiness beginning in 1990.

The print period: 1990 to 2001

The *Nation's Business* (1989 circulation 850,000) ran a short, but telling piece in February 1990 on problem sleepiness (Schaefer 1990). Subtitled 'Managing insomnia', readers were alerted to the deterioration of 'problem-solving and decision-making abilities' that accompany acute daytime sleepiness (1990: 132). *Fortune* (1989 circulation 755,000) followed with a lengthy discussion of 'The executive insomniac' (Kiechel 1990). '[I]n any given year upwards of 50 million Americans have trouble sleeping'. Moreover, 'go-getter Type A personalities suffer sleeplessness in disproportionate numbers' (1990: 183).

Arguably, the most important vehicle for launching sleepiness into popular culture is a December 1990 cover story in *Time*, a magazine that circulated to 4,500,000 people in 1989. 'Drowsy America' (Toufexos and Dolan 1990) announced in unsparing terms the contemporary problems with sleepiness. It is 'as threatening as a heart attack . . . Drowsiness [is] a leading cause of traffic fatalities and industrial accidents . . . Inadequate sleep [is] a major factor in human error'. Moreover, '[w]eariness corrodes civility and erases humor'. And finally – and, appropriately, considering this list of troubles—Dr. Charles Pollak, head of the sleep disorder center at Cornell University considers 'sleepiness one of the least recognized sources of disability in our society' (Toufexos and Dolan 1990: 79–81). 'Millions of Americans are chronically sleep deprived', the article continues. A quote from Dr. William Dement, director of Stanford University's sleep center explains: 'Most Americans no longer know what it feels like to be fully alert. . . . They go through the day in a sort of twilight zone' (1990: 80).

Time concludes its cover story on sleepiness with a strong normative message:

What is needed most of all . . . is a fundamental change in Americans' thinking about the necessity of sleep. A difficult task, yes. But not impossible . . . Wake up, America—by getting more sleep (Toufexos and Dolan 1990: 81).

In all, 11 articles on daytime sleepiness were posted in *The Reader's Guide* in 1990 (see Figure 1). From 1990 through to 2000 the problem of sleepiness resounds through popular literatures. *The Guide* posts 224 citations on the many aspects of problem sleepiness during this 11-year period. A bar graph nicely illustrates the marked increase in coverage of this issue from 1990 to 2000.

In addition, from 1990 to 2000 the *Washington Post* published 46 articles on sleep disorders, the risks of drowsy drivers, and sleepiness and workplace performance. Seventeen of these articles discuss hypersomnia or excessive daytime sleepiness as a growing public health problem. The *New York Times*

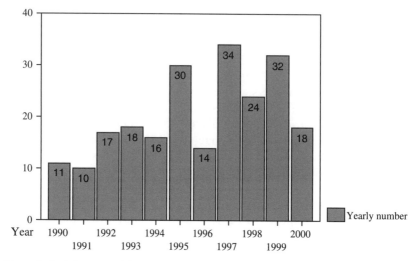

Figure 1 Articles on problem sleepiness appearing in *The Reader's Guide*, 1990–2000

did not ignore sleep disorders and problem sleepiness after 1990, publishing 39 stories on these and related topics between 1990 and 2000. *The Times,* it is worth noting, devoted more space to editorials about the dangers of somnolent people than the *Post.*

Importantly, during this period the textual message that 'excessive sleepiness is a public health problem' is circulated in both *general reader* and *targeted reader* periodicals. The likelihood that problem sleepiness is effectively communicated as a public and personal health issue is increased to the extent that coverage occurs in both types of publications.

Interpreting general and targeted coverage

Imagine general reader coverage as a bass line of a music score and targeted reader coverage as the melody. Booming in a deep voice, for example, is the *USA Today Magazine* (1993 circulation 249,000) announcing its headline 'The great American sleep debt' (Williams 1993) to anyone in the general population. Or, *US News and World Report* (1993 circulation 4,500,000) declaring 'Americans asleep at the wheel' (Steinberg 1993) to its mass audience. In that same year a more subtle voice lilting above the boom of the general periodical targeted specific populations with similar messages. Tailored to its specific audiences, *Working Woman* (1993 circulation 560,000) profiled a woman suffering with excessive sleepiness in 'Diary of a mad insomniac' (Heller 1993) and *Men's Health* (1993 circulation 1,200,000) urged men to take sleep hygiene seriously in 'Choose to snooze' (Lafavore 1993).

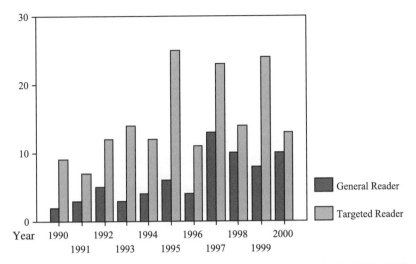

Figure 2 Articles on problem sleepiness in general and targeted media, 1990–2000

This working relationship between the booming message to the general reader and the more tailored message to a select reader runs throughout this 10-year period. In 1994, for example, *The New York Times Magazine* (1994 circulation 1,700,000) published a feature piece entitled 'America's falling asleep' (Brody 1994). A sleep expert concludes on a dramatic note: 'There is more sleepiness in more people more of the time than ever before, and the consequences of human error have never been more serious' (1994: 65). Also in 1994, *The Ladies Home Journal* (1994 circulation 5,000,000) published a biographical sketch of 'The exhausted woman' (Hickey 1994), echoing the general message of the *NY Times Magazine* as it applies to the lives of career women. 'Women', it notes, 'are increasingly disabled by chronic sleepiness' (1994: 86).

The complementary voices of general and targeted texts (Figure 2) are working together to make excessive sleepiness a fragment of social consciousness with a modicum of authority over people's lives. Moreover, they help account for the noticeable gap between self-diagnosis with a sleep problem and physician-diagnosis and treatment.

The rhetorical authority of magazines and newspapers in the prosaic mental work of ordinary people is increasingly salient, due in part to the often contingent, fortuitous character of once solid institutional centres of control. The 'problem of excessive daytime sleepiness', it would appear, is emerging in print media as a personal and public health issue in spite of its general disregard by clinical medicine. But print media are only a part of the bibliography of textual authority on sleepiness. The World Wide Web is competing with if not surpassing, newspapers and magazines in organising conduct around the problem of sleep.

The web period and excessive daytime sleepiness: 1997–2002

In 1993, fewer than three per cent of American households were accessing the World Wide Web (WWW). By 2000, 42 per cent of American households were connected to the Web (US Census Bureau 2001). And the Web, it is safe to say, is awash with healthcare information. Cotten records estimates of health websites ranging from '10,000 . . . to close to 20,000' (2001: 321). The considerable range in this estimate stems, in part, from the absence of anything like a *Reader's Guide* for the Internet. The sheer volume and protean character of the WWW precludes any reasonable attempt to catalogue its contents. Although a reliable and functional bibliography of web-based health and illness information is not possible at this time, a growing number of lay people are nevertheless accessing it for their personal use. Presaging this discussion, Cotten sites a recent article suggesting that Internet health and illness information is likely to challenge physicians' control of the distribution and interpretation of medical knowledge (2001: 325).

Sleepiness is a frequent topic in at least one major news site: Cable Network News Interactive or CNN Interactive (CNNI) (*http://www.cnn.com/ HEALTH*). From 1997 to 2000, CNNI and CNBC together posted at least 31 stories on problem sleepiness. As early as 1995, CNNI was posting occasional headlines like 'Sleep problems are costly, dangerous' (23 October) and reminding readers that 'sleepy people are accidents waiting to happen'. Between 1995 and 1996, CNNI posted five articles on sleepiness. By 1997, however, sleepiness appeared with considerable regularity on the CNNI site with at least one account a month appearing on the 'Health Story Page' with titles like 'Lack of sleep America's top health problem, doctors say' (17 March). While it is difficult to pinpoint the exact number of websites dedicated to sleep problems, three popular search engines (Google, Ask Jeeves and Dogpile) found a total of 32 addresses (there are probably more) dedicated to sleepiness and its associated problems. Importantly, these sites provide continuous conduits between current research on sleep and sleepiness and the Internet public. The British Sleep Society, for example, seeks to improve public health by promoting education and research into sleep and its disorders (*http://www.sleeping.org.uk*). The Sleep Well, a website developed by the Stanford University Sleep Research Center, encourages visitors to search medical journals on-line for timely information on sleep problems (*http://www.stanford.edu/~dement*). 'Sandman', a digital librarian, 'is trying to consolidate all the information available by [sleep] disorder to make it easier to find the information you are looking for' (*http://www.sleepnet.com*).

But the Internet is doing more than consolidating information on problem sleepiness and reinforcing and complementing the authority of printed texts. It is also emphasising a particular way of making sense of daytime sleepiness. No longer just an unwelcome somatic state, daytime sleepiness is being transformed into a distinct medical disorder.

Excessive daytime sleepiness: from symptom to disorder

Type the word 'sleepy' or 'sleepiness' into any search engine and a majority of the 'hits' will portray this somatic state as some variation of 'Excessive Daytime Sleepiness'. The National Sleep Foundation, for example, defines 'Excessive Daytime Sleepiness [EDS] [as] a condition in which an individual feels very drowsy during the day and has an overwhelming urge to fall asleep . . .' (*http://www.sleepfoundation.org*). The Yahoo health web page defines EDS as a 'significant sleep disorder and is different from fatigue' (*http://www.health.yahoo.com/*). MeritCare Health System reminds visitors to its site that 'excessive daytime sleepiness . . . can have serious conse-quences such as auto accidents . . . poor school performance . . . work-related accidents' and more (*www.//meritcare.com*). The British Sleep Foundation Home Page reminds its viewers: 'Drivers falling asleep at the wheel cause about 20% of major road accidents in Britain and these accidents result in a higher rate of death and serious injury as sleeping drivers don't brake or swerve. These are avoidable deaths' (*http://www.britishsleepfoundation.org.uk*).

It is reasonable to assume that the legitimacy of rhetorical authority is likely to increase by amplifying the moral valence of its textual lessons. Cephalon Pharmaceuticals devotes an entire site to EDS, defining it as 'feel-ing drowsy and tired and having to sleep during the day . . . People with EDS frequently doze, nap, or fall asleep in situations where they need to be or want to be fully awake and alert' (*http://www.daytimesleep.org*). Finally, EDS has made its way to at least one Internet bibliographic resource. Thinkquest defines it as a 'disorder whereby the victim experiences drowsi-ness during the day and has an overwhelming urge to fall asleep. . . .' (*http://.library.thinkquest.org*).

Clinically, excessive sleepiness is typically identified as a possible sign or symptom of narcolepsy or obstructive sleep apnoea, two sleep disorders with long histories. Someone with conspicuous daytime sleepiness might be examined to determine the presence of one or the other of these disorders (Mahowald 2001). The Internet, in collaboration with print media, however, is redescribing excessive daytime sleepiness as a separate, discrete pathology, cleaving it from narcolepsy and sleep apnoea and encouraging people to view it as a singular problem. Examine the several definitions of EDS offered above; not one of them refers to it as a symptom. It is discussed, rather, as a discrete medical issue. The National Sleep Foundation (NSF), for example, promotes excessive daytime sleepiness as a distinct pathology in several ways. 'EDS' is listed first among its catalogue of sleep disorders posted on its web page, standing alone as a singular pathology. Moreover it is not referred to as a 'symptom' of an underlying sleep disorder; it is described, rather, as 'associated' with other, more prominent, sleep disorders, particu-larly narcolepsy, but also sleep apnoea and restless leg syndrome, among others (*http://www.sleepfoundation.org*).

A telling piece of rhetorical evidence is also apparent in this shift to EDS as a unique pathology, to wit, the emergence of the acronym EDS. Shortcuts to the familiar, acronyms in medical nosology are used to denote diseases or syndromes (TB, AIDS, or CJD), not symptoms. Promoted to an acronym, excessive daytime sleepiness or 'EDS' assumes a more singular identity as a bona fide medical disorder. But there is more than a lingual shift at work here.

Dozens of websites on EDS now include a subjective, Likert measure of excessive sleepiness to self-test for EDS. The Daytime Sleepiness Test, also known as the Epworth Sleepiness Scale, is a subjective measure of relative states of sleepiness. Simple to administer and score, it is found on websites and publications of major sleep advocacy and research organisations, as well as pharmaceutical companies marketing sleep-related drugs (see web pages for The Stanford University Sleep Clinic, Cephalon, Inc. and the National Sleep Foundation). Even the cable news CNNI posted The Epworth Sleepiness Scale on its health page (*http://www.cnn.com/HEALTH/indepth.health/sleeping.conditions/test*). A scalar measure designed to be self-administered might easily assume a somatic reality against which a number becomes a meaningful piece of evidence about the relative presence or absence of a particular disorder. The disorder in question, of course, is excessive daytime sleepiness.

Summary

Excessive daytime sleepiness is represented in the popular media as a distinct medical disorder marked by a diminished level of vigilance at socially inappropriate times. Moreover, it is characterised as morally inappropriate signaling the need for personal, if not civil, intervention. Importantly, problem sleepiness is being fashioned and deployed as a legitimate medical disorder by popular media. The idea of EDS and its accompanying symptoms is mediated more by magazines, newspapers, and the Internet than by practising physicians. Excessive daytime sleepiness as a medical disorder, in other words, is emerging in non-medical arenas as ordinary people access the images and grammar of popular media, cast in the rhetoric of medicine, to examine their own sleep behaviours.

In its '2001 "Sleep in America" Poll', the National Sleep Foundation surveyed the sleep habits and experiences of a representative sample of adults in the US. Among its many suggestive conclusions is the sizable proportion of respondents who report experiencing excessive sleepiness during the day. Indeed, a total of 40 per cent of US adults apparently suffer from mild to severe EDS. Over half of this group (22%) report recurring symptoms of EDS from a 'few days a week' to 'every day' (NSF 2001: 84). Respondents were also asked to rank their Internet use from 'Rarely/Never' to 'Heavy'. It is worth noting that 42 per cent of adults reporting 'daytime sleepiness at least a few times a week' made 'Light' to 'Heavy' use of the Internet (2001: 29).

Medical sociology in a Panoptical and post-Panoptical society: a case for both-and

In a shot across the bow of modern sociology, Alain Touraine asks us to abandon the word 'society' as anything more than a convenient description of a country or a state, as in 'British' or 'American society' (1998: 119). 'Society' is an increasingly meaningless term, he reasons, if it is meant to describe a more or less self-regulating, normative system, characterised by a close fit between social actors and institutions. Touraine is writing about those regions of the world saturated with digital and print media whose economies are increasingly globalised. His counsel, while highly provocative, would seem premature. Routine roles firmly grounded in institutions still exercise considerable jurisdiction over people's lives. But alongside this now familiar version of authority is a second more discursive version. The once-firm presumption that there is a 'right' way to be in the world – to work, fashion a family or get sick, for example – softens as people cobble together facts, data, and expert opinions to configure their own versions of work, family and sickness. It is with this protean social milieu in mind that Ulrich Beck encourages us to revisit our conventional 'units of analysis' to see what new and unfamiliar sense we might make of them (2000: 25).

Zygmunt Bauman (2000) deploys an idea first advanced by Beck, the 'zombie institution', to account for modern systems of social control that are simultaneously dead and alive. A zombie institution is alive in so far as it is embodied in visible social arrangements, but it is also dead (or dying) in so far as its authority to guide, shape and predict human choices diminishes (2000: 6). The emergence of zombie institutions signals 'the end of the era of mutual engagement . . . between the supervisors and the supervised' and the beginning of what he calls a *post-Panopticon history* (2000: 11). It is a short step between these observations on contemporary history and the idea of rhetorical authority inspired by Dorothy Smith, Arjun Appadurai and others who write about the increasing salience of print and digital texts in the co-ordination of human affairs. Consider medicine, if only briefly, as a zombie institution: the medical gaze will continue, but not in the near-perfect form of a Panoptical society.

To be sure, the institutional authority of medicine remains a potent factor in the day-to-day lives of ordinary people, but illustrated in this inquiry into sleep and sleepiness is an alternative authority expressed in the voices of print and digital media. This second, rhetorical authority, is reaching into the mundane lives of people fashioning what will count as a personal health issue. The idea or culture of medicine will continue to exercise a powerful hold over our lives. But this power is likely to be more discursive and less personified than routinely found in the physician-patient encounter. This new history invites a new look at some of the core concepts in medical sociology. Consider briefly the sociology of diagnosis and the classical distinction between illness and disease.

Contemporary literatures on these two concepts emphasise medicine as a powerful social institution, bounded by tradition, law and mysterious expertise. A Panopticon arrangement, modern medicine names diseases, labels people and prescribes and proscribes patient behaviours. Phil Brown (2000), for example, in a now seminal article, makes a persuasive case for a sociology of diagnosis. Assuming the early modern, Panopticon idea of institutions, he writes, medical diagnosis is 'based on the dominant biomedical framework . . . the socialization of medical providers, especially physicians, [and] the professional and institutional practices of the health-care system . . .' (2000: 78). With a strong voice, Elliot Mishler affirms Brown's Panopticon version of modernity: 'Diagnosis', he writes, is the 'voice of medicine', in contrast to the 'voice of the life-world' (cited in Brown 2000: 82).

The case of excessive daytime sleepiness hints at an evocative idea, to wit, the 'voice of medicine' and the 'voice of the life-world' are beginning to converse outside the once solid container of institutionalised medicine. '[T]he voice of medicine', it appears, is escaping into a contemporary world of porous institutions increasingly affected and affecting one another in a delightful, if maddening, exchange of digital, video, and print media. In a post-Panopticon history, sociologists are encouraged to re-examine the social locations of medical knowledge, to question the modernist assumption that it is exclusive to hierarchical, systemic arrangements. Medical knowledge, of course, is still found in the institution of medicine and we should not ignore this important area of inquiry, but we should also seek it outside its institutional matrix in less solidified, more casual and contingent venues. A person who self-diagnoses with EDS after taking the Epworth Sleepiness Scale found in a magazine article or on a website does not by herself threaten modern medical authority; but she is exercising, if only momentarily, an alternative authority, one worth investigating.

Open almost any textbook in medical sociology and you will encounter a distinction between illness and disease. In one highly respected text, illness is defined as 'laypersons' notions', that express 'people's diverse experiences' (Freund and McGuire 1991: 159–60). Disease, on the other hand, is the province of biomedical knowledge administered by physicians (Freund and McGuire 1991: 204). In a Panopticon world, physicians assign disease languages to bodies, and ordinary people experience their diseases as illnesses. Importantly, even when Freund and McGuire critique the naturalist assumptions of biomedicine by reminding readers that disease, like illness, is also socially constructed, it is physicians who do the constructing and lay people who experience the illness (1991: 204).

Calling attention to the socially constructed make-up of disease is indeed worth the effort. But in addition to this modernist critique, we are invited, at this point in history, to consider how the traditional dichotomy between disease and illness, so central to modern medical sociology, is being reconfigured. Excessive daytime sleepiness is a 'disease' fashioned by popular media, and communicated directly to ordinary people outside the institutional encounter between physician and patient. Coached and informed by a persuasive rhetorical authority, ordinary people are claiming to know something valid, that is, medical, about the nature of the body.

From this vantage point, EDS is more than a subjective appraisal of discomfort or suffering – more than an illness in other words – it is also a theory, an explanation, a way of making medical sense of the body. Indeed, an increasing number of 'diseases' are fashioned and deployed by popular media in spite of their contested status in institutional medicine. Among the more well known are Gulf War Syndrome, multiple chemical sensitivity, chronic fatigue syndrome and third stage Lyme Disease (for a recent discussion of contested diseases see Brown, Kroll-Smith and Gunter 2000). As we examine the nomenclatures of disease floating about in multiple media, appealing to general and targeted groups alike, we are witness to a rhetorical form of authority discernibly different from Foucault's Panopticon medical gaze (1995: 191). And we are invited to revisit our classic distinction between illness and disease, not to debunk it, but to rethink it.

In sum, submitted here is not an *either-or* distinction between institutional and rhetorical authority or Panopticon and post-Panopticon moments in time. It is, rather, an invitation to a *both-and* way of thinking. Consider it a modest call to be adventurous, to look for new and novel social arrangements emerging alongside the familiar ones coded in our common sociological vernacular.

Note

1 With a few exceptions, sociologists have ignored sleep and sleepiness. Little is known about dormant cultures and their various social arrangements. There are hints, however, that dormancy and soporific bodies are emerging as legitimate topics of social and cultural inquiry (Two recent examples are Kroll-Smith 2000 and Williams 2002).

References

Appadurai, A. (1996) *Modernity at Large*. Minneapolis: University of Minneapolis Press.
Bain, P., Baldry, C. and Taylor, P. (1999) Sick Building Syndrome and the industrial relations of occupational health, *International Journal of Employment Studies*, 4, 125–48.
Bauman, Z. (2000) *Liquid Modernity*. Cambridge: Polity Press.
Beck, Ulrich (2000) *What is Globalization?* Cambridge: Polity Press.
Brody, J. (1994) America's falling asleep, *The New York Times Magazine*, 24 April, 64–5 + 3.

Browman, C.P., Sampson, M. and Krishnareddy, S. (1982) The drowsy crowd, *Psychology Today*, 16, 35–8.

Brown, P. (2000) Naming and framing: the social construction of diagnosis and illness. In Brown, P. (ed) *Perspectives in Medical Sociology*. Prospect Heights, IL: Waveland Press.

Brown, P., Kroll-Smith, S. and Gunter, V. (2000) Knowledge, citizens, and organizations: an overview of environments, diseases, and social conflict. In Kroll-Smith, S., Brown, P. and Gunter, V. (eds) *Illness and the Environment, a Reader in Contested Medicine*. NY: New York University Press.

Cochet, P. (1982) Dealing with trouble sleep, *Business Week*, October, 132–3.

Coleman, R.M., Roffwarg, H.P. and Kennedy, S.J. *et al.* (1982) Sleep-wake disorders based on polysomnographic diagnosis: a national comparative study, *Journal of the American Medical Association*, 247, 997–1003.

Cotten, S.R. (2001) Implications of internet technology for medical sociology in the new millennium, *Sociological Spectrum*, 21, 319–40.

Ezzy, D. (2000) Illness narratives: time, hope and HIV, *Social Science and Medicine*, 50, 605–17.

Fairclough, N. (2001) Global capitalism and critical awareness of language, *http://www.schools.ash.org.au/litweb/norman1.html*, (accessed 06.05.2002).

Foucault, M. (1995) *Discipline and Punish*. New York: Vintage Books.

Fox, S. and Rainie, L. (2000) *The Online Health Care Revolution: how the Web Helps Americans Take Better Care of Themselves*. Washington, DC: Pew Charitable Trusts.

Frank, A. (1995) *The Wounded Story Teller*. Chicago: University of Chicago Press.

Freund, P. and Meredith, M. (1991) *Health, Illness, and the Social Body*. Englewood Cliffs, NJ: Prentice-Hall.

Frost, R. (2001) *Selected Poems*. NY: Barnes and Noble.

Giddens, A. (1991) *Modernity and Self-Identity*. Stanford: Stanford University Press.

Gretchen, K., Berland, M.D. and Elliott, M. (2001) Health information on the Internet, *Journal of the American Medical Association*, *http://jama.ama-assn.org/issues/v285n20/joc02274.html*, (accessed 01.05.2002).

Haponik, E.F., Frye, A.W. and Richards, B. (1996) Sleep history is neglected diagnostic information, *Journal of General Internal Medicine*, 11, 759–61.

Heller, K. (1993) Diary of a mad insomniac, *Working Woman*, 18, 72–3 +2.

Hickey, M.C. (1994) The exhausted woman, *Ladies' Home Journal*, 111, 86 +2.

Kiechel, W. (1990) The executive insomniac, *Fortune*, 122, 183–5.

Kroll-Smith, S. (2000) The social production of the drowsy person, *Perspectives on Social Problems*, 12, 89–109.

Kroll-Smith, S. and Floyd, H. (1997) *Bodies in Protest*. NY: New York University Press.

Lafavore, M. (1993) Choose to snooze, *Men's Health*, 8, 38–9.

Love, A. (1986) The sleep disease, *Forbes*, 131, 156–8.

Lukachko, A. (1999) Estrogen and health: how popular magazines have dealt with hormone replacement therapy, *http://www.acsh.org/publications/reports/estrogen.htm*, (accessed 3.05.2002).

Mahowald, M. (2001) What is causing excessive daytime sleepiness? *Postgraduate Medicine*, *http://www.postgradmed.com/issues/2000/03_00/mahowald.htm*, (accessed 15.05.2002).

Meissner, H., Reimer, A. and Santiago, S.M. *et al.* (1998) Failure of physicians documentation of sleep complaints in hospitalized patients, *Western Journal of Medicine*, 169, 146–9.

Muir, K. (1996) *Macbeth by William Shakespeare.* NY: Thomason Learning.

National Cancer Institute (2001) Communicating cancer research, *http://www.cra.nci.nih.gov/1_communicate_research/understanding_risk.html*, (accessed 15.05.2002).

National Sleep Foundation (2001) *Sleep in America Poll.* 1522K. St., NW, Washington DC 20005.

Phillips, D.P., Kanter, E.J. and Bednarczyk, B. (1991) Importance of the lay press in the transmission of medical knowledge to the scientific community, *The New England Journal of Medicine*, 325, 1180–3.

Pisetsky, D. (1995) *Book of Arthritis.* NY: Fawcett Columbus Press.

Rorty, R. (1989) *Contingency, Irony and Solidarity.* London: Cambridge.

Rovner, S. (1984) Waking up on sleep, *Washington Post*, 30 March, D5.

Schaefer, K. (1990) Sweet dreams, *Nations Business*, 78, 66.

Smith, D. (1993) *Text, Facts, and Femininity.* London: Routledge.

Steinberg, D. (1983) Americans, asleep at the wheel, *US News and World Report*, 114, 406–07.

Toufexos, A. and Dolan, B. (1990) Drowsy America, *Time*, 136, 78–85.

Touraine, A. (1998) Sociology without society, *Current Sociology*, 46, 119–43.

US Census Bureau (2001) *Home Computers and Internet Use in the United States: August 2000. Report # P23-207 September.* Washington, DC: Economics and Statistics Administration.

Weld, N. (1983) A nation of sleepy heads, *Science News*, v. 104, p. 4.

Williams, D. (1993) The great American 'sleep debt', *USA Today Magazine*, 122, 1–3.

Williams, S.J. (2002) Sleep and health: sociological reflections on the dormant society, *Health*, 6, 173–200.

Wise, N. (1990) Sleep debt, *New York Times*, 15 May, C1.

Woznicki, D. and Case, A.G. (1994) Nutritional accuracy in popular magazines (1990–1992), *http://www.acsh.org/publications/priorities/0603/accuracy/html*, (accessed 12.05.2002).

Chapter 8

Bio-phobias/techno-philias: virtual reality exposure as treatment for phobias of 'nature'

Joyce Davidson and Mick Smith

Introduction

Since its inception Sociology as a discipline has sought to explain in terms of social causes the conditions and characteristics of that 'modern' society with which it has been so intimately associated. In looking to social, rather than naturalistic or psychological, explanations, health sociologists have highlighted the role of society in *framing*, *constructing* or, in its most socio-logically deterministic form, actually *producing* various categories of mental illness. Whatever their differing ontological implications these approaches share an emphasis on the *mediating* role of social space(s). They agree that society is not just the passive backdrop against which individual mental health problems arise but is an active player in shaping, transmitting and transforming individuals' healthy and unhealthy perceptions of the world around them, including their perceptions of the 'natural' (that is, the non-human) world.

From these sociological perspectives, phobias like arachnophobia cannot then be understood simply in terms of an individual's panicked reaction to spiders. There must also be some 'social' reason why spiders in particular are the kind of (natural) things that are framed, constructed or produce fear or loathing. This paper argues that bio-phobias are, at least in part, a result of modern society's ideological obsession with separating, controlling, ordering and subjugating an unruly nature through artifice. Control, however, is never complete and the inevitable return of this *socially repressed nature* in various apparently uncontrollable manifestations, such as spiders, bats, thunder and so on, intrudes upon and threatens the prevailing cultural logic, precipitating fearful reactions from susceptible individuals who have inter-nalised these social relations. Phobias are then *socially* mediated anxieties.

The emergence of a new technologically-mediated 'cyberspace' posited as something separate from the 'realities' of social or natural spaces and its increasingly frequent use in the treatment of phobias thus has a number of important implications for the sociology of mental health and for sufferers themselves. One danger is that naturalistic and psychological assumptions are transferred to the treatment regimes provided within this new medium without taking into account the importance of social spaces as contributory factors mediating the appearance and prevalence of the conditions to be treated. A related problem is that technologically-mediated treatments seem to mirror this same modernist social project of cultural control over nature.

Indeed they could be seen as taking modernity's artificially mediated cultural separation from, and subjugation of, nature to new extremes. If this is so, then the 'technical fix' that cyberspace might purchase for some individuals may come at the social cost of widening an increasingly fearful void between nature and culture. This may have implications for the future prevalence of bio-phobias and possibly for the future of nature itself.

The study draws on 40 in-depth, semi-structured interviews with users (recruited through the NPS) and 10 providers (recruited using purposive sampling) of both statutory and non-statutory treatment services, including cognitive behavioural, holistic massage, counselling and hypno-therapies. All interviews were audio-tape recorded and transcribed verbatim with interviewees' permission. All interviewees have been given pseudonyms. Interview material was supplemented with data collected during five extended observational sessions in the NPS headquarters and from less formal sources, such as conversations with phobia researchers and NPS volunteers. Additionally, and of particular relevance for this paper, research visits were made to investigate use of two different forms of 'VR therapy' for phobias. The first was to clinical psychologist Paul Abeles, working with 'Spider Phobia Control' (Spider PC) in the Psychiatry Department of Manchester's Booth Hall Children's Hospital. The second meeting was with members of the 'Equator' team of computer scientists and clinical psychologists, led by Mel Slater, at the Computing Sciences Department of University College London. Following 'indexing' of material thus collected (Pope, Ziebland and Mays 2000) and in-depth reflection on emergent themes, data were subjected to an ongoing process of critical discourse analysis (Capps and Ochs 1995).

The nature of phobias and phobias of nature

Anecdotal as much as clinical evidence suggests that we all know someone who has an apparently 'irrational' fear of some*thing*, be it spiders, birds, mice or thunder. There is, however, an important distinction to be drawn between 'sub-clinical' *fears* and more debilitating *phobias*. Many of us dislike heights, or flying, or find that some insect or other 'gives us the creeps', but such fears are unlikely significantly to curtail our ability to pursue 'normal' everyday activities. Phobias entail an altogether different level of reaction, including convoluted and highly restrictive patterns of avoidance, in an attempt to remain free of the experience of sheer *panic* that often characterises confrontation with the phobic object (Antony *et al.* 1997).

Phobias are among the most common mental health problem presented at the level of primary care; MIND estimates there are currently 10 million sufferers in the UK, a figure including significantly more women than men. Gelder *et al.* (1996: 170) estimate lifetime prevalence rates to be 13 and four per cent respectively. Specific Phobias, as defined by the most recent edition of the Diagnostic and Statistic Manual of Mental Disorders (APA 1994: 405) involve a marked and persistent fear of clearly discernible, circumscribed objects or situations. Interestingly, despite the predominantly urban and technologically mediated existence that characterises modern societies, specific phobias tend to be focused on what might be regarded as 'natural' objects and situations, rather than specific technologies or elements of city life (Arrindell 2000). As Merckelbach et al. (1996: 338) remark 'survey studies have consistently found that, in the general population, some fears (e.g. the fear of snakes) are far more prevalent than others (e.g. fear of electricity)'. A rank order of children's fears similarly shows that 'the most common fears were concerned with the dark, spiders and thunderstorms', and that of those children deemed to meet the full criteria for specific phobias 'animal phobias appeared to be the most common type' (Muris et al. 1999: 815).

The prevalence of highly specific natural stimuli is mirrored in the four major categories used for diagnostic purposes, namely, animal type natural environment type (e.g. vertigo), blood-injection-injury type and situational type (e.g. claustrophobia) (APA 1994: 406). Apparently non-natural phobias, for example of dentists or doctors, may in fact be more closely tied to specific 'natural' elements like blood and/or to what the individual deems to be a risk of potentially invasive or injurious practices to their body. Frederikson et al. (1996: 37) have also argued that situational and natural-environment phobia types cluster together and may 'share a common underlying theme' which would fit with an understanding of phobias like vertigo and claustrophobia as spatially or environmentally mediated reactions (see also Davidson 2000). Even those phobias associated with technical phenomena, such as methods of transportation, tend to be spatially mediated and articulated (fears of being suspended 'high and away from earth' in an aeroplane, or 'trapped underground' in a train (Marks 1987)). While not all phobias are directed at natural objects or situations (some phobias encountered throughout this research included, for example, jewellery, broken dolls and buttons) these non-natural fears remain relatively rare. (On further analysis even the jewellery phobia actually seemed connected to fears of dirt and infection.)

This somewhat bizarre pattern has led some practitioners to develop naturalistic evolutionary accounts of phobias, as genetically-coded responses to potentially dangerous species/situations – snakes or heights are obvious examples (Marks and Nesse 1994). But such explanations are undermined by the fact that fears appear to be culturally induced and culturally reinforced (Fredrikson et al. 1997). Young children tend not to show fearful responses to spiders or snakes (Field et al. 2000). There is also evidence that specific phobias are culturally variable (Davey et al. 1998). Evolutionary and naturalistic approaches also find it difficult to explain the objects of certain common phobias, such as feathers, pigeons or moths, or adequately to account for the gender bias shown in many examples (Merckelbach et al.

1996). In any case, a serious phobic response where the person may freeze or suffer a panic attack is hardly likely to confer a selective advantage, quite the opposite. Someone with a spider phobia would find it impossible to search for edible grubs, collect berries or inhabit a cave.

Even if we discard evolutionary accounts of the origins of specific phobias there might be other 'naturalistic' explanations. Issues around aetiology receive substantial clinical attention, though interviewees themselves vary in their desire to explore or discuss the possible cause(s) of their phobia. Some clearly pin-point a specific adverse and often childhood event, such as terror of a thunderstorm, having a spider fall on them in the bath, or being chased or bitten by a dog (Forsyth and Chorpita 1997). But, with the exception of immediately painful experiences like dog-bites, there is a certain circularity in such arguments unless we also take pre-given cultural associations into account and many sufferers remain deeply puzzled by the source of their fear. Personal exposure to potentially phobic objects can actually be inversely related to the degree of fear felt, as a study of fear of storms and hurricanes in Antillean and Belgian children reveals (Muris *et al.* 2002). For all these reasons it seems that the fear of certain 'natural' things is primarily a culturally mediated phenomenon. Although the phobia sufferer's fears are focused on natural objects, these objects themselves have to be understood in terms of their place (or lack of place) in the specific set of social relations that characterise modern societies and sensibilities.

There is no need here to enter the complexities of debates about the social construction of nature (Eder 1996). Ideas of nature/human relations clearly differ from society to society and over time (MacCormack and Strathern 1989, Thomas 1984). For present purposes we need only note that modernity is frequently characterised by the ubiquity and importance it attaches to a distinction between nature and culture and by the use of technology to order, control and transform nature for cultural purposes on a previously unimaginable scale. As Castree (2001: 6) argues, 'this ontological separation of the natural and the social has, since the European Enlightenment, been associated with other dualisms organising our thought, such as rural-urban, country-city, and wilderness-civilisation' (see also Plumwood 1993). (This nature/culture dichotomy is, of course, also reflected in the distinction between the social and natural sciences themselves.) The figures of Francis Bacon and Rene Descartes are frequently invoked as exemplifying or even initiating this scientific/technological dream of subduing 'external' nature (Merchant 1990). As Coates (1998: 72) states, '[t]he goal of what Max Scheler in the 1920s dubbed *Herrschaftswissen* ("knowledge for the sake of domination") was manipulation and mastery. With Bacon, the question "what is nature?" became inseparable from "what can we do with nature"?' Max Horkheimer (1974: 97) too speaks of modernity's association with 'an empty nature degraded into mere material, mere stuff to be dominated'. As Seidler (1998) argues, the need to control the outer world is mirrored by control over the psyche:

we witness the reduction of nature to matter which is largely to be explained through the discovery of scientific laws. Progress is identified with the control and domination of an external nature just as it is in relation to inner natures. Just as outer nature is there to be controlled, since it is governed through external laws, so our inner natures also have to be controlled if we are to exist as rational selves (1998: 15).

Interestingly, interviewees almost invariably identify a perceived lack of control over natural objects/situations as a key factor. It seems to be creatures' propensity to act as unpredictable sources of autopoietic activity that makes them appear as being(s) so out of control. These specific objects/situations might thus be seen as a source of 'danger' in Mary Douglas's (1993) terms precisely because they conflate the controlling (in both senses) ideological categories of modernity's social order. This paper thus first sets out to demonstrate that bio-phobic objects do indeed represent a substantial threat to the sufferer's sense of 'ontological security' and self-*control* before turning to the issue of treatment and new media technologies.

Bio-phobias and the control of nature

Apart from the higher incidence of specific phobias in women there seem to be no discernible predictive patterns. For example, social class or 'race' – or 'types' of personality – all seem equally prone to bio-phobias, supporting our contention that they are mediated through generalised cultural conditioning. As one therapist explains, it can affect 'anybody, yea. I can't say that I've seen any similarities at all because I've seen young teenagers and older people you know in their seventies and across the board [. . .] no pattern'. Phobics are certainly not generally 'irrational' or even belong to especially anxious kinds of individuals as Anita, a sufferer, explains:

> I'm not a fearful woman. I'm quite, quite tough really and this is the thing that, that I find so extraordinary because I mean I've, I've gone through some very tough times. I've coped with it, I've brought up four children. I'm not frightened of things and yet I can't reason myself or be logical about this [thunder] and that's *so* awful.

Sufferers frequently report taking great pains to 'reason' with themselves and about their phobic responses. They may be 'rational', 'strong', 'sensible', 'level-headed', 'well-balanced' in every other aspect of their lives, but when dealing with their phobic object, they can find themselves 'entirely without resources'. Monica continues:

> I think it's very important for the people to whom you are presenting your findings in your research, that the sense of being, the point at

which you are being *frightened*, the point of the panic attack, is a point where a lot of what happens in the rest of your life, other kinds of rational understanding and other kinds of rational competence, is just wiped away.

Monica's statement suggests that something radically alters at the point of panic. As previous research has shown (Davidson 2000, 2001), in the throes of a panic attack it is not just 'rational competence', but the sufferer's entire sense of self and her place in the world that comes under threat. Panic entails a significant shift in the dynamic, mutually constitutive *relations* between (internal) subject and (external) object. That is to say, this transformation entails absolute, unthinkable terror, along with a repositioning of the perceived locus of *control* from the individual to the phenomenon she fears. This theme of 'loss of control' and the horror it provokes appears time and again in phobic narratives. Clearly, a sense of having some command over our circumstances and environment is crucial to the maintenance of one's ontological security (Giddens 1997) and during the moment of panic, this simply falls away.

Interviews with sufferers suggest that it is often the *unpredictability* of the phobic object that threatens our sense of mastery so acutely. The *noise* of wind, for example, or the *movement* of insects, is capricious. Susie illustrates this when she explains the unpredictable direction and speed of spiders' movements 'totally freaks me out. Because I don't know which way, I don't know how fast, so I can't, for myself, I don't even know my escape route because I don't know where that thing is going'. Referring to birds rather than spiders, Sandra makes a strikingly similar point: 'They're not predictable as to where they are going to land and I think that's what scares me the most about them'. Monica's statement also highlights the unpredictability that she attributes to her phobic object:

What frightens me about lightning is the sense of um, I suppose not knowing where it will strike. I mean there's, there's a sense of being hunted about lightning and my feelings about it, which I suppose is part of what frightens me. I just find it a very very powerful and very unknowable power.

Issues of control and containment emerge strikingly in other narratives, demonstrating a need to keep the natural object separate from sufferers at all costs. For example, when Nadia describes 'unpredictability' of movement as that which bothers her most about her feared natural objects – frogs, lizards and mice – I ask her why, in that case, she thinks her phobia doesn't extend to spiders. Her answer is illuminating;

I think with spiders they're more, you can contain them a bit more. If I put something over them, say if I put a flowerpot over it, its gonna stay there. But a frog might sort of, my fear would be that it would jump about and a mouse, it wouldn't contain it at all.

Maryanne, too, is unequivocal about exactly why thunder is for her, utterly intolerable, and interestingly, she communicates this by drawing comparisons with her much more *manageable* fear of spiders and mice. She explains that, with these latter creatures,

> you can get [one] in a box and contain it, right [. . .] But this [thunder] I can't control it no matter what I do. [. . .] I can't catch thunder and lightning and put it in a nice big pot and say 'right shoo, go away', it just doesn't happen.

In each case, the issue seems to be that their own particular phobic object cannot be contained or controlled. This, we would argue, reflects modernity's dominant cultural logic in seeking to separate and control the natural sphere. We like to experience 'nature' on our own limited terms, visiting rather than *dwelling* in what now passes for natural spaces, for example, country or city parks, forests or farms, zoos and aquariums, or (for the more adventurous) eco-tourist holiday destinations. For most of us, nature is packaged and perused at our convenience. It is only allowed to enter the cultured – and *cleansed* – space of our homes under very particular and circumscribed (potted, pictured, petted) circumstances. Nature is something to be kept apart from, and is 'other' than, our supposedly cultured selves.

Increasingly, such attitudes towards nature mean that our homes are subject to almost obsessive decontamination rituals, as we are encouraged (by advertising, industry, associated social mores, etc.) to adopt and apply ever more toxic solutions to the problem of maintaining our household's sanctity. The possible physiological implications of such an enthusiastic approach to the removal of all 'matter out of place' (Douglas 1993) – *e.g.* allergies, asthma, immuno-suppression, etc. – are increasingly well documented, but what of the consequences for our *mental* health? What does this conceptual and physical separation from the natural world *mean* for contemporary selves and society?

The kinds of concretised and citified lifestyles we lead are likely to foster unreasonable beliefs about the extent to which we can control the non-human environment. Such attitudes encourage us to imbue potentially intrusive natural agents with menacing symbolic powers. The spider or thunderstorm serve as cipher for that which we cannot contain and control. It is (depending on one's theoretical predilection) a 'condensation' or 'projection' of fears we cannot deal with. (As Annette says of her wasp phobia, 'I probably put all my anxiety and worry into silly little things that fly around'.) The severity of phobic reaction seems to relate to how far the sufferer imagines the (natural) object can intrude on the (cultural) realm. Monica again epitomises this when she says 'I mean I think that we um, it is nature that, that frightens us because for a lot of us it's an issue about control and we can't control it'.

Conventional approaches to treatment

Experiences of treatment vary widely, but in the UK diagnosis by a National Health Service General Practitioner (GP) would typically result in referral to specialist service providers. Referral to a clinical psychologist or clinical nurse specialist currently involves a wait of approximately six to 12 months. The most likely course of treatment provided will be Cognitive Behavioural Therapy (CBT) involving between 6–12, weekly sessions of 45–60 minutes in the therapist's office (Lovell and Richards 2000). During this time, patient and therapist use a collaboratively constructed form of graded exposure therapy to work through a hierarchy of anxiety-provoking tasks, starting with the most manageable and gradually building towards the most difficult. A clinical nurse specialist illustrates the principles underlying the graded exposure aspects of CBT:

> so you'd start with – 'right, what we hope to achieve today is that you can see a live spider without going out of the room or without panicking, or you might want to touch a dead one', or whatever. And so you would start of with maybe saying the 's' word, writing it down, you know, then showing them some pictures, getting a dead one out of the drawer, because I've always got one in there. And if you, if you were planning it you would maybe having a live one to hand somewhere. [. . .] And actually go from one stage to the other, and you overcome each stage [. . .]. It works on the principle of habituation. You know your anxiety goes up but it can't stay up there indefinitely and it will sooner or later come down (Susan).

The thinking behind this approach is clear; if the person can gradually be brought face to face with their fears, in a controlled and relatively safe environment in the presence of a trusted professional, they can learn to *control* rather than avoid their anxiety. As one clinical psychologist interviewee explains, CBT aims to achieve this by addressing the

> three ways the phobia affects them; behaviour, that's mainly avoidance; physiological – heart rate, sweating, it affects people in different ways, and obviously the cognitive. Negative thoughts popping into your mind, negative ways of interpreting them. [This approach is about] trying to get them to have a sense of how it's affecting them, to get them to take control (Peter).

Part of this process of taking control entails sufferers learning to *measure* their fear, using scales provided by their therapist, often referred to as 'subjective units of distress' (SUDS). As a second clinical psychologist interviewee highlights the point of CBT is to

> give them the means to cope with that anxiety, you know, relaxation, breathing, [. . .] the notion that you are actually able to control yourself physically and you have that power, and panic is not something that is going to sweep across and wipe you out (June).

Gauging and reacting to the severity of their symptoms in this way involves taking a calculating, 'scientific' approach to phobic distress. CBT involves a highly rational and controlling approach to 'unreasonable' phobic responses (raising important questions about the 'rationalist' model of subjectivity it deploys (Davidson 2002)). It can be experienced as a very 'harsh' therapy (Nicky, NPS manager), but, according to the clinical literature, can also be highly effective in treating Specific Phobias (Chambless and Gillis 1993, Clarke and Fairburn 1997). It offers a 'no nonsense' approach that emphasises the control of the rational agent – no matter what the context, cause or focus of the phobia:

> It doesn't matter because if you can't find what the cause was, it's irrelevant, it's still there [. . .]. So if, if they don't know why they've got a snake phobia, or a height phobia, a wart phobia, a wind phobia, whatever the phobia is, it's irrelevant. You just treat that they've got one. That's the fact of the matter (Susan).

Certain phobic objects are, of course, more difficult to capture, contain and bring to the therapist's office to facilitate controlled exposure. Although the therapist can encourage patients to imagine themselves in increasingly anxiety-provoking situations this tends to be far less effective than in vivo exposure. One interviewee who has experienced difficulty receiving appropriate treatment for her phobia of thunder draws attention to this limitation:

> And I said, up until the day comes that I actually come here and it's thundering I said you can't really see what I'm like. I said and if it is thundering on the day I'm supposed to come, I said you won't flaming see me cause I won't come out the sodding house.
> So I can't win (Maryanne).

Until recently technical simulations of phobic objects have been of limited use because while they may be 'uncomfortable' to experience they don't usually have the immediacy of the 'real' thing. Several interviewees in this project, like Anita, have tried audio and audio-visual recordings of thunderstorms:

> I did buy myself one, a tape of a thunderstorm to try and sort of desensitise or try to, and I didn't. It didn't work because I knew it was

a, only a tape. [. . .] I knew I was alright really you know. I couldn't put myself into, into believing that it was real so it didn't work.

Similarly, she can watch a thunderstorm on television because 'It's just in a screen'. New media however seem to offer the very real possibility of both more extensive control and more immediate presentation of phobic simulations during treatment.

Techno-philias: towards virtual reality

In May 2002, one of us (Joyce) interviewed clinical psychologist Paul Abeles about research he has conducted using a computerised CBT programme for the treatment of arachnophobia. This package, named Spider Phobia Control (Spider PC), developed by Whitby and Alcock (1994) 'recreates a traditional in vivo exposure hierarchy using a series of computer-generated spider images' (Abeles 2001: 165). It allows the user to encounter four types of spider (each assumed to be increasingly threatening) and make minor adjustments to the on-screen spider's size, as well as the speed and manner of its movement.

In a written case study Abeles describes how 'CBT is particularly well suited to interactive computer programs because it is highly structured with well-delineated procedures, targets specific behaviours and symptoms, and proceeds in a systematic fashion' (Abeles 2001: 164). In our interview he further argued that a computer-based approach may even have certain advantages over traditional exposure because of increased control and containment:

> In everyday life, for someone with a phobia, you're always confronted with the possibility of things right high up the hierarchy, you know, real spiders. [. . .] But with this hierarchy you can systematically just change one thing so that the increased anxiety will be contained, because you know what's going to happen next.

As the emphases we have added to Abeles' statements below show, this 'controlling' aspect seems vital for successful treatment:

> The person, in order for them to learn to, take *control* of their own anxiety, to cope, you need to be in *control* of that situation. It's important for the person doing the treatment to make sure you've got absolute *control* over what's going to happen, against real life, when you're not in *control*. Think of dog phobia, if you've got a dog in the room, you can't get the dog not to bark, or whatever. With a spider, it could just run off. So from the point of view of the clinician, using the [computer] programme, they have a chance to *control* their fear, but also perhaps an experience of *controlling* the thing that they are *scared* off, externally.

Abeles makes plain that he finds the package very valuable and that computer technology holds real promise for the improvement of this area of mental health service provision. During our discussion, he does, however, draw attention to what he perceives to be limitations associated with the programme's abstraction from 'real life', and reports that it works most effectively when backed up by *actual* embodied exposure:

> I think for some people, it could be enough, just to have the programme. But from my study, it would appear that you do need to do some in vivo work, non-virtual work as well. The computer work is definitely exposure, you're going up the hierarchy, you're learning skills, practising, but then those skills need to be applied to the non-virtual environment.

Abeles recognises then, as do sufferers, that the way that the screen operates as a visual two-dimensional intermediary clearly limits the effectiveness of this simulated reality. Like others, he has pondered the implications of more 'life-like', multi-sensual elements (*e.g.* scurrying *sounds, textured* images) leading towards a more complete Virtual Reality.

Virtual reality therapy for phobias

> Phobia desensitization, it seems, is a perfect match for virtual reality because it provides a more practical, controllable means for facilitating conventional therapy for this type of disorder (Mahoney 1997: 52).

A substantial number of researchers are currently working on the development of virtual reality therapies for Specific Phobias (see Carlin *et al.* 1997, Rothbaum *et al.* 1995). Virtual Reality (VR) has been described as a technology that 'integrates real-time computer graphics, body tracking devices, visual displays, and other sensory inputs to immerse individuals in a computer-generated virtual environment' (Emmelkamp *et al.* 2002: 509). As one of us (Joyce) discovered during a visit to the Computing Science Department at University College London, virtual reality simulations certainly can provoke anxiety similar in nature and intensity to everyday life.

Following initial discussions with clinical psychologists and computer scientists involved with the 'Equator' research team, led by Mel Slater[1], I was led to 'the cave' for a demonstration of simulations used to treat acro(height)phobia. I had already been told that:

> People do seem to respond to virtual reality, even though they know it's not real, they respond as if it is. So, you stand over a virtual cliff, you know there's no cliff there, but you still, some people, still exhibit the symptoms of vertigo (Mel).

The acrophobia simulation I was exposed to was described as 'the pit' and involved physically entering a 'room', wearing a 'headtracker', a pair of goggles that made sense of high-resolution images projected onto the floor and three walls. Together, these technologies create the VR environment, making it appear as though a square of floor was dropped around 20 feet from the middle of the room. Moving tentatively towards this 'pit', 'my' perspective and perception of distance, depth and so on changed appropriately. The headgear 'tracked' the movement of my body within the simulation, and adjusted the projected images accordingly, such that the drop was experienced as increasingly frightening the closer I became. I recall feeling taken aback by how 'realistic' the experience actually *felt*. The tape recorder I had left running picked up some comments made during the demonstration:

Joyce: Something that makes this, I can imagine more useful, for me anyway, is that your *body* is still there. I had imagined virtual reality to be a very *disembodied* experience where you're sort of expected to project yourself into that environment. But I can still see my feet. I can look down and be part, you're still physically here, not having to imagine you're part of the environment.

Mel: That's the advantage of this system, that's right.

My verbal expression of visceral unease when I reach 'the edge' and peer over the side into the pit was also recorded:

Joyce: Oh my god right that's really quite unpleasant. Jeez
Mel: What's unpleasant? Seeing the pit?
Joyce: *Yes.*
Mel: Even though you know there's not one there?
Joyce: Yeah. Not happy about that at all.
Mel: It's amazing, that you know there's not one there, but your body still reacts as if there is.

The researchers are keen to get users involved in this project at an early stage to help them develop the technology appropriately. This is appreciated by the NPS, and increases the chances of the treatment that emerges from their research being 'user-friendly'. Mel explains:

Effectively we want to provide, if you like, virtual knobs, that the phobic person in there can turn up the knob a bit to make them a bit more anxious, or turn it down a bit. We want to know what those knobs should be.

Team-member Daniela Romano then makes the fascinating suggestion – in light of our concern with bio-phobias – of using a VR '*natural* environment', as somewhere users could be gradually introduced to the technology in a pleasant and even relaxing way. She describes her vision of a controllable natural environment, such as, you know, a virtual environment, which is absolutely controllable. You know the amount of grass, the amount of trees, the sound is controllable. I think, this might be a first starting environment, and then it can trickle, bring in the difficult elements, you know, add something, change the light, would be my idea. So that, from a natural environment we could move to, anything you like (Daniela)[2].

Here then we have the possibility of a simulated VR version of the 'natural' where even the characteristic unpredictability of those 'difficult elements' are themselves subject to control (see also Abeles 2001, Carlin et al. 1997, Hoffman et al. in press). This has obvious therapeutic advantages and Emmelkamp et al. (2002: 514) who tested similar technology claim success in 'the first study in which the effects of VR exposure were compared with the golden standard of treatment for specific phobias (exposure in vivo) in a between-group design'. The team replicated in VR the experience of walking around the university plaza, a fire escape and the university roof garden. In a fascinating (though philosophically suspect) use of language, they claim that:

In this study, patients in the VR exposure condition were exposed to *exactly the same* three situations as were used with patients in the exposure in vivo conditions (Emmelkamp et al. 2002: 514, emphasis added).

Leaving aside issues of Baudrillardian complexity, the point Emmelkamp et al. make is that treatment by VR seems to be 'as effective as exposure in vivo on anxiety and avoidance' (2002: 509) behaviour. Despite its problematic ontological status, VR can provide realistic feeling situations and clearly has some potential as an effective modifier of phobic behaviours. However, even if VR works as well as its proponents claim and is as cost effective and as therapeutically convenient as they imagine, it still raises wider issues about such treatments' relation to the social medium of everyday life.

VR and (un)natural relations

If, as we have argued, specific phobias are largely about the lack of control over natural intrusions into individualised experiences of modern social space then VR seems to provide a mechanism (a technology) and a medium (cyberspace) for re-asserting that control through behaviour modification. VR seems to be the perfect controlled environment; in 'VR, you have total control of complex stimulus presentation [...] This is a psychologist's dream' (Albert Rizzo quoted in Mahoney 1997: 56). It also 'seems to offer the space for unconstrained, omnipotent experience, as well as providing a "protective shield" affording insulation from "external reality" ' (Robins 1996:10). After all, Lajoie asks (1996: 165), '[w]hat is cyberspace if not the ultimate protective shield against the threat posed by otherness?'.

But if this otherness is nature itself, and if phobias of bats, birds, wasps and so on are just specific 'projections' of this fear of modernity's unruly 'other', then the limited horizons of this kind of technological fix become apparent. Unless, with the naïve Prometheanism of certain extreme proponents of VR, we believe that it can become a genuine replacement reality (see Lajoie 1996: 164), a totally artificial environment in which we might 'live', then nature will always be with us. Unless we buy into the ideology of complete control then we have to recognise that nature will continue to 'intrude' into our well-ordered social existence and our individual lives in one form or another, often when we least expect it. Recent environmental problems like BSE, the depletion of the ozone layer and so on might be seen in this light as unforeseen social consequences of attempts to impose control over nature (Beck 1993, Smith 2001). Insofar as human existence remains 'natural' there will always be inescapable consequences of existence, most notably our own individual death. Despite our best efforts, we are not, nor ever will be, in 'complete' control. Given the fact that we cannot (yet) live full time in the 'control-space' of VR (Doel and Clarke 1999: 264), might it not be a better idea to learn to deal with *not* being in total control? Wouldn't such an approach to our place in the (real) world be more, well, realistic?

In other words, as with all technological interventions, there is a need to see the bigger (social) picture here. VR may prove to be an effective therapy for some individuals. But, on the societal scale, the use of a technology so heavily imbued with the ideology of command and control over nature through the creation of artificial (nature-free) spaces *might actually recapitulate the problem rather than provide a solution*. To 'fix' someone's fears of spiders or snakes may indeed be a worthwhile project, but there are innumerable objects/situations onto which a fear of nature itself can be transferred, germs, prions, our own bodies. The growth of bio-phobias may be a consequence of our social alienation from nature and if so a genuine understanding of this *disorder* will require us to look at our society's relations to nature as a whole. There is a real danger that in re-asserting the necessity for control we are furthering the questionable modernist social project of mastering a nature we don't understand, don't care for, and fear. In this light the experiences of the 'ingeniously' named 'Miss Muffet', being treated for spider phobias by researchers at the Human Interface Technology Laboratory at the University of Washington might be instructive:

Eventually, after getting used to them, Miss Muffet could tolerate holding and picking up virtual spiders without panicking. She could pull the spider's legs off (initially this occurred accidentally, and then deliberately at the experimenter's request).
(*http://www.hitl.washington.edu/research/exposure/*)

While pleased for her recovery, we want to close by suggesting that VR-land's ultimate solution to nature's unpredictable movements should give us cause for concern, and by posing an uneasy question: Is de-sensitisation to natural 'otherness' the answer, or perhaps part of the technologically mediated problem?

Acknowledgement

Research funded by National Health Service Postdoctoral Research Fellowship RDO/35'12.

Notes

1   Mel explains 'one of the goals of the Equator project is to understand . . . and to build relationships between physical reality and virtual reality'. www.cs.ucl.ac.uk/research/equator/projects/digitalcare/
2   '[T]he very term "cyberspace", with its etymological link through "cyber" to the Greek *kybernan* (meaning to control or steer), displays a certain fixation on the construction of a "control-space" ' (Doel and Clarke 1999: 264).

References

Abeles, P. (2001) One session treatment of girl with spider phobia using computerised exposure. Unpublished case study.
American Psychiatric Association (1994) *DSM IV*: Diagnostic and statistical manual of mental disorders (4th Edition), Washington, DC.
Antony, M.M., Brown, T.A. and Barlow, D.H. (1997) Heterogeneity among specific phobia types in DSM-IV, *Behaviour Research and Therapy*, 35, 12, 1089–100.
Arrindell, W.A. (2000) Phobic dimensions: IV. The structure of animal fears, *Behaviour, Research and Therapy*, 38, 509–30.
Beck, U. (1993) *Risk Society: towards a New Modernity*. London: Sage.
Capps, L. and Ochs, E. (1995) *Constructing Panic: the Discourse of Agoraphobia*. Cambridge: Harvard UP.
Carlin, A.S., Hoffman, H.G. and Weghorst, S. (1997) Virtual reality and tactile augmentation in the treatment of spider phobia: a case study, *Behaviour, Research and Therapy*, 35, 153–8.
Castree, N. (2001) Socializing nature: theory, practise and politics. In Castree, N. and Braun, B. (eds) *Social Nature: Theory, Practice, and Politics*. Oxford: Blackwell.
Chambless, D.L. and Gillis, M.M. (1993) Cognitive therapy of anxiety disorders, *Journal of Consulting and Clinical Psychology*, 61, 248–60.
Clarke, D. and Fairburn, C.G. (1997) *Science and Practice of Cognitive Behaviour Therapy*. Oxford: Oxford University Press.
Coates, P. (1998) *Nature: Western Attitudes Since Ancient Times*. Cambridge: Polity Press.

Davey, G.C.L., McDonald, A.S., Hirisave, U., Prabhu, G.G., Iwawaki, S.J., Ching, I., Merckelbach, H., de Jong, P.J., Leung, P.W.L. and Reimann, B.C. (1998) A cross-cultural study of animal fears, *Behaviour, Research and Therapy*, 36, 735–50.

Davidson, J. (2000) A phenomenology of fear: Merleau-Ponty and agoraphobic life-worlds, *Sociology of Health and Illness*, 22, 5, 640–60.

Davidson, J. (2001) Pregnant pauses: agoraphobic embodiment and the limits of (im)pregnability, *Gender, Place and Culture*, 8, 3, 283–97.

Davidson, J. (2002) 'All in the mind?' Women, agoraphobia and the subject of self-help. In Bondi, L. (ed) *Subjectivities, Knowledges and Feminist Geographies*. Colorado: Rowman and Littlefield.

Doel, M.A. and Clarke, D.B. (1999) Virtual worlds: simulation, suppletion, s(ed)uction and simulacra. In Crang, M., Crang, P. and May, J. (eds) *Virtual Geographies: Bodies, Space and Relations*. London and New York: Routledge.

Douglas, M. (1993) *Purity and Danger: an Analysis of the Concepts of Pollution and Taboo*. London: Routledge.

Eder, K. (1996) *The Social Construction of Nature*. London: Sage.

Emmelkamp, P.M.G., Krijn, M., Hulbosch, A.M., de Vries, S., Scheumie, M.J. and van der Mast, C.A.P.G. (2002) Virtual reality treatment versus exposure in vivo: a comparative evaluation in acrophobia, *Behaviour Research and Therapy*, 40, 509–16.

Field, A.P., Argyris, N.G. and Knowles, K.A. (2000) Who's afraid of the big bad wolf: a prospective paradigm to test Rachman's indirect pathways in children, *Behaviour Research and Therapy*, 39, 1259–76.

Forsyth, J.P. and Chorpita, B.F. (1997) Unearthing the nonassociative origins of fears and phobias: a rejoinder, *Journal of Behavioural Therapy and Experimental Psychiatry*, 28, 4, 297–305.

Fredrikson, M., Annas, P., Fischer, H. and Wik, G. (1996) Gender and age differences in the prevalence of specific fears and phobias, *Behaviour, Research and Therapy*, 34, 33–9.

Fredrikson, M., Annas, P. and Wik, G. (1997) Parental history, aversive exposure and the development of snake and spider phobia in women, *Behaviour Research and Therapy*, 35, 1, 23–8.

Gelder, M., Gath, D., Mayou, R. and Cowen, P. (eds) (1996) *Oxford Textbook of Psychiatry* [3rd Edition]. Oxford: Oxford University Press.

Giddens, A. (1997) *Modernity and Self-Identity*. Cambridge: Polity Press.

Hoffman, H.G., Garcia-Palacios, A., Carlin, C., Furness, T.A. and Botella-Arbona, C. (in press) Interfaces that heal: coupling real and virtual objects to cure spider phobia. *International Journal of Human-Computer Interaction*.

Horkheimer, M. (1974) *Eclipse of Reason*. New York: Seabury Press.

Lajoie, M. (1996) Psychoanalysis and cyberspace. In Shields, R. (ed) *Cultures of Internet: Virtual Spaces, Real Histories, Living Bodies*. London: Sage.

Lovell, K. and Richards, D. (2000) Multiple access points and levels of entry (MAPLE): Ensuring choice, accessibility and equity for CBT Services, *Behavioural and Cognitive Psychotherapy*, 28, 379–91.

MacCormack, C. and Strathern, M. (eds) (1989) *Nature, Culture and Gender*. Cambridge: Cambridge University Press.

Mahoney, D.P. (1997) Virtual therapy nets real results: virtual exposure to fears helps to overcome phobias, *Computer Graphics World*, 20, 12, 52–6.

Marks, I.M. (1987) *Fears, Phobias and Rituals*. New York and Oxford: Oxford University Press.

Marks, I.M. and Nesse, R.M. (1994) Fear and fitness: an evolutionary analysis of anxiety disorders, *Ethology and Sociobiology*, 15, 247–61.

Merchant, C. (1990) *The Death of Nature: Women, Ecology and the Scientific Revolution*. San Francisco: Harper and Row.

Merckelbach, H., de Jong, P.J., Muris, P. and van der Hout, M.A. (1996) The etiology of specific phobias: a review, *Clinical Psychology Review*, 16, 4, 337–61.

Muris, P., Schmidt, H. and Merckelbach, H. (1999) The structure of specific phobia symptoms among children and adolescents, *Behaviour Research and Therapy*, 37, 863–8.

Muris, P., Meesters, C., Merckelbach, H., Vershuren, M., Geebelen, E. and Aleva, E. (2002) Fear of storms and hurricanes in Antillean and Belgian children, *Behaviour Research and Therapy*, 40, 459–69.

Plumwood, V. (1993) *Feminism and the Mastery of Nature*. London and New York: Routledge.

Pope, C., Ziebland, S. and Mays, N. (2000) Analysing qualitative data. In Pope, C. and Mays, N. (eds) *Qualitative Research in Health Care*. London: British Medical Journal.

Robins, K. (1996) Cyberspace and the world we live in. In Dovey, J. (ed) *Fractal Dreams: New Media in Social Context*. London: Lawrence and Wishart.

Rothbaum, B.O., Hodges, L.F., Kooper, R., Opdyke, D., Williford, J.S. and North, M. (1995) Effectiveness of Computer-generated (virtual reality) graded exposure in the treatment of acrophobia, *American Journal of Psychiatry*, 152, 626–8.

Seidler, V. J. (1998) Embodied knowledge and virtual space. In Wood, J. (ed) *The Virtual Embodied*. London and New York: Routledge.

Smith, M. (2001) *An Ethics of Place: Radical Ecology, Postmodernity, and Social Theory*. New York: SUNY.

Thomas, K. (1984) *Man and the Natural World: Changing Attitudes in England 1500–1800*. Harmondsworth: Penguin.

Whitby, P. and Allcock, K. (1994) Spider phobia control, Wales: Gwent Psychology Services.

Chapter 9

Healthy viewing: the reception of medical narratives

Solange Davin

Introduction: screening medical narratives

When Norman Felton was put in charge of development at the CBS network in 1959, one of his aims was to create a medical drama. But senior executives at first rejected the idea. 'Sick people in hospital is something you don't want to put on television. People have enough trouble during the day!' they objected[1]. They could not have been more mistaken. Medical dramas won instant acclaim, and, 50 years on, the genre has reached epidemic proportions. From selfless surgeons to egotistical consultants to emergency room anti-heroes, physicians occupy a place of honour on the small screen. In Great Britain, the US drama *Dr. Kildare* remained in the top 10 favourites for five years in the 1960s (Philips 2000), *Peak Practice*, made by the British network ITV, reached ratings of 13 million (Hallam 1998) and *Casualty*, the BBC1 flagship medical drama, first made in 1986, continues to attract over 10 million followers, according to the BBC (news.bbc.co.uk/1/hi/entertainment/tv_and_radio/1749007.stm). Medical themes have also been popular in the UK in factual genres, from the 1958 ground-breaking documentary *Your Life in Their Hands* through well-known series like *Horizon* and *Panorama* to the sarcastic 1990s *Trust Me I'm a Doctor* (all BBC programmes). Yet the reception of (fictional and factual) health and illness narratives on television has been neglected by researchers. Little is known about the responses of these substantial audiences to images of sickness[2] despite the fact that television is known to be a prime source of medical information for the public (Karpf 1988, Kitzinger 1998). How televised representations of health and illness contribute to spectators' knowedge thus needs urgent attention, particularly as the medium is increasingly prevalent. This paper begins to fill in the gap by reporting on two reception studies, one of the American drama *ER* and the second of parallel illness storylines in a documentary and a soap opera, whose purpose was to collect hitherto-lacking data on the interpretations[3] of medical narratives on television.

ER as a source of medical information

The first study presented in this paper draws on letters received in response to advertisements in British and French television magazines[4] asking viewers why they watched *ER*, a wording which enabled respondents to discuss the broadcast in their own terms. One hundred and 33 women and 62 men replied, of whom just under half were British, aged between 12 and 84 and from a diverse range of backgrounds – students, unemployed, doctors, nurses, clerks, housewives, etc. (including six viewers who disliked *ER*). The data were analysed manually. After repeated readings, an open coding procedure (Strauss and Corbin 1990) was applied in order to generate themes grounded in the letters rather than imposed *a priori*. The categories which emerged were further scrutinised in order to discern similarities and differences between interpretations, and sub-classifications were drawn accordingly. The limitations of the study are acknowledged – more women than men participated and self-selected informants may respond differently from a random sample. The aim of the project was to examine responses to medical narratives in the light of recent reception studies demonstrating the complexity and subtlety of viewers' interpretations (*e.g.* Hill 1999, Turnock 2000).

ER is a fast-paced American medical drama which follows the lives and loves of a group of health professionals working on an emergency ward in Chicago. It was conceived in the late 1970s by Michael Crichton, best known for his films *Jurassic Park* and *Coma*. Although he never practised, Crichton is a qualified physician and the first *ER* scenarios were inspired by his casualty training. In its first season *ER* was hailed as the highest-ranking drama in US media history with 35 million viewers (Pourroy 1996). It has since become a quasi-cult show in over 60 countries, including the UK with more than four million fans (reported in Radio Times) and France with five million (*http://www.t7j.com/audiences.php*).

Most viewers, as may be expected from its international fame, described *ER* as quality entertainment, perhaps the best medical drama yet. They enjoyed its swinging rhythm of action and emotion, triumph and defeat, chaos and calm, joy and sorrow:

Each episode seems to take you on a roller-coaster ride, laughing one minute, crying the next . . . It shows life at both ends of the spectrum (British woman, 53, housewife).

They tried to predict forthcoming plots and wrote their own happy-ending scenarios. They looked forward to their weekly meetings with regular characters and to the gradual discovery of their complex personalities:

I am interested in all the characters because we discover new facets in each episode. He who seemed perfect shows weaknesses and he who seemed abominable is 'redeemed'. . . (French woman, 27, teacher).

But *ER* is no mere distraction. In line with the current *infotainment* trend, it was simultaneously perceived by informants as a trustworthy source of information on topics which they were eager to know more about, from 'the intricacies of the profession, what goes into the training, the ethics, the negligence, the politics, etc.' (British woman, 38), to 'what an operation looks like' (French man, 62, hotel manager). In addition, a dozen informants explicitly thought of the drama in terms of a documentary:

> We find it a very realistic series, that is, in the sense of 'documentary', which is very rare and interesting (French woman, 49, switchboard operator).

This should not be surprising since *ER* has many attributes usually associated with documentaries: the scripts are written by doctors who also supervise the filming, the medical stories are based on real emergency cases reported by health professionals, the main actors have familiarised themselves with real casualty procedures, the medical equipment is genuine, and the Steadycam cameras give an impression of impromptu, of real life (Pourroy 1996).

What did viewers learn from a popular entertainment show to which they attributed informative properties? Although the production team refused to indulge the public's unquenchable thirst for medical knowledge and to provide explanations for the medics' actions (Pourroy 1996), just under half the informants reported acquiring data on physiology, symptoms, diseases, treatments, the practice of medicine:

> A cancer can cause a broken leg, I did not know that at all (French woman, 19, Baccalaureate student).

Some believed that the production team wanted to raise awareness of health risks old (drug abuse, smoking, HIV infection) and new, and remembered some of the dangers brought to their attention:

> I liked the episode where a student gets a shock allergy from latex gloves. It informs you about an increasingly common allergy (French woman, 48, GP).

Moreover, like *Casualty*, *ER* may 'help to prepare viewers for the experience of witnessing such scenes, or for going into hospital themselves' (Buckingham 1997: 224):

> I had never seen such glasses. Now if I go to casualty I won't be surprised if they wear glasses or a green or blue gown or gloves (French man, 27, computer programmer).

This information-gathering process is not specific to *ER*. Medical knowledge is extracted from other fictional broadcasts. Kingsley (1993) reports that some fans diagnosed their own diseases from *Casualty* and claims that it has taught millions about the ins-and-outs of medicine. Incidental findings show that soap operas can convey useful data: a woman became pregnant after hearing about ovulation prediction kits in the US soap *All My Children* (Rogers 1995). The famous American serial *Dallas* provided details on amniocentesis (Rapp 1988) and the British soap opera *Coronation Street* on mental illness (Philo 1996). Guidance about drugs and safe sex was gleaned from a range of soaps by Willis's (1990) adolescents. The pedagogic potential of fiction has been acknowledged and legitimised by the use of soap operas in health promotion campaigns (see below) and in schools (Grahame and Simons 1998), of police series for police training courses (Simon and Fejes 1987), and of *ER* in universities:

> My neighbour, who did his internship at [name of hospital], told me that tutors recommend ER and discuss the episode the following day (French woman, 41, sales assistant).

Some medical dramas have (had) educational ambitions (and so have British-made soap operas, as will be seen below). The mission of early British ones was to help 'overcome the pre-war attitude of the public to hospitals as institutions, as places to be avoided at all costs' (Karpf 1988: 183), with positive results: *Emergency Ward 10* was praised by the British Medical Association for helping allay these fears (Kingsley 1988). From the beginning, *Casualty* has included medical and first-aid hints and its motto has been 'educating while entertaining' (Kingsley 1993: 86).

These objectives match viewers' taste for such *mélanges*. From the farmers who, in 1950, chose a format of soap opera to receive agricultural advice (a choice which led to the creation of the ongoing BBC radio soap *The Archers*) (Kingsley 1988) to the young people who, more recently, called for information about contraception and safe sex to be disseminated in soap operas (BAC 1999), viewers – particularly adolescents who seem strongly resistant to didactic approaches (Gavin 2001) – have consistently restated their preference for 'edutainment' (*e.g.* Bouman, Mass and Kok 1998). For many, a good series is one which simultaneously 'entertains and addresses their problems' (Elkamel 1995: 228).

ER as a vehicle for social knowledge

It is not only medical knowledge which was acquired from *ER*. Social concerns have long been a key attraction of 'professional dramas' (dramas whose main protagonists are lawyers, doctors, police officers) (Dientsfrey 1976), and *ER* is no exception. Viewers were alert to the social issues evoked in the show. First, they learnt about the organisation of health care. The informants who addressed the subject compared the day-to-day functioning of US and British/French health systems. They were especially struck by the differential roles of the emergency wards:

Many of the non-urgent patients would not be in casualty in England.
They would have gone to their GP (British woman, 38, legal secretary).

At a broader level, some informants contrasted the Welfare State ethos of
free care for all to the American health market where a few underfunded
state hospitals are the only provision available to the many without private
insurance:

> They show the problems of social cover in the US, the lack of money in
> hospitals, the treatments chosen because they are cheap, the patients sent
> away because they cannot pay for their treatment . . . (French woman, 33,
> travel agency clerk).

These informants agreed that the former is superior, with one striking
exception:

> Whoever has been to casualty in France can only wish they could go to
> Chicago to be treated. They don't have to wait for hours . . . (French man,
> 23, architecture student).

Second, because *ER* takes place in a state hospital, it is ideally situated to
reveal aspects of American society which are commonly erased from entertainment. Around a quarter of respondents, observing the ongoing flow of
unemployed and/or homeless patients taking refuge in *ER*, commented on
this depiction of poverty, violence, exclusion, and contrasted it to the socially
and economically healthy country portrayed in 'Beverly Hills-style serials
like Dallas' (French woman, 44). *ER* was praised for its 'non-PC approach'
(British woman, 36, nurse) which discloses the flip-side of *Dallas-Dynasty*'s
America:

> We keep seeing patients who need help from social services, children's
> bodies full of bullets, abused children. It seems to me that ER is a rich
> and realistic portrait of American society (French woman, 17, high
> school pupil).

A few informants feared that these images of healthcare rationing and of
daily hardship for the less wealthy may prove to be a preview of their own
country when these problems reach the European side of the Atlantic.

These remarks add a political touch to the reception of *ER* which echoes
that produced by the young *EastEnders* viewers who interpreted the long-
lasting BBC1 soap opera in political/ideological terms even though the
'kinds of judgements which are invited are more frequently moral rather
than ideological ones – that is, judgements which relate to the rights and
wrongs of *individual* behaviour, rather than to broader social issues' (Buckingham 1987: 174).

Deceptive documentaries

In view of the linking of *ER* to documentaries, it seems somewhat ironic that respondents in a follow-up project should express scepticism towards the genre. The objective of this study was to compare the reception of medical narratives in a fictional storyline ('Peggy's breast cancer' in *EastEnders*, Peggy being a long-standing central character) and in a factual narrative, a 50-minute Channel 4 documentary following a patient and her husband through the stages of her fight against breast cancer.

Advertisements were placed in several locations (libraries, shops, etc.) and 24 British women were recruited and interviewed individually[5] after viewing the programmes. The interviews were 'ethnographic', as defined by Spradley (1979), conversation-like, encouraging informants to speak in their own words and to broach topics of interest to them rather than those pre-determined by the researcher. Interviews were taped and transcribed verbatim and submitted to the same coding procedures as the *ER* data. The study was the first of a series examining men and women's responses to fictional and factual television narratives of (male and female) cancers and was designed to explore women's interpretations of portrayals of breast cancer. Men's responses are therefore not included.

Despite documentaries' traditionally high status (somewhat tarnished in recent years by several 'faked documentary' scandals (see Maddox 1999)), most informants were cautious. Their circumspection was based on two objections. Documentaries[6] are misleading: first, because the camera, often seen as a mechanical, neutral device, as the eye-which-never-lies, does indeed lie: it lies by omission, by not telling the whole story, by presenting snippets of a broader picture, portions of which are erased. Thus they are incomplete, partial (in both senses of the term) constructions:

> She did not fall to pieces or apparently she did not . . . But you
> don't know if she is schooled beforehand or if it is edited.
> We don't know about the editing and we are left with the positive
> bits (Teacher, 36).

Secondly, the presence of cameras is enough to lure even the most genuine protagonists into being tempted to playact, to adopt a false persona:

> It is a realistic documentary but you are aware that the family was being
> watched. Hence they are not quite being themselves. I wonder what goes
> on off camera (Receptionist, 52).

Most women repeatedly wondered about the 'off camera' and 'the editing', sometimes speculating as to what had (perhaps) been removed from the screen, and documentary images were said to be fragmentary and artificial.

They cannot be taken for a full and faithful reproduction of real life. These arguments were corroborated by the husband of the patient who features in the documentary, who agreed to discuss the making of the programme (16 May 2000):

> It is a story. There is so much selection of material . . . They filmed 60 hours over four months. So it's only part of the whole story [. . .] There were cameras outdoors and inside. I could not see them but it was very artificial. I was very conscious of them. It was almost like acting . . .

Thus, viewers were critical of the documentary genre but not of the documentary side of *ER*. This may be because the former's reputation for objectivity and honesty raises both viewers' expectations and their vigilance and propensity to look for flaws, as this quote from the second study suggests:

> I know that it is a documentary and that they say what they think is the case but I am more inclined to question it because I know that doctors have different viewpoints. While, funnily enough, when it comes to *EastEnders*, I did not think that at all. I just felt 'that's what they say'. There is a difference. With documentaries you are more likely to question things because it's a different process when you watch documentaries. And I think it calls for different kinds of responses. A soap you will accept more easily (Company director, 64).

Anticipating entertainment from *ER*, viewers, surprised and delighted to find useful material, may therefore be more lenient. Thus, form and content are intertwined: expectations about form may affect the perception of content. This phenomenon was also visible when viewers criticised *ER* excesses (notably the 'unbelievable number of serious cases in each episode' (British woman, 53, housewife) and the speed at which they were treated) but discounted their implausibility on the grounds that these exaggerations were not due to mistakes, sloppiness or deception, but were necessary if the requirements of good drama are to be met. In spite of these recurrent unrealistic elements, *ER* therefore remains realistic.

This is not to say that viewers dismissed documentaries. But, although only four informants mentioned using documentary information, it is worth noting that two reported conducting a verification procedure beforehand:

> I changed my diet and my family's diet, all on the basis of information from television, mostly documentaries about how things affect you. You consider what they say and you go to the sources to confirm your impressions and then you change. That's my experience (Office administrator, 49).

Continuous serials as a pedagogic resource

Soap operas began on American radio in the 1930s. Sponsored by manufacturers of domestic products eager to target housewives, they soon acquired a
'feminine drivel' label which followed them when they appeared on television[7].
In contrast, in British public service culture, many soaps have had (partly)
pedagogic objectives (see Anger 1999, Buckman 1984). The radio soap *The
Archers* was sponsored by the Department of Agriculture and designed to
disseminate farming advice (Kingsley 1988). Tony Holland, the *EastEnders*
script-editor, was adamant that 'we are not going to duck any social issues.
Our stories would deal with all the contemporary problems of London's
East End' (quoted in Geraghty 1994: 34), and many have indeed figured in
the serial, from abuse to xenophobia through sickness (schizophrenia, HIV/
AIDS, spina bifida, depression, infertility, alcoholism, cancer, etc.). Equally, Phil
Redmond, the creator of *Brookside*, a soap produced by the British network
Channel 4, aspired to 'contribute to any continuous social debate . . .'
(quoted in Gottlieb 1993: 40). In the 1990s, *Brookside* became the backbone
of the literacy campaign of the British Department of Education (Grahame
and Simons 1998).

   Some stigma still surrounds soap operas, as this quote suggests: 'I dismiss
Casualty as a soap with all these sentimental stories, not a medical drama'
(British woman, 23, shop assistant), but most respondents in the second
study gave them more credit than they gave documentaries. They believed
soaps to be an effective vehicle for communicating (health) advice:

> Getting information through the soaps is a good way of doing it. It's a
> sort of health education, if you like. With information about illnesses
> (Teacher, 53).

One must be wary, however, of lumping programmes into genres, and of
attributing to them *a priori* properties. Not all programmes are equal. One
viewer in this study trusted *EastEnders* more than *Coronation Street* which,
she thought, treated all subjects in a trivial and caricatured fashion (but of
which she nevertheless remained a devoted fan). In terms of health promotion,
such questions need to be tackled at the formative research stage.

   Furthermore, informants can be ambivalent. One woman, talking about
soaps in general, claimed that networks are too preoccupied with ratings to
worry about accuracy ('If they get desperate, if the ratings drop, they'll put
on anything' (Administrative assistant, 44)), but was nevertheless convinced
that they are good educative tools because they foster identification.

   The 'emotional' information-gathering tactics of identification is one of
four reasons given by interviewees for the usefulness of continuous serials.
Soap opera characters were described as 'very identifiable with' by several
women, a quality enhanced by regular viewing, some added, and which rendered

the narratives closer and more relevant. Identification also occurred with *ER*. Twenty-three correspondents identified with medical students, with whom they felt a strong empathy due to a perceived shared status of newcomer on the ward:

> Spectators are thrown into the whirlwind of the situations with the students. They could be the spectator who has crept inside the emergency department. Their beginners' eyes are ours (French man, 19, college student).

Viewers and students alike were novices, ignorant of casualty practices, learning together through a process of trial and error, making mistakes together, failing and suffering ('I suffered with him throughout his training' (French man, 39) one person wrote), succeeding and rejoicing together. Thanks to these medics-to-be, thrilled spectators could join a (virtual) course in emergency medicine, penetrate into a hitherto mysterious hospital and discover how it functions:

> We can go in the parts of the hospital which are prohibited to the public and to families, operating theatres and others (French man, 28, administration worker).

Emotional tactics may perhaps partly explain why some informants reported becoming aware through entertainment such as *ER* of issues like violence in the USA which have repeatedly made news(paper) headlines in recent years and which are therefore already well known.

This is especially pertinent to health promotion because, contrary to the long-held belief that new knowledge directly leads to behaviour modification (*i.e.* once informed that their conduct may be dangerous, rational listeners will stop/alter it), responses to health messages may have more to do with emotions than cognition (*e.g.* Frankham 1991).

ER viewers also made use of a ludic strategy[8]: a dozen people played games with the narratives, turning them into a mystery or a quiz. Once aware of patients' symptoms/injuries, they attempted to predict the diagnoses, tests and treatments they would receive:

> My favourite sport is to guess the diagnosis as soon as they admit them and tell us the injuries (British woman, 54, nurse).

In so doing, they collected material about symptoms and syndromes, the weaknesses of diagnostic techniques etc.

Secondly, these shows have vast followings (*EastEnders*, for example, with 17–18 million followers (Ruddock 2001, and *ER* with fans in over 60 countries) and exposure to messages is accordingly high. Further, their continuity requires multiple intersecting narratives, each episode chronicling a variety of plots. This mosaic style alleviates the impact of taxing illness storylines by adding a dose of light relief:

> *EastEnders* was easier to take than the other one. It is putting its message across without being gruelling (Housewife, 54).

Finally, continuous serials include much duplicated material as characters consider and reconsider their plight, discuss it with friends, seek advice, etc. Many informants thought that repetition enhanced assimilation and recollection, a suggestion confirmed by research (*e.g.* Rogers and Singhal 1990).

One should also notice that all the viewers who broached the topic took it for granted that serious matters like sickness were addressed by the networks in a conscientious fashion, irrespective of genre. Many trusted producers' and/or directors' professionalism and sense of duty, and considered that broadcasting medical narratives without expert input and thorough research would be irresponsible and unacceptable:

> They could not give false information about something as sensitive and important for women's health. They'd have to get it right. The research would have to be done. I believe what they say, I really do (Classroom assistant, 40).

This was endorsed by an *EastEnders* researcher whom I interviewed (9 November 1999 at the BBC Elstree Studios), who confirmed that although drama sometimes takes precedence over realism, oncology nurses and consultants were involved in the making of the 'Peggy's cancer' episodes:

> For the Peggy story, we co-operated with [name of oncology hospital] and with cancer nurses and with [name of cancer charity]. Peggy's story is based on a case study [. . .] Sometimes it's a story decision, for example the waiting room where Peggy and Frank are alone, rather than a full room. This way we can focus on the characters. But we follow the medical guidelines. We did check the information.

Two viewers were more cynical. While believing that most medical information in the media is correct, they had little faith in producers' integrity and/or respect for viewers. A more likely motivation, they suggested, was their fear of poor ratings and of court cases should the information prove incorrect. In a sense, it was ultimately on themselves, on the power of the public to forsake and/or take to task a network, that these informants' confidence rested.

Moreover, there was no agreement about what *EastEnders* was meant to be communicating. As with *ER* and the documentary, contradictory opinions were articulated: some, for instance, claimed that Peggy's initial refusal of surgery and subsequent consent promoted patients' choice and agency while others argued that it illustrated that doctors' advice, especially in serious cases, should be adhered to, and that she had wasted precious time. That such diversity in interpretations is unexceptional[9] is illustrated by two further examples from the second study. When talking about the documentary, ten informants speculated about the (perceived) aloofness of the patient's husband when she broke the news to him that her cancer was spreading. They suggested diverse reasons for his detachment, reasons which reflected their differing perceptions (not least diverging perceptions of the two protagonists), experiences, opinions, beliefs, etc.: His remoteness befits his ongoing lack of support for his wife. He only expresses himself when directly questioned. He is unable to open up emotionally. He cannot handle the issue. He is worried that his wife cannot handle the issue. The ongoing strain has become overwhelming and he wants nothing more to do with the situation. He is embarrassed at being filmed in such an intimate situation. He is angry with his wife for consenting to filming.

Similarly, six women were puzzled by the patient's sudden decision to move house, of whom four imagined possible motivations, with equally disparate results: she wants to be busy so that she forgets about her disease; she needs a house with better facilities for when she becomes more ill; she would like to see her family settled before she goes; she wishes for a fresh start away from the home where she became sick.

Viewers' attribution of pedagogic qualities to ongoing melodramas echoes the findings of health promotion campaigns in developing countries which have demonstrated their efficacy[10]. This success can be explained by the fact that they possess features known to promote learning (in addition to those cited above by informants – popularity, identification, repetition) which may be absent from large-scale publicity campaigns (see Davin 2000 for further details and references). For example, despite occasional frightening items, serials tend to have reassuring themes:

We love *ER* in a security way. We want to believe that it will be the same when we go to *ER* ourselves (French woman, 24).

Such a positive approach has been found more fertile than fear-inducing methods which have had poor overall results (Montazeri, McGhee and McEwen 1998). Furthermore, didactic exhortations, more often than not, fail to alter people's habits because they tend to be perceived as moral lessons and/or social control which prompt rejection (*e.g.* Plant and Plant 1994). Broadcasts like the 1990s series, moulded in postmodern uncertainty, encourage audiences to reflect on contemporary issues, to weigh the pros and cons of various solutions, to reach their own conclusions:

There is no demonstration. We are not told 'such and such is bad'. We are shown facts and behaviours. It is for us to think about it (French man, 33).

Enabling spectators to engage in debate may have more impact than prescriptive messages: post-viewing discussions were crucial to the success of soap-supported campaigns in developing countries, as indicated by Singhal and Rogers (1999). Finally, (perceived) authenticity is key to viewers' willingness to accept and take advice on board. Realism is the first requirement of good 'edutainment' (Elkamel 1995) and, as previously seen, many viewers have confidence in the realism of serials.

This dual role of hybrid broadcasts resonates with the 'new' theories of education (see Meyer 1997, MacMahon 1997). While the transmission of information (intended or not) is reminiscent of 'old' top-bottom 'good Samaritan' transfer models, the audiences in these studies are by no means empty vessels passively awaiting to be filled, but active interpreters processing and evaluating programmes in an intricate fashion. Their ability to be in two seemingly incompatible viewing modes at once – cognitive *and* emotional, distant *and* involved, informing *and* enjoying themselves – questions established dichotomies and befits the recent 'travelling' or 'growing' theories of learning which mix 'couch' metaphors (relaxed, undemanding viewers) and 'desk' ones (engaged, attentive viewers) (MacMahon 1997), and where programmes are 'treats designed to motivate more than to instruct' (Buckingham 1983: 97), to stimulate spectators to seek further knowledge about a topic. Some of these shows, like *ER*, are indeed inspiring:

I am fascinated by medical terms. I have the most incredible curiosity. I keep asking all sorts of questions to my medical student friends (French man, 26, translator).

This is particularly true of adolescents, some of whom were inspired to enter medical school:

My daughter has just started studying medicine partly because of the series, and she is not the only one [French woman, 49, pharmacist].

Similarly, registrations in law schools shot up after *LA Law* (Winckler 2002) and the number of men's applications to enter nursing schools raised dramatically following the portrayal of male nurses in *Casualty* (Hallam 1998).

Conclusion

The studies presented in this paper show that *ER* was perceived both as quality entertainment and as a reliable source of knowledge from which the public gathered medical and social information. Viewers used emotional (identification) and/or ludic (game-playing) strategies to collect this knowledge. In the second project, many informants described soap operas as efficient pedagogic tools because they reach massive audiences, they are 'easy to take' and they allow identification and repetition which enhance learning. On the other hand, most expressed caution about the documentary – and documentaries in general – which were criticised for being incomplete and artificial.

Despite their limitations, these findings indicate that real viewers do not resemble the caricatures of 'passive, ignorant and undiscerning sponges' (Gauntlett 1995: 10) which have informed some areas of Media Studies until recently (Gauntlett 1995). Real viewers are sophisticated, astute, insightful and media-literate. They produce complex, multi-layered, sometimes contradictory and/or unexpected interpretations. They ascribe their own genres to programmes. They read and use broadcasts according to their mood and wants at a particular moment. They generate meanings in their encounters with flexible texts, meanings which cannot be predicted by content analysis of broadcasts alone. The success of health promotion through continuous fiction is precisely rooted in a recognition of the public's impressive abilities and diversity. It is by empathising with characters, by assessing the dis/advantages of different courses of action, by discussing storylines with relatives and friends, by filling in the blanks, by creating narratives, by playing games with the stories, etc., that viewers engage with, and learn from, broadcasts.

Producers of early radio soaps and CBS executives had little insight into their public's tastes, and the situation has barely changed (*e.g.* Espinosa 1982, Gripsrud 1995). Equally, in academia, despite some reception research, knowledge of real viewers' responses to the small screen remains limited. Like producers, who make gratuitous suppositions about imagined television consumers such as 'the Huddersfield housewife' (Karpf 1988: 228), scholars are prone to fabricate audiences from their own readings (the 'viewer-in-the-text') and/or from preset sociological categories ('women', 'working-class people', etc.). Furthermore, reception continues to be routinely overlooked in the social/human sciences. Cancer research is a case in point: lay conceptions of the disease (*e.g.* Payne 1990, Balshem 1993, Oakley *et al.* 1995) have been examined, and so have media discourses (*e.g.* Freimuth *et al.* 1984, Clarke and Robinson 1999, Seale 2001), but, with one exception (Henderson and Kitzinger 1999), the link between the two has been neglected – how do viewers use media representations to formulate their notions of cancer? The reception of health and illness narratives needs further research, particularly since viewers rely heavily on television for their medical knowledge, as noted in the introduction.

Finally, theories of reception may benefit from a multi-disciplinary approach (see Davin forthcoming, 2005). Media Studies do not have the monopoly of reception. Interpretation is a salient topic too in health promotion, in literary criticism, in the public understanding of science, and sociologists, psychologists and education specialists have paid attention to the phenomenon. *ER* fans, Shakespeare enthusiasts and health advice listeners all employ equally intricate reading and meaning-making processes. More co-operation and communication between fields which may at first sight appear largely unconnected would benefit scholars involved in reception research in all domains.

Notes

1 Norman Felton was interviewed in a documentary, *Playing Doctor*, part of a BBC1 'Docs on the Box' week-end (09.06.1996).

2 Apart from Buckingham's (1997) book on young people's interpretations of diverse programmes which includes a few pages on *Casualty*, and Bouman, Mass and Kok's (1998) article on a Dutch 'hospital serial', no reception work on medical dramas is, to my knowledge, available (although one may arguably include the work of Tulloch and Moran (1986) on the Australian 'rural medical soap' *A Country Practice* and of Tulloch and Lupton (1997), part of a small upsurge of studies prompted by the 1980s AIDS crisis and which also includes episodes of *A Country Practice*).

The reception of documentaries has not feared much better. Few studies are available and they have primarily focused on social/environmental matters. Only Hoijer (1992) explored a Swedish science magazine on social/medical aspects of AIDS.

3 Although space lacks to address the topic, the definition of 'interpretation' is an important issue. There have been debates as to whether 'interpretation' is limited to denotation or whether it encompasses connotation and evaluation (*e.g.* Corner 1992). But, as Rorty (1989: 98) remarked, 'there is no point at which you can draw a line between what we are talking about and what we are saying about it'. 'Interpretation' is used in this article in its widest sense.

4 This study began as a comparison of British and French viewers. Its rationale was less national identity than the differences between the number of, enthusiasm for, and familiarity with, medical dramas between the two countries (which have been relatively rare in France and, until *ER*, have attracted little interest), which suggested possible variations in interpretations. Cross-cultural differences, however, failed to appear. The themes evoked by British and by French correspondents, and their comments, parallel each other.

Personal information in informants' letters was sketchy. Nationality was not specified and was attributed according to the correspondent's address. Some respondents may therefore (conceive themselves to) be neither British nor French. However, in the Europe of 2002, the notion of national identity is increasingly blurred – what does it mean to be British, and what is, for example, the relation of Britishness to Englishness, to Scottishness, etc.? (my article at *http://wjfms.ncl.ac.uk/ER.htm* addresses both the lack of cross-cultural differences and national identity). Full details of the study are available in Davin (forthcoming, 2003).

5 Individual interviews avoid the risk of conformity inherent in group interviews (*e.g.* Kitzinger and Miller 1992) and ensure higher levels of privacy and confidentiality. They provide opportunities for probing ambiguous replies and for acquiring 'thick' knowledge, and they give informants scope to enlarge on their replies (Tulloch and Lupton 1997).

As is common in media research, informants occasionally spoke in the 'third person' (Davison 1983), imagining how others might react. Most comments, however, remained rooted in the first person.

6   Although conversations began by focusing on the documentary in question, informants soon generalised to 'documentaries'.

7   Many soaps also cover 'masculine' issues and try to appeal to both genders. Two celebrated British soaps, *Brookside* and *EastEnders*, have been described as 'male soaps' (see respectively Geraghty 1994: Chapter 8 and Kingsley 1988). In terms of reception, alleged gender differences may in part be due to methodology. For instance, while men admit to enjoying 'women's shows' in questionnaires (*e.g.* Tulloch and Moran 1986), they tend to deny it in peer groups (*e.g.* Buckingham 1997). New technologies may both motivate, and provide a justification for, men to take part in such studies. Most of the 62 men who answered the advertisement in the *ER* study did so by e-mail, and some stated that it was the e-mail address which had encouraged them to reply.

8   This is not to say that viewers do not use other strategies – they almost certainly do – but that identification and game-playing were the only two used and/or mentioned in these studies.

9   This diversity is partly due to the fact that texts are full of gaps (see Iser 1995). Viewers' familiarity with media grammar ensures that most of these blanks are automatically filled in (notably space and time compression without which most programmes would be impossible – for instance, a character leaves home and in the next take is at the office. Viewers know that time has elapsed and that s/he has travelled). Other gaps (*e.g.* unstated reasons for characters' actions) incite viewers to exercise their imagination, as can be seen in the examples in the main text.

10   See Nariman (1993) for the basic principles of melodrama-based health promotion, and Singhal and Rogers (1999) for a review of campaigns. These books also address the ethics of covert messages.

References

Anger, D. (1999) *Other Worlds*. Toronto: Broadview.

BAC (Brooks Advisory Centre) (1999) *When you meet someone you really like, you don't think of AIDS . . .* London: Brooks Advisory Centre.

Balshem, M. (1993) *Cancer in the Community*. Washington: Smithsonian Institution Press.

Bouman, M., Mass, L. and Kok, G. (1998) Health education in TV entertainment, *Health Education Research*, 13, 4, 503–18.

Buckingham, D. (1983) *Teaching Through Television*. London: Inner London Education Authority.

Buckingham, D. (1987) *Public Secrets*. London: British Film Institute.

Buckingham, D. (1997) *Moving Images*. Manchester: Manchester University Press.

Buckman, P. (1984) *All for Love*. London: Secker and Warburg.

Clarke, J. and Robinson, J. (1999) Testicular cancer: medicine and machismo in the media, *Health*, 3, 3, 263–82.

Corner, J. (1992) Meaning, genre and content. In Curran, J. and Gurevitch, M. (eds) *Mass Media and Society*. London: Arnold.

Davin, S. (2000) Medical dramas as a health promotion resource, *International Journal of Health Promotion and Education*, 38, 3, 109–12.

Davin, S. (forthcoming 2003) *La médecine dans le salon: urgences et ses spectateurs*. Pairs: L'Harmattan.

Davin, S. (forthcoming 2005) *New Approaches to Television Criticism*. Exeter: Intellect Books.

Davison, W.P. (1983) The third-person effect in communication, *Public Opinion Quarterly*, 41, 1, 1–15.

Dientsfrey, H. (1976) Doctors, lawyers and other television heroes. In Newcomb, H. (ed) *Television – the Critical View*. London: Penguin.

Elkamel, F. (1995) The use of television series in health education, *Health Education Research*, 10, 2, 225–232.

Espinosa, P. (1982) The audience in the text, *Media Culture and Society*, 4, 77–86.

Frankham, J. (1991) AIDS – it's like one of those things you read about in the newspapers. In Schostack, J.F. (ed) *Youth in Trouble*. London: Kogan Page.

Freimuth, S., Greenberg, R., De Witt, J. and Romano, M. (1984) Covering cancer, *Journal of Communications*, 34, 62–62.

Gauntlett, D. (1995) *Moving Experiences – Understanding Television's Influences and Effects*. London: John Libbey.

Gavin, J. (2001) Television teen drama and HIV/AIDS, *Continuum: Journal of Media and Cultural Studies*, 15, 1, 77–95.

Geraghty, C. (1994) *Women and Soap Opera*. Cambridge: Polity.

Gottlieb, V. (1993) *Brookside*: Damon's YTS comes to an end. In Brandt, G. (ed) *British Television Drama in the 1980s*. Cambridge: Cambridge University Press.

Grahame, J. and Simons, M. (1998) Remission Impossible, *The English and Media Magazine*, 38, 36–40.

Gripsrud, J. (1995) *The Dynasty Years*. London: Routledge.

Hallam, J. (1998) Gender and professionalism in television's medical melodramas. In Moody, N. and Hallam, J. (eds) *Medical Fictions*. Liverpool: John Moores University Press.

Henderson, L. and Kitzinger, J. (1999) The human drama of genetics: 'hard' and 'soft' media representations of inherited breast cancer, *Sociology of Health and Illness*, 21, 5, 560–578.

Hill, A. (1999) *Shocking Entertainment*. Luton: University of Luton Press.

Hoijer, B. (1992) Socio-cognitive structures and television reception, *Media Culture and Society*, 14, 583–603.

Iser, W. (1995) Interaction between text and reader. In Bennett, A. (ed) *Readers and Reading*. London: Longman.

Karpf, A. (1988) *Doctoring the Media*. London: Routledge.

Kingsley, H. (1988) *Soap Box*. London: Macmillan.

Kingsley, H. (1993) *Casualty*. London: Penguin.

Kitzinger, J. (1998) Resisting the message. In Miller, D., Kitzinger, J., Williams, K. and Beharell, P. (eds) *The Circuit of Mass Communication*. London: Sage.

Kitzinger, J. and Miller, D. (1992) 'African AIDS': the media and audience beliefs. In Aggleton, P., Davies, P. and Hart, G. (eds) *AIDS: Rights, Risks and Reason*. London: Falmer Press.

MacMahon, J. (1997) Imaginary learners. In Meyer, M. (ed) *Educational Television*. Luton: John Libbey.

Maddox, B. (1999) How trustworthy is television? *British Journalism Review*, 10, 2, 34–38.

Meyer, M. (1997) Introduction. In Meyer, M. (ed) *Educational Television*. Luton: John Libbey.

Montazeri, A., McGhee, S. and McEwen, J. (1998) Fear-inducing and positive images strategies in health education campaigns, *International Journal of Health Promotion and Education*, 36, 3, 68–75.

Nariman, H. (1993) *Soap Opera for Social Change*. Westport: Praeger.

Oakley, A., Bendelow, G., Barnes, J., Buchanan, M. and Husain, N. (1995) Health and cancer prevention, *British Medical Journal*, 310, 1029–33.

Payne, S. (1990) Lay representations of breast cancer, *Psychology and Health*, 5, 1–11.

Philips, D. (2000) Medicated soap. In Carson, B. and Llewellyn-Jones, M. (eds) *Frames and Fictions on Television*. Exeter: Intellect.

Philo, G. (1996) *Media and Mental Distress*. London: Routledge.

Plant, M. and Plant, M. (1994) *Risk-takers*. London: Routledge.

Pourroy, J. (1996) *Behind the Scenes at ER*. London: Ebury Press.

Rapp, R. (1988) Chromosomes and Communication, *Medical Anthropology Quarterly*, 2, 2, 143–143.

Rogers, D. (1995) Daze of our lives. In Dines, G. and Hunez, J. M. (eds) *Gender, Race and Class in the Media*. London: Sage.

Rogers, E. and Singhal, A. (1990) Afterword. In Atkin, C. and Wallack, L. (eds) *Mass Communication and Public Health*. London: Sage.

Rorty, R. (1989.) *Contigency, Irony and Solidarity*. Cambridge: Cambridge University Press.

Ruddock, A. (2001) *Understanding Audiences*. London: Sage.

Seale, C. (2001) Sporting cancer: struggle language in news reports of people with cancer, *Sociology of Health and Illness*, 23, 3, 308–329.

Simon, R. and Fejes, F. (1987) Real police on television supercops. In Berger, A. (ed) *Television in Society*. New Brunswick: Transaction Books.

Singhal, A. and Rogers, E. (1999) *Entertainment-Education*. Mahwah, NJ: Erlbaum.

Spradley, J. (1979) *The Ethnographic Interview*. New York: Holt Rinehart and Winston.

Strauss, A. and Corbin, J. (1990) *Basics of Qualitative Research*. London: Sage.

Tulloch, J. and Lupton, D. (1997) *Television, Aids and Risk*. London: Allen and Unwin.

Tulloch, J. and Moran, A. (1986) *A Country Practice*. Sydney: Currency Press.

Turnock, R. (2000) *Interpreting Diana*. London: British Film Institute.

Willis, P. (1990) *Moving Culture*. London: Gulbenkian Foundation.

Winckler, M. (2002) *Les miroirs de la vie*. Paris: Le Passage.

Chapter 10

'About a year before the breakdown I was having symptoms': sadness, pathology and the Australian newspaper media

Rob Rowe, Farida Tilbury, Mark Rapley and Ilse O'Ferrall

Introduction

Much has been written about what has been described as the false and negative construction of 'mental illness'[1] in the media, and the consequent stigmatisation of the 'mentally ill'. Media coverage frequently focuses on violence and crime by the mentally ill, and is said to be the most influential source of public views about mental illness. So stigmatising, it is said, is the effect of negative media coverage that there is growing pressure for more 'accurate' and less stereotypical reporting of mental illness and associated issues (Allen and Nairn 1997, British Psychological Society 2000, Deifenbach 1997, Hazelton 1997, Hyler *et al.* 1991, Philo 1996, Wahl 1992).

While much has been written about mental illness and the media generally, little research is available on the representation of 'depression', a condition receiving increasing attention. Using a discourse analytic approach (Wetherell and Potter 1992, Edwards and Potter 1992) we investigated the construction of 'depression' in Australian newspapers during the year 2000. We identify three broad discursive repertoires and significant features of reporting styles, and explore their functions and effects. Unlike the negative portrayals of other mental illnesses, depression is constructed more ambiguously. It is rarely associated with violence, and where it is, the focus is generally on self-harm. We conclude that apparently distinct discourses work together to produce depression as a widespread and growing phenomenon affecting the lives of individuals, and in need of management through appropriate political, medical, psychological and social-structural interventions.

Methodology

A search of the print media in Western Australia (WA) for articles mentioning depression in the year 2000 was conducted using the Healthwatch electronic database operated by the Health Department of WA. The database contains full text articles from local and state newspapers in WA, and *The Australian*, the national daily. A keyword search for 'depression' was undertaken. In total, 49 articles appeared in the year 2000 in the newspapers extracted by the database.

Analysis

A systematic thematic analysis which identified significant features of both the form and content of articles was undertaken (Lupton 1994, Riffe *et al.* 1998). Particular attention was paid to the ways in which depression was constructed as a taken-for-granted category of illness, and the category memberships cited for speakers reported in the articles. Content analysis was complemented by a discursive approach, focusing on the textual construction of particular versions of reality. To this end, an examination of the discursive repertoires and of specific linguistic devices employed to produce such versions as solid and factual, was undertaken (Edwards 1997, Potter 1996). Following Sacks (1992), then, we examine in detail perspicuous instances of the construction of depression in the WA media, instances which produce depression as a taken-for-granted medical category.

Whose voice?

Access to the media is not equally available to all (Gurevitch *et al.* 1982) and the media tend to use 'experts' whose reputations and qualifications add weight to the argument being made, influence the way events are interpreted, and set the agenda for future debate (van Dijk 1991). Generally, the media provide little coverage of the opinions and experiences of members of the public, apart from occasional reference to add a personal dimension or to provide human interest (Fowler 1991). In the case of mental health issues this tendency would seem to be consistent, with news journalism students specifically taught to give prominence to expert voices, and to include occasional real-life exemplars to generalise the purportedly factual information provided[2]. But, as Foucault (1970) points out, what is now the commonplace idea that there should be professional, fact-based, expertise in human subjectivity – which carries greater epistemic weight than everyday experience – is a remarkably recent historical development.

In the case of depression, those deemed qualified to speak tend to be medical professionals, researchers and politicians. Of the 49 articles analysed, 45 referred to experts in some way – academics, researchers, politicians, bureaucrats or members of the legal or medical profession. Even those writing Letters to the Editor more often than not used their expert status to warrant their views, including their position as 'President of the xxyy Association of Psychiatrists' or 'Director of xxyy Anger Management Clinic' in their signatures. Competition between the entitlements of such categories (Potter 1996) are evident in some articles, such as Extract 1 below, where different professionals vie with each other as legitimate 'expert' commentators.

Extract 1: Mental illness help narrow: psychiatrists (*The West Australian*, 16 March 2000: 34)

The Royal Australian and New Zealand College of Psychiatrists said the government's depression initiative did not go far enough.

'The government has missed an important opportunity to look at the whole area of mental illness and the stigma which it continues to carry in our society', the group's president, Jonathon Phillips said. [. . .] Mr Kennett said he was happy with the early political support for the National Depression Institute he was setting up with the Federal Government. [. . .] 'I have been very gratified by the universal support that I and the initiative have received', he said. 'After the announcement, I spoke to Kim Beazley, I spoke to premiers around the country, including my successor, and all have committed themselves fully to this initiative'. [. . .] Dr Phillips said the government was to be applauded for putting mental health on the political agenda.

'However, let's not limit ourselves', he said.

The President of the Royal Australian and New Zealand College of Psychiatrists has the weight of his organisation and its members behind him, arguing the case for more money for mental illness generally. The politician/bureaucrat rallies support by quoting several politicians from both sides of the political fence as backing the initiative. The use of professional and political credentials clearly stake a claim to ownership of the problem. Crediting the government for focusing on mental health, while criticising the exact form of that focus, is an example of 'minimal agreement' which positions Dr Phillips as a reasonable expert, willing to make concessions and recognise shared ground. What is left unsaid is as important as what is said in this article – the dispute is about the extent and scope of medical management, not about the value of the clinical categories and management approaches generally.

The pragmatics of the media's material selection must be acknowledged at this point. News is produced in routine ways: official news sources tend to monopolise newspapers due to increased time pressures on journalists resulting in less investigative reporting and an increase in the straightforward reproduction of media releases from interested parties. If the current data are anything to go by, stories on 'depression' in the Australian press appear to have very few possible sources:

• press releases from government agencies;
• extracts from the medical media;
• press releases provided directly to newspapers by researchers.

Likewise, the sifting process which occurs in the production of news stories tends to privilege the voices of professionals. The opportunity for controversy is a significant factor in news choices, and the media will often attempt to canvass alternative points of view, generally from another expert, to make their story appear 'balanced' and hence objective, as the above example illustrates.

The media also preferentially select stories characterised by drama, immediacy, human interest and simplicity, together with topics relevant to society's élites, stories about common or unusual things, and stories which are negative (Lupton 1994, Galtung and Ruge 1981). This process has produced an association between mental illness and crime and violence to others, with up to three-quarters of coverage being about these issues (Deifenbach 1997, Philo 1996). The construction of depression is quite different. The focus is on the effect of depression on the individual with the condition rather than on others, and therefore on medical and bureaucratic management by experts. Only one article of the 49 mentioned harm to others (a murder). On the other hand, over a third mentioned self-harm or suicide.

It is extremely rare for the voice of lay persons diagnosed with depression to be heard, and their views are never canvassed in relation to the claims of the medical or bureaucratic experts. Only seven articles referred to lay people's views, and where depression from the point of view of the 'ordinary person' is presented, as we see in Extract 2, the supposedly lay message is supportive of expertise.

Extract 2: The Anxiety Epidemic (*The Sunday Times*, 29 October 2000: 6)
Ian Ewart, 37, suffered a breakdown last year.
He blamed work-related stress as a catalyst.
'About a year before the breakdown I was having symptoms', he said.
'I started getting tired, unable to deal with the stresses that I used to deal with. [. . .] Then I started having panic attacks. I felt so run down I wasn't able to cope with even the basics'.
'This is the stage where you should seek help, but I didn't'.
Eventually Ian went to his doctor, who told him to take time off work.
'I took two weeks off and just lay in bed', he said. [. . .] The experts say anxiety, when it becomes unmanageable, is central to all breakdowns.

Direct quotations from the individual sufferers are interlaced with statements, ostensibly of fact and advice, by unnamed experts. The privileging of medical or bureaucratic experts and the lack of voice of the lay person, produces depression as a condition outside the realm of everyday comprehension and within the domain of those with special knowledge and expertise. Ownership of the problem is thus vested in the hands of the experts rather than ordinary people.

Discursive repertoires

Depression was constructed via three broad discursive repertoires – the biomedical, the administrative/managerial and the psycho-social. While it would be easy to see these discourses as mutually exclusive, with the biomedical discourse attached to the position of medical expert, the psycho-social discourse associated with the patient or lay person, and the administrative/ managerial discourse the domain of the bureaucrat and politician, there are significant overlaps in their articulation. We wish to emphasise that discourses cannot simply be read off social positions in this manner, nor vice versa (Wetherell and Potter 1992, Silverman 1996). While each discourse will tend to support the interests of a particular group, complementarities exist because the boundaries of the groups, and therefore their interests, are not fixed.

The biomedical discourse
Seventeen of the 49 articles which mentioned depression attributed it to a biological cause, and many others noted the utility of pharmacological treatments, implying (via quite fallacious logic as Healy (1997) has pointed out) some involvement of biochemical derangement or imbalance. Of the articles sampled, testosterone, brain chemistry, genetics and hormonal deficiencies were specifically mentioned as biological causes.

   As with many other forms of unwanted conduct, representations of depression in the media are heavily invested with medical or disease-related terminology and scientific jargon. Over the years, deviance from behavioural and emotional norms has come to be identified as an illness, within the purview of the medical profession (Sontag 1978). The metaphor of mental 'illness' has become a reality (Ross 1989) and instead of anxiety or depression being described as being *like* a disease, they become reified as *actual* diseases. For example, in an extremely common textual practice in our sample, we find 'depression' characterised as being like 'many other common medical disorders (for example, diabetes, hypertension, asthma)' ('Dubious mindset of depression program', *The Australian*, 17 March 2000: 14), and therefore in need of research and treatment by medical professionals (Hansen, McHoul and Rapley 2003). By virtue of this process, metaphorical constructions of human experience become solidified and taken for granted. Extract 3 illustrates this taken-for-grantedness of talk about unhappiness *qua* illness or disease.

   Extract 3: Blues assault chief in call to revise GP pay (*The West Australian*, 25 October 2000: 39)
   Changes to the way general practitioners are paid for treating patients with depression is a key to tackling it, according to the man who will head a national assault on the illness. [. . .] Mr Kennett [. . .] would seek to promote community awareness of depression, improve patient management and increase clinical research.

Of importance here is the terminology used. Terms such as illness, treatment, patients *with* depression (our emphasis) and patient management construct misery/depression within an 'objective' medical discursive field. 'Patients with depression' are clearly 'ill' in a way that the construction 'people who are very unhappy' are not. The term 'clinical research' further acts to produce images of white coats, laboratories, and randomised controlled drug trials. It is presumed that 'depression' is treatable by GPs. By relying on the common-sense knowledge that when one is sick one goes to a doctor to be made well, the text need not justify this account of toxic sadness, for the connection of depression with sickness and doctors acts rhetorically as an explanation, rather than simply a description (Sacks 1992).

Also significant are the different degrees of agency ascribed to patients and medical professionals. GPs 'treat' depression, and they 'manage' patients. Prospective and, later, identified patients, on the other hand, are passive, needing their 'awareness' increased, and to be 'managed'. These idioms (re)produce the patient as powerless – their agency is explicitly denied. They are expected passively to accept biomedical diagnosis and treatment advised by medical professionals, who have the power to provide such diagnosis and advice simply by virtue of their status as professionals.

Paradoxically, despite the use of scientific and medical terminology, the biomedical discourse is characterised by a lack of precision. Biological causes of depression were articulated using a rhetorical device described as the 'studied use of vagueness' (Augoustinos, et al. 1999, Edwards and Potter 1992), with few articles providing detail of the biochemistry putatively involved, or of exactly how biology 'produces' the feelings, thoughts and behaviours associated with depression. For instance, the health advice column in *The West Australian* on 18 October (2000: 6) features a reader asking about the difference between clinical depression and 'feeling a bit down'. The doctor who replies begins with a disclaimer, stating that 'depression can be hard to diagnose even for the experts' but in the next sentence advises that 'if you think you may be depressed you *must* go and see your doctor' (our emphasis). Again the contrast is striking: a vaguely specified admission of the difficulty of diagnosis, followed by an imperative direction to see a doctor for help. An obvious question is – if the experts cannot diagnose it, what is the point of going to one? The rest of the answer gives neither a clear definition (' "Clinical depression" is just a popular new term to separate real medical depression from everyday blues') nor a discussion of biological causes or mechanisms, despite advising the writer that 'you must get rid of the idea that you must have a reason to be depressed – that's not true and sometimes depression just comes'.

Such systematic vagueness works in a number of ways to position the hypothesised biochemical causes of emotions – as a known or given reality – as factual. First, lack of explication constructs it as so obvious that the exact biochemical mechanism need not be explained. Second it reinforces the expert's position *as* expert, and the reader as either not needing proper explanation because of the expert's expertness, or because of their own inability to understand the technicalities of the biochemical processes.

The administrative/managerial discourse
One third of the articles emphasised health care management and administration issues and the question of how to improve the recognition and management of depression generally. As we have seen above, one of the key foci
in 2000 was the launch of the beyondblue (sic) depression initiative – a
national institute to increase public awareness and undertake research. This
was the topic of three-quarters of all articles referring to 'depression' in *The
Australian*. However, while this bureaucratic response to unhappiness has
clearly had an impact on the number of pieces on depression in 2000, our
interest here is more in the construction of the issue than in the amount of
coverage given to it.

That is to say, stories on the beyondblue initiative are not the only way in
which the administrative/managerial discourse makes its appearance. Many
articles primarily constructing depression via biomedical or psycho-social
discourses framed the issue within the larger context of the administrative/
managerial discourse. Articles, for example, refer to the financial cost of depression to society in terms of lost productivity and health care costs, suggesting
that structures, services and resources need to be changed to improve health
'outcomes'. The inadequacy of current service provision was a common
theme, as exemplified in the argument of an expert from the National Drug
and Alcohol Research Centre. In an article about the relationship between
depression, drink and drugs, this expert is reported as saying that people
who have both drug or alcohol and 'mental health' problems are at risk of
'falling through the cracks', and a reconsideration of how the health services
should operate is needed ('Depression tie to drink, drugs', *The Australian*,
2 September 2000: 6).

This discourse draws on the corporatist tropes of management. Indeed
across the texts sampled, discussing what is supposedly a devastating individual psychological/biochemical problem, lexical items such as the following
were routinely deployed: the long term, the big picture opportunities, health
promotion, private sector, political agenda, solutions, health services, screen-
ing, outcomes, chief executive, medical workforce, improving skills, patient
management, health policy, bulk-billing arrangements, high through-put,
national programmes, announcements, appointments, generate funds, advocacy, measures, models, multi-million dollar campaign, public arena, cost-
cutting strategy, quality of care, services, implementation, contracts, burden
of disease, official launch. These linguistic forms frame depression as
another technical problem in need of improved management systems. And
yet within this rather sterile bureaucratic language is a subtle implication of
panic evident in the construction of depression as an 'epidemic', 'a rising
tide' against which a 'national assault' needs to be launched, a 'major health
problem' producing widespread 'disability' which needs to be 'tackled'. Such
extreme case formulations (Pomerantz 1986, Edwards 2000) justify the focus
of bureaucratic attention on the condition as requiring new initiatives, interventions and resources.

Given that responsibility for mental health management exists within a bureaucratic system with both medical and political aspects (Turner 1995), it is perhaps not surprising that media framings are strongly interlaced with discussions of problems in existing structures, and what can be done to improve these through new initiatives. Such discussions occasionally entail debate about where the causes of depression lie – in brain biology or in social structures which produce difficult life situations. The following extract, from a Letter to the Editor by a research GP, illustrates this point.

Extract 4: Keep a level head on depression (*The Australian*, 21 March 2000: 18)
On another note, the major determinants of depression and suicide, like many complex public health problems have as much to do with social factors as they do with health. It is seductive to think that a 'medical/ health' solution will fix the problem. Unfortunately, a single portfolio response to the problem of depression and suicide will fail unless we address social issues such as youth and long-term unemployment, fair access to education, support for families, gambling and drug policy.

This is the final paragraph of a discussion of the best ways to manage the 'major public health problem' of depression, noting changes to rebate systems to reduce over-servicing by psychiatrists and time pressures on GPs. We note the implicit assumption that sufferers must be managed by those in professional positions who will provide appropriate treatments (biomedical, psychological or social structural), administered through appropriate services, within appropriate funding structures. The individual, and any agency which they may be thought to have, is entirely absent.

The psycho-social discourse
As has been noted, the psycho-social discourse tends to emphasise psychological and social bases for unhappiness, and focuses on the human experience of depression. Rather than emphasising the role of professionals, clinicians and researchers, the focus is on social critique: life circumstances, social, cultural and political conditions and other factors that increase human misery.

As such, the language used tends to be much softer, with emotion words more common. For example, in an article with the headline 'Youth fit but stressed: study' the author of a report on the mental health of Australian youth says 'we know that there are certain groups who are vulnerable to the ill effects, the pressures, the seduction and the harm associated with contemporary society' (*The West Australian*, 25 January 2000: 3). Here clearly is a different way of thinking and talking about depression, one less enmeshed in biology, and more focused on emotional states and interactional influences.

Societal or personal change and a personal, individual, inability to adapt are common themes. Likely culprits identified explicitly in the articles include social and work stresses, lack of role models, unhappy childhoods, jealousy, bereavement, relationship breakdowns, marital difficulties, redundancy, lack of access to education, gambling, drugs and alcohol, loss of religious faith, loss of social connections, unemployment, farming insecurities for those in rural communities, the gap between rich and poor, and a lack of laughter. A connection between increasing rates of depression and the increasing social difficulties of modern life was a common theme.

It is interesting to note that speaking of depression in this manner occurs more often in *The Australian* and community-level newspapers, than in *The West Australian*, the State daily. Articles in *The Australian* included those critical of the medicalisation and politicisation of depression, critiques of social inequalities and world economic events such as globalisation. Coverage of depression in local community papers tended to focus on adverse life circumstances (poor harvests, heavy schedules) or psychological factors (low self-esteem, difficulties in dealing with stress) as causes. Several of these articles were specifically designed to promote public health, and mentioned local mental health initiatives such as public talks, social skills programmes and self-help groups. Despite the focus on social causes of distress, these articles do not question the definition of depression as a mental illness. For example, in an article relating the increase in depression to an economic downturn in rural communities, the co-ordinator of a Community Depression Project notes that people need to be 'educated' to 'recognise the signs' of the 'condition at an early stage, and to seek help [from the] many avenues of treatment' ('Rural downturn aids depression', *The Great Southern Herald*, 24 May 2000: 5).

Intersecting discourses

Among a number of interesting observations which emerge from the analysis, the almost equal coverage of biomedical and psycho-social explanations for depression is surprising. It is easy to assume that the biomedical discourse attaches to the position of medical expert, so the privileging of expert opinion in media coverage will ensure a predominance of biomedical explanations. This is clearly not the case in our sample. Of note also is the frequent coalescence of the three discourses, which are sometimes juxtaposed as opposing approaches, and sometimes interlaced with each other into a complex whole.

The following article in the national daily, *The Australian*, illustrates this clearly. It reports research indicating that a combination of psychotherapy and anti-depressants is the best treatment for 'chronic' depression.

Extract 5: Medicine and talk work best for depression (*The Australian*, 27 May 2000: 11)
A combination of psycho-therapy and anti-depressant medicine is the best treatment for people suffering from chronic depression, according

to a study published recently by the *New England Journal of Medicine*. Of 681 patients receiving the two-pronged course of treatment in the study, which was conducted at Brown University in Washington, 85 per cent showed positive results.
'This is the first time that combination therapy has proven so much more effective than either medication or psychotherapy alone', wrote lead researcher Martin Keller. [. . .] 'The findings offer hope for a vast number of patients suffering from chronic forms of major depression', Keller said.

The story is newsworthy as it is the first time, we are told, that the combination of therapies has been proved to be more effective than one or the other alone. The article is presented scientifically, with the use of both technical terminology and statistical data. The source of the published research is cited, together with the number of participants and specific details of study design and findings. The research is called an 'experiment', the course of treatment 'two-pronged', and positive results referred to as an 'improvement rate' (although once again diagnostic tools and measures are not mentioned). As befits scientific research, opinion quoted is that of medical experts.

The final third of the article is structured as fact provision, with information on depression rates and the biological pathways involved being straightforwardly presented. This is clearly a treatable medical condition. The conclusion states the type of anti-depressant medication used in the trial, SSRIs (selective serotonin reuptake inhibitors), giving Prozac as an example of this type of drug. This section appears to be directly taken from drug company promotion literature, as it not only describes the biochemical action thought to produce depression unproblematically, but also because it includes prevalence figures from the US, rather than Australia. The final paragraph is highly technical, explaining that:

Serotonin is a natural chemical in the brain known as a neurotransmitter, the activity of which can be boosted by SSRIs, which act by inhibiting its reabsorption by brain cells.

The exact operation of this mechanism, and how it should affect emotions, is left entirely unspecified. Technical language stands in for explanation, yet all the directly attributed quotes in the story (five in all) focus on the positive outcomes for patients and use an emotional rather than a scientific tone. For example, the second quote from the lead researcher, states that for some of the participants 'it was the first time in more than 20 years that they could sustain pleasure and function fully at work and with families and friends'. Such a framing provides a more human side to the condition than would be expected in a strictly scientific and biomedical discourse, providing an insight into the personal difficulties sufferers may have. It also makes clear that the expert seeks only the best interests of patients.

Likewise, despite the scientific construction of most of the language in the report, extreme case formulations abound. The researcher uses superlatives, referring several times to this research as being 'the first time' such an improvement has been noted, offering hope to a 'vast number' of patients. A similar construction occurs in other articles, such as the article headlined 'Beat the blues', which notes that 'with hundreds of young people falling victim to depression each year, health professionals are desperate to find a means of helping teenagers . . .' (*The West Australian*, 13 September 2000: 6). Such constructions, along with the alarmist quasi-militaristic language (hundreds, falling victim, attack, fight, desperate) found in much of the media coverage of depression, stake a unique claim for expert involvement with depression. It imbues the specialists – in this case the health professionals – with importance and credibility, presenting them as saviour figures who are, by definition, not only capable of providing help, but who are also desperate to help, implying their moral expertise and commitment. These extreme case formulations and articulations of concern function to claim expertise, constructing the researcher as enthusiastic, caring and knowledgeable, while denying agency to the 'sufferers' who require assistance to solve the problem.

So we see an interesting discursive overlap – with the journalist using objective scientific language to present the results, the researcher using emotive language to stake a claim to humanitarian concern, and the actual content of the article being about medical research. This last can be read as offering support to both the psycho-social discourse and the biomedical one, and providing an evidence-base for a change in management practices.

Similarly, in 'The Anxiety Epidemic' (*Sunday Times*, 29 October 2000) two sufferers' stories of depression and anxiety are reported, with an emphasis on contributing factors (work-related stress, domineering fathers, unrequited love, job loss) and treatments (medication, talk therapy). While the piece offers a rare example of depressed people voicing their experience, the journalist defers to experts and psychiatrists to provide accurate information about their disease, in an article peppered with reference to experts and research. The reader is informed, for example, that 'experts agree it is never right to treat a major depressive episode solely with drugs. Adequate treatment usually requires a combination of drugs and therapy'.

Talking about depression as physical disorder, be it related to some form of genetic anomaly or dysfunctional brain chemistry with medication the only cure, is clearly a partisan position. Indeed this is shown by the 'show concession' (Antaki and Wetherell 1999) in the piece – appearing to give ground by admitting that talking therapies may also be required. This works to provide an added degree of credibility to the biological argument, and provides a convenient 'out' when explaining why biological treatments might have failed. Interestingly, the two sufferers' stories each reach a climax of misery which is solved by their going to their doctor and getting medication. For example Ian 'says':

Extract 6: The Anxiety epidemic (The Sunday Times, 29 October 2000: 6)
I still thought I could cure myself, that it was all work related and I just
needed some peace . . . but . . . I realized how desperate I was . . . By 9 am
I was at my doctor, who prescribed anti-depressants as well as therapy.

In a familiar media device, the voice of both of these lay people, who identify drug therapy as important in their treatment, is deployed to *buttress* the
essentially medical argument advanced by the piece (see Leudar and
Thomas 2000).

Another example of this discursive polyphony, illustrative of the futility
of attempting to connect specific discourses to particular social positions,
comes from an article about a woman whose husband committed suicide
'after a long battle with depression' ('White wreaths mark grim toll', *The
West Australian*, 9 November 2000: 38). Julie talks about the general lack
of understanding and the stigma attached to mental illness, saying 'if Ian
had [sic] diabetes it would have been acceptable'. She is reported as going
on to say, in a straight biomedical account, that 'a mental illness such as
depression is caused by a chemical imbalance in the brain yet diabetes is
more acceptable in our society'. Recognition of psycho-social issues is
minimal, apart from the assertion that a more accepting society might
have prevented the man's suicide. And the entire article is framed within
the administrative/managerial discourse, reporting on a 'consumer-driven'
initiative to commemorate, regularly and publicly, deaths from mental
illness-related suicide and to push government to provide more services for
family and friends. It concludes with a response from the State Health
Minister claiming more services have been provided and suggesting the
community has an important part to play in reducing suicide.

The effect is polyphonic, with the three discourses intersecting, in this case
in the reported speech of a lay person. Clearly, lay people sometimes reproduce the biomedical discourse. There may be a number of reasons for this.
The biomedical discourse has been pervasive in its influence, particularly
when one considers the types of experts given voice in public forums, resulting in extraordinarily high levels of positivity of the discourse of the biomedical science (Foucault 1994, Hansen *et al.* 2003). Indeed – as writers such
as Smail (1998) have suggested – it is also arguable that the biomedical
explanation for mental illness is successful precisely as a way of legitimising
personal troubles, by making them biological. Thus, as in the above
example, the biomedical approach becomes a strategy for destigmatising
mental 'breakdown' (Karp 1996) – it is just another illness anyone can 'get'.

Finally, it was common for medical practitioners to use the psycho-social
discourse – in *Extract 4* ('Keep a level head on depression', *The Australian*,
21 March 2000) we heard a GP arguing that depression had as much to do
with social as health factors, and needed a generalised response including
better access to education, employment and family support, rather than a
single portfolio response. That such a statement should come from a GP is

extraordinary if one assumes the biomedical discourse attaches solely to the position of medical expert. While it is entirely possible that this letter was published *because* it came from a medical expert, it is illustrative of the ways in which the different discourses are drawn upon by a variety of social actors. The language of the administrative/managerial discourse is also evident in the discussion of the major determinants of complex public health problems which need more than a 'single portfolio response'. It combines with a message which points to social factors such as employment and access to education, which influence wellbeing. And it comes from a medical doctor, who accepts that depression and suicide are medical issues that doctors should be concerned with, and government should manage. The discourses coalesce to produce doctors and bureaucrats as pivotal in tackling this problem.

Discussion and conclusion

There are a number of features of this analysis worth further consideration. We have noted that depression is covered in a taken-for-granted manner where – while definitions and explanations are sidelined – direct comparison with other, genuinely biological, illnesses is made; where medico-scientific language is used to account for lived experience; where agency resides in medical practitioners and politicians rather than members of the public; and where the expertise of medical, research and bureaucratic experts is not questioned, but in fact promoted. As such, in the media texts sampled here, depression is simultaneously an underdetermined and overdetermined concept, being ill-defined and contentious, but also taken for granted as a mental illness in need of cure through biological, psychological or social-structural means.

The media act, albeit subtly, as a site of contestation where debates which parallel those in the 'scientific' literature play themselves out. The debate between biomedical and psycho-social discourses can be seen as simply another instance of the nature/nurture debate about human behaviour. Those with a stake in maintaining the dominance of the biomedical discourse occasionally make concessions to alternative positions, in order to sustain that position of dominance. This can be seen, for example, in the use of the psycho-social discourse in tandem with medicalised conceptions of epidemics and cures: indeed the tactical incorporation (and subsequent neutralisation) of moral accounts of misery and madness into now-dominant biomedical/ psychiatric accounts has a long history (Boyle 2002). It is also a useful strategy for diverting responsibility if biomedical treatments fail.

A further shared feature of all three discourses is their locus of agency. The biomedical discourse constructs depression as biological illness and therefore as treatable through medical means; the psycho-social discourse constructs it as a sign of the times, and therefore treatable through changing social structures and/or by providing people with the (internal) resources to cope; and the administrative/managerial discourse constructs depression as another phenomenon needing to be managed through more organised politicobureaucratic means. None questions the definition or existence of depression as an individualised, reified, condition.

So what does it all mean? We wish to argue, along Foucauldian lines, that the biomedical and the psycho-social discourses are not necessarily competing, nor indeed that one may sensibly be seen as offering resistance to the other, if a broader view of the expert project is taken. Indeed it may be argued that both biomedical and psycho-social discourses are subsumable under an overarching administrative/corporatist discourse of the late modern subject (Rapley and Ridgway 1998). Further, as Nikolas Rose (1999) has argued, the current trend toward psychopharmacological solutions for existential problems has resulted in a biopolitics of life itself and of how life should be lived, a situation he terms ethopolitics. Under such a politics, the psy professions function to provide persons with techniques by which to judge themselves and to guide persons in the ways in which to act upon themselves in the name of improvement (Rose 1999, 2001). Of course, it is not simply the pharmacological approach to depression that produces such an ethopolitics, but that the psycho-social discourse *also* lends itself to the stipulation of appropriate ways of acting and being – in this instance to what Wierzbicka (1999) has identified as the American imperative of 'obligatory happiness'. Mental health promotion initiatives, be they formal governmental endeavours, or informal efforts – the newspaper advice column, the magazine problem page, or the talk-back radio show – produce and promulgate ideal ways of living to which all should aspire and which failure to achieve renders the subject liable to diagnosis and therapy (Hansen *et al.* 2003, Turner 1995). Strategies based on 'self-work' are often provided to support such initiatives, strategies in many respects similar to the magic bullets prescribed by psychiatrists and general practitioners for similar 'conditions'. The overlap in discourses makes sense when seen as part of this larger project to determine and to specify appropriate ways of being, and appropriate pathways to treatment. The media thus construct depression as a condition about which something must be done, where control of the definition, diagnosis and treatment is located outside the individual.

This study has examined a number of devices in the print media's production of very particular ways of understanding depression. Devices such as the use of scientific jargon and pseudo-physical analogies which construct depression as *naturally* falling into the domain of medical experts, the studied use of vagueness which produces depression as a scientific, medical condition in no need of cogent definition and explanation, the reproduction of experts' extreme case formulations which cement their position as authoritative, legitimate and concerned – all function to produce, and specifically to pathologise – what is also describable (in human terms) as 'malignant sadness' (Wolpert 1999).

Whilst, for the purposes of our analysis here, it has been useful to differentiate the three discourses identified, in practice, these ways of talking about depression act to produce and to facilitate the same outcome – the identification, monitoring and surveillance of socially troublesome emotion states, and the possibility of acting upon those states. Media stories about depression, at least in Australia, then offer a useful pedagogic vehicle for the dissemination of contemporary technologies of the self.

Acknowledgement

Financial support for this project from Healthway is gratefully acknowledged.

Notes

1   We place 'mental illness' in scare quotes here to indicate that this notion, like 'depression' itself, is not to be taken for granted. For reasons of aesthetics these quotation marks are omitted from the text from here on. They should, however, be inserted by the reader.
2   We are grateful to an anonymous reviewer for this point.

References

Allen, R. and Nairn, R. (1997) Media depictions of mental illness: an analysis of the use of dangerousness, *Australian and New Zealand Journal of Psychiatry*, 31, 375–81.
Antaki, C. and Wetherell, M. (1999) Show concessions, *Discourse Studies*, 1, 1–32.
Augoustinos, M., Tuffin, K. and Rapley, M. (1999) Genocide or a failure to gel? Racism, history and nationalism in Australian talk, *Discourse and Society*, 10, 351–78.
Boyle, M. (2002) *Schizophrenia: a Scientific Delusion?* 2nd Edition. London: Routledge.
British Psychological Society (2000) *Understanding Mental Illness: Recent Advances in Understanding Mental Illness and Psychotic Experiences*. Leicester: The British Psychological Society.
Deifenbach, D. (1997) The portrayal of mental illness on prime-time television, *Journal of Community Psychology*, 25, 3, 289–302.
Edwards, D. (1997) *Discourse and Cognition*. London: Sage.
Edwards, D. (2000) Extreme case formulations: Softeners, investment, and doing non-literal, *Research on Language and Social Interaction*, 33, 347–73.
Edwards, D. and Potter, J. (1992) Discursive psychology. In McHoul, A. and Rapley, M. (eds) *How to Analyse Talk in Institutional Settings: A Casebook of Methods*. London: Continuum, Sage.
Edwards, D. and Potter, J. (1992) *Discursive Psychology*. London: Sage.
Foucault, M. (1970) *The Care of the Self: The History of Sexuality, Volume 3*. Trans. Robert Hurley. London: Penguin.
Foucault, M. (1994) *The Order of Things: An Archaeology of the Human Sciences*. New York: Vintage Books.
Fowler, R. (1991) *Language in the News*. London: Routledge.
Galtung, J. and Ruge, M. (1981) Structuring and selecting news. In Cohen, S. and Young, J. (eds) *The Manufacture of News*. London: Constable.

Gurevitch, M., Bennet, T., Curran, J. and Woollacot, J. (1982) *Culture, Society and the Media.* London: Methuen.

Hansen, S., McHoul, A. and Rapley, M. (2003) *Beyond Help: A Consumer's Guide to Psychology.* Ross-on-Wye: PCCS Books.

Hazelton, M. (1997) Reporting mental health: a discourse analysis of mental-health related news in two Australian newspapers, *Australian and New Zealand Journal of Mental Health Nursing*, 6, 73–89.

Healy, D. (1997) *The Anti-depressant Era.* Cambridge: Harvard University Press.

Hyler, S., Gabbard, G. and Schneider, I. (1991) Homicidal maniacs and narcissistic parasites: stigmatization of mentally ill persons in the movies, *Hospital and Community Psychiatry*, 42, 1044–8.

Karp, D. (1996) *Speaking of Sadness: Depression, Disconnection and the Meanings of Illness.* London: Oxford University Press.

Leudar, I. and Thomas, P. (2000) *Voices of Reason, Voices in Sanity: Studies of Auditory Hallucinations.* London: Routledge.

Lupton, D. (1994) *Moral Threats and Dangerous Desires: AIDS in the News Media.* London: Taylor and Francis.

Philo, G. (1996) The media and public belief. In Philo, G. (ed) *Media and Mental Distress.* London: Longman.

Pomerantz, A. (1986) Extreme case formulations: a way of legitimizing claims, *Human Studies*, 9, 219–29.

Potter, J. (1996) *Representing Reality: Discourse, Rhetoric and Social Construction.* London: Sage.

Rapley, M. and Ridgway, J. (1998) Quality of life talk: the corporatisation of intellectual disability, *Disability and Society*, 13, 451–71.

Riffe, D., Lacy, S. and Fico, F. (1998) *Analyzing Media Messages: Using Quantitative Content Analysis in Research.* Mahwah, New Jersey: Erlbaum.

Rose, N. (1999) *Governing the Soul: the Shaping of the Private Self.* London: Free Association Books.

Rose, N. (2001) The politics of life itself, *Theory, Culture and Society*, 18, 6, 1–30.

Ross, M. (1989) Psychosocial ethic aspects of AIDS, *Journal of Medical Ethics*, 15, 74–81.

Sacks, H. (1992) Lecture 12: Category bound activities; Programmatic relevance; hinting; being 'phoney'. In Jefferson, G. (ed) *Lectures on Conversation* (Volumes 1–2). Oxford: Basil Blackwell.

Silverman, D. (1996) *Interpreting Qualitative Data: Methods for Analysing Talk, Text and Interaction.* London: Sage.

Smail, D. (1998) *The Origins of Unhapiness.* London: Harper Collins.

Sontag, S. (1978) *Illness as Metaphor.* New York: Straus and Giroux.

Turner, B. (1995) *Medical Power and Social Knowledge.* London: Sage.

van Dijk, T. (1991) *Racism and the Press.* London: Routledge.

Wahl, O. (1992) Mass media images of mental illness: a review of the literature, *Journal of Community Psychology*, 20, 343–52.

Wetherell, M. and Potter, J. (1992) *Mapping the Language of Racism: Discourse and the Legitimation of Exploitation.* Hertfordshire: Harvester-Wheatsheaf.

Wierzbicka, A. (1999) *Emotions across Languages and Cultures: Diversity and Universals.* Cambridge: Cambridge University Press.

Wolpert, L. (1999) *Malignant Sadness: the Anatomy of Depression.* London: Faber and Faber.

Notes on Contributors

Kerry Chamberlain is a Reader in Health Psychology at Massey University, where he teaches research methods and health psychology and researches physical health. His research interests focus on social processes in health, with current research focussed on the relation of food and health, the medicalisation of food, the direct marketing of pharmaceuticals, and the role of media in health. He is the editor (with Michael Murray) of *Qualitative Health Psychology: Theories and Methods* (Sage 1999), and (with Gary Reker) of *Exploring Existential Meaning* (Sage 2000), and the author (with Antonia Lyons) of *An Introduction to Critical Health Psychology* (Cambridge, forthcoming).

Joyce Davidson is Post-Doctoral Research Fellow in the Institute for Health Research at Lancaster University, England, U.K., and will be Assistant Professor of Geography at Queen's University, Kingston, Ontario, from August 2003. Her research and teaching focus on geographies of emotion and embodiment, and her publications include the forthcoming (2003) *Phobic Geographies: The Phenomenology and Spatiality of Identity* (Aldershot: Ashgate Press).

Rosemary Davidson has recently completed her PhD on *Representations and lay perceptions of inequalities in health: an analysis of policy documents, press coverage and public understandings* at the MRC Social and Public Health Sciences Unit at Glasgow University. This included focus groups with participants from a wide range of social backgrounds in addition to a media analysis. She has previously co-authored an article on 'Funding research through directed programmes: AIDS and the human genome project in the UK' (*Science and Public Policy* 1998; 25: 141–216).

Solange Davin is an independent researcher. Her interests include medical narratives on television, the anthropology of health and illness, cross-cultural issues, the philosophy of science, literary criticism, identity. She is the author of *La médecine dans le salon: Urgences et ses spectateurs*, to be published in 2004 by L'Harmattan, and of numerous articles. She is currently preparing two edited books. The first applies literary criticism theories to television and the second focusses on medical dramas.

James Gillett is currently an Assistant Professor in the Health Studies Programme and the Department of Sociology at McMaster University. His interests include cultural representations of health and illness, expertise and lay knowledge, and the use of communication media.

Lesley Griffiths (B.Sc.Econ, Ph.D) leads the Centre for Health Economics and Policy Studies at the University of Wales, Swansea. Her interests lie in the area of qualitative research, particularly in narrative and discourse analysis and the application of these methods to a range of areas. She has carried out research for a variety of funders, including ESRC, The Nuffield Trust and The National Assembly for Wales.

Angie Hart is Principal Lecturer at the Centre for Nursing and Midwifery Research, University of Brighton. She has a background in medical social anthropology and sociology and has published widely on social relationships and organisational issues within health and social care. Her most recent publications include 'Inequalities in Health Care Provision: The Relationship between Contemporary Policy and Practice in the Maternity Services in England' (2002, with R. Lockey, *Journal of Advanced Nursing* 37(5) 485–93) and 'Views of Heads of Midwifery on electronic patient records' (2003, with F. Henwood and A. Jones). *British Journal of Midwifery* 11(1) 53–57.

Flis Henwood is a Senior Research Fellow in the Social Informatics Research Unit, University of Brighton, UK. She is a social scientist with over 20 years experience working on the relationship between technology and society. She has published widely in the areas of gender and techology and, more recently, health informatics. She has co-edited two books: *Technology and In/Equality: Questioning the Information Society*, Routledge, 2000, and *Cyborg Lives? Women's Technobioghraphies*, Raw Nerve Press, 2001.

Darrin Hodgetts was a Lecturer in Media and Communications at the London School of Economics and Political Science. Darrin is now a Lecturer in Community Psychology at Waikato University. He has published a number of articles on the role of media in the negotiation of public understandings of health, illness, and unemployment. Darrin is currently researching images of homelessness and symbolic exclusion.

David Hughes (B.A., M.A., Ph.D) is a professor in the School of Health Science at the University of Wales Swansea and spent 2002–03 as a visiting professor at Mahasarakham University, Thailand. His current research interests include comparative health care systems, resource allocation and the health care division of labour. He is co-author (with Davina Allen) of *Nursing and the Division of Labour in Healthcare* (Palgrave, 2002), and co-editor (with Donald Light) of *Rationing: Constructed Realities and Professional Practices* (Blackwell, 2002).

Kate Hunt is a Senior Research Scientist and head of the Gender and Health programme at the MRC Social and Public Health Sciences Unit at Glasgow University. She has published widely, topics including: social and gender inequalities and health, cultural constructions of gender and health, gender blindness in epidemiological research, and lay understandings of health and illness (including of inequalities in health, coronary heart disease, inheritance and professional and non-professional constructions of 'family history'). Kate is co-editor of *Gender Inequalities in Health* (Open University Press).

Jenny Kitzinger is Professor of Media Studies at the School of Journalism, Media and Cultural Studies, Cardiff University. Her research addresses media representations of health, science and 'risk' (e.g. genetics, breast cancer, infant feeding) and the media and sexual violence. Jenny is co-editor of *Developing Focus Group Research* (Sage) and co-author of *The Mass Media and Power in Modern Britain* (Oxford University Press) and *The Circuit of Mass Communication in the AIDS crisis* (Sage).

Steve Kroll-Smith is a Professor of Sociology and Head of the Department of Sociology at The University North Carolina at Greensboro. Among his recent books are *Illness and the Environment, A Reader in Contested Medicine* with Phil Brown and Valerie Gunter (New York University Press, 2000) and *Environmental Illness, The Struggle Over Medical Knowledge* (New York University Press, 1997). He is currently finishing a book with Valerie Gunter for Sage Press titled *Perilous Communities, A Study of Environmental Conflicts*.

Ilse O'Ferrall is manager of the Eastern Perth Population Health Unit and holds a visiting lectureship at the School of Public Health, Curtin University, and visiting research fellowship at Murdoch University. Her applied research interests include the health needs of socially disadvantaged groups, women's health and alcohol harm minimisation.

Mark Rapley is Associate Professor of Psychology at Murdoch University. His work applies discursive psychology to questions of power, examining the interactional and rhetorical production of persons with intellectual disabilities, the 'mentally ill' and Aboriginal Australians. His most recent books are *Quality of Life Research: A Critical Introduction* (Sage 2003) and, with Susan Hansen and Alec McHoul, *Beyond Help: A Consumer's Guide to Psychology* (PCCS Books, 2003). He is a foundation member of the Australian Institute for Ethnomethodology and Conversation Analysis and convenor of The Murdoch Symposium on Talk-in-Interaction.

Robert Rowe is an educator who has worked in classroom, administrative, school psychology, and IT positions. His areas of research interest include self-empowering models of adult mental health rehabilitation. The current paper arose from his postgraduate research and was part of a larger project between Murdoch University and Royal Perth Hospital exploring understandings of depression among ethnic minorities. It provided a baseline whereby mass media representations of depression could be compared with representations in ethnic media and understandings of ethnic communities.

Clive Seale took up a post as Professor of Sociology at Brunel University, London in September 2003, having worked at Goldsmiths College, University of London for the previous ten years. His research focuses on topics in medical sociology, including work on the experience of dying and the popular media representation of illness, health and health care. He is author or editor of numerous books and articles, including *Constructing Death: The Sociology of Dying and Bereavement* (Cambridge University Press, 1998), *The Quality of Qualitative Research* (Sage 1999) and *Media and Health* (Sage 2003).

Julie Smith has a background in the politics of mind. She read for an MA in the socio-cultural applications of psychoanalytic theory at Goldsmiths, University of London and studied subjectivity and social exclusion at doctoral level within the Social Work Department at Brunel University. She was a part-time researcher on the project reported in this volume for 18 months, undertaking a large proportion of the first interviews with women.

Mick Smith is Reader in Sociology at the University of Abertay Dundee, Scotland, U.K. and will be Associate Professor of Geography and Environmental Studies at Queen's University, Kingston, Ontario, from August 2003. He has published widely on issues relating to place and ethical feelings. His most recent publications include *An Ethics of Place: Radical Ecology, Postmodernity and Social Theory* (2001) (New York: SUNY) and *The Ethics of Tourism Development* with Rosaleen Duffy (2003, forthcoming) (London: Routledge).

Farida Tilbury is lecturer in Sociology and Community Development at Murdoch University. Her research interests include race, ethnicity and identity, health, discourse analysis and methodology. She has published articles and book chapters on rhetorical devices used to produce racist and anti-racist arguments, Derridian notions of identity as applied to New Zealand identity talk and the sociology of everyday life.

Sally Wyatt is an Associate Professor in the Department of Communication Studies and The Amsterdam School of Communications Research (ASCoR), University of Amsterdam. She is also President of the European Association for Studies in Science and Technology (EASST). Her research interests include the social relations of non-use of the Internet, and their representation. Together with Flis Henwood, Nod Miller and Peter Senker, she edited *Technology and Inlequality, Questioning the Information Society* (Routledge, 2000).

Index

lay beliefs 43, 44; and making sense of policy change 41, 44; moral dilemmas surrounding 50–1, 52; privatisation of 46–7; public anxiety over 40–1; quality of treatment/social standing link 49; resource allocation/access to 48, 50–2; responsibility, personification, dilemmas of 50–4; and state mismanagement 46, 48; and superiority of public system 48; trickle-down theories 40

Healthy Living Centres   27

Healy, D.   164

Hill, A.   5

HIV/AIDS, autobiography sites   97–9; dissent sites 101–2; expertise sites 99–100; making sense of 103–5; and media activity/Internet use 92–5, 102–3; moral panic concerning 92; normalisation process 92; and organising of people with 94; research on 93, 95–7; self promotion sites 100–1; treatment of 92–3

Holland, T.   150

Horkheim, M.   129

HRT, and the media   110–11; reasons for research 79–80; recruitment/interview focus 80; results of study 80–8; study 79

Information for Health (1998)   75

informed patients, and availability of information   74; and doctor/patient relationship 74, 75, 76, 88; emergence of 74–5, 89–90; and empowerment 75–6; and HRT study 79–80; information for choice/information for compliance 76; and information literacy 82–6, 89; and the Internet 76–9; lay/expert differences 86–7, 89; and privileging of bio-medical knowledge 76; and quality/targeted information 75; results of HRT study 80–8; and rights agenda 89; and taking responsibility 81–2, 86, 87–8

Internet   14–15, 74; and excessive daytime sleepiness 118, 121; and HIV/AIDS sites 94–102, 103, 104, 105; and patient empowerment 76–9; as primary source of knowledge 111; use of 81–2, 83–6

Journal of the American Medical Association   111

Karpf, A.   7, 10, 13

Kingsley, H.   145

Kitzinger, J. 7–8

Kroll-Smith, S.   123

Langer, J.   5, 8

lay/expert differences, and informed patient   86–7, 89; and the media 161–2, 163, 171; and use of knowledge 109–10

Lupton, D.   76, 88, 104

Massé, R.   76

media, access to   161; as arenas for struggle 58; and experts 161–2; and fashioning of narrative 109–10; and formation of lay beliefs 41; and HIV/AIDS activism 92–5, 103, 104–5; and lay persons 163, 171; and material selection 162–3; and political favouritism 58; relationship with policy-making 21; as salient source of knowledge 110–11; sources 58; structure of 3–4; text/programme analysis 58

media/health, audience   4–6; data collection 13; geographical bias 12; health risks 15–16; health-promotion campaigns 15; interaction 1–3; Internet studies 14–15; media representations 16; policy issues 13–14; political aspects 13; representation vs production/reception 12–13; representations 6–12; understanding 4–12; written vs image 13

medical dramas *see Casualty*; *ER*

medical sociology   121–3

Medline   85

mental illness   160; administrative/managerial view 166–7; analysis 161; bio-medical view 164–5, 172, 173; coverage of 172; discursive repertoires 163–8, 172–3; intersecting discourses 168–72; and the media 161–3, 172, 173; and obligatory happiness 173; psycho-social view 167–8, 171–2, 173; research methodology 160; self-work strategies 173; and sidelining of definitions/explanations 172; terminology 164–5

Merckelbach, H.   128

Miller, D.   13

MIND   127

Morley, D.   5

narrative, as communal process   43; confessional 11; dangers of modern life 8, 9; individual use of 109; and lay belief research 44–6; life stories/mediation of socio-cultural 54–5; and the media 109–10; medical dramas 143–9, 154–5; and negotiation of responsibility for healthcare 46–54; oppositions 6, 7–11; professional/lay heroes 10–11; retold, reframed, abstracted 52–4; and role of television 42–3; soap operas 150–4; socio-cultural aspects 43–4; tabloidisation 6–7; template 7–8; twitch/reversal 6; victims 10; villains/freaks 9–10

National Cancer Institute (NCI)   110

National Health Service (NHS)   57; and contract negotiations 62; public policy management 59–60; public/private domains 59–62

National Sleep Foundation (NSF)   108